The Powers of Sound and Song in Early Modern Paris

Perspectives on Sensory History

Books in the Perspectives on Sensory History series maintain a historical basis for work on the senses, examining how the experiences of seeing, hearing, smelling, tasting, and touching have shaped the ways in which people have understood their worlds.

Mark Smith, General Editor
University of South Carolina

EDITORIAL BOARD

Camille Bégin
University of Toronto, Canada

Martin A. Berger
Art Institute of Chicago, USA

Karin Bijsterveld
University of Maastricht, Netherlands

Constance Classen
Concordia University, Canada

Kelvin E. Y. Low
National University of Singapore, Singapore

Bodo Mrozek
University of Potsdam, Germany

Alex Purves
University of California, Los Angeles, USA

Richard Cullen Rath
University of Hawaii, USA

The Powers of Sound and Song in Early Modern Paris

Nicholas Hammond

The Pennsylvania State University Press
University Park, Pennsylvania

Library of Congress Cataloging-in-Publication Data

Names: Hammond, Nicholas, 1963– author.
Title: The powers of sound and song in early modern Paris / Nicholas Hammond.
Description: University Park, Pennsylvania : The Pennsylvania State University Press, [2019] | Series: Perspectives on sensory history | Includes bibliographical references and index.
Summary: "An interpretation of early modern Paris demonstrating that sound was as important as vision during the reign of Louis XIV. Discloses myriad ways in which sound generated an interpenetration of elite and popular culture, revealing complex acoustic dimensions of class, politics, sexuality, and punishment"—Provided by publisher.
Identifiers: LCCN 2019025597 | ISBN 9780271084718 (cloth)
Subjects: LCSH: Songs, French—France—Paris—17th century—History and criticism. | City sounds—France—Paris—History—17th century. | Paris (France)—History—Louis XIV, 1643–1715. | Paris (France)—Civilization—17th century.
Classification: LCC ML1427.2.H36 2019 | DDC 780.944/36109032—dc23
LC record available at https://lccn.loc.gov/2019025597

Copyright © 2019 Nicholas Gascoigne Hammond
All rights reserved
Printed in the United States of America
Published by The Pennsylvania State University Press,
University Park, PA 16802-1003

The Pennsylvania State University Press is a member of the Association of University Presses.

It is the policy of The Pennsylvania State University Press to use acid-free paper. Publications on uncoated stock satisfy the minimum requirements of American National Standard for Information Sciences—Permanence of Paper for Printed Library Material, ANSI Z39.48–1992.

Contents

List of Illustrations [vi]
Acknowledgments [vii]
Author's Note [ix]

INTRODUCTION [1]

PART I THE POWER OF SOUND [7]
1. The Sounds of Paris [9]
2. Singers and Listeners [31]
3. *Informé de tout*: Sound and Power, 1661–1662 [59]

PART II CHAUSSON'S SONG [93]
4. The Death and Afterlife of Jacques Chausson [95]
5. Guitaut, Condé, and the *Cordon bleu* [125]
6. Different Worlds [145]

CONCLUSION [161]

Appendix [165]
Notes [169]
Bibliography [188]
Index [197]

Illustrations

1. Manuscript detail from *Chansonnier Maurepas*   [2]
2. Nicolas Guérard, "L'Embaras [sic] de Paris"   [19]
3. Eighteenth-century engraving of the Samaritaine water pump   [20]
4. Gérard Audran, "Guillaume de Limoge"   [34]
5. Jacques Lagniet, "L'Apollon de la Grève"   [37]
6. Jacques Lagniet, "Le Savoyard"   [42]
7. "Brunel dit Bétancourt conduit au supplice"   [109]
8. Map of Paris (1675) by Jouvin de Rochefort   [126]
9. François de Poilly, "Chevalier de l'Ordre du Saint-Esprit"   [129]
10. Diagram of the Cross of the Ordre du Saint-Esprit   [130]

Acknowledgments

The supportive and encouraging voices of colleagues and friends have formed part of a long-lasting and invaluable conversation during the writing of this book. I am especially grateful to Tom Hamilton, whose intellectual generosity and enthusiasm helped me negotiate terrain that had hitherto been unfamiliar to me. Jonathan Rees, who tracked down and arranged the tunes of many street songs, has been inspirational in bringing the Pont Neuf to auditory life. It has been a privilege to work with him (viol) and the other members of the period instrument group Badinage: Katie Bray (mezzo-soprano), Naomi Burrell (violin), Leo Duarte (oboe and recorder), and Tom Foster (percussion). Grants by the British Academy, the Cambridge Arts and Humanities Research Grant, and the Cambridge Arts and Humanities Impact Fund were all essential in setting up the Parisian Soundscapes project, which helped fund the establishment of the website (www.parisiansoundscapes.org), together with the transcription, arrangement, performances, and recording of songs by Badinage. Emilia Wilton-Godberfforde and Ella Johnston have both assisted me enormously with the website and with the transcription of manuscripts. Librarians at Cambridge University, the Bibliothèque Nationale in Paris, and especially the Archives of the Château at Chantilly were unfailingly helpful in tracking down documents and images. Of the many excellent scholars who work in the area of sound studies, John Romey, Una McIlvenna, and Éva Guillorel have gone beyond the call of duty in their willingness to share their ideas and offer help. Jonathan Patterson offered useful suggestions regarding villainy and justice in the early modern period, and George Revill alerted me to interesting writings on sound studies in the field of cultural geography. Sarah Kay, who asked me to contribute to a volume; Delphine Denis, who invited me to speak at her seminar at the Sorbonne; Gary Ferguson; and Joan DeJean have been very generous with their suggestions and intellectual inspiration. In the latter stages of this book, Jeffrey Merrick gave valuable advice and was happy to share unpublished work with me. I have always enjoyed conversing with Paul Scott, whose insights and knowledge of early modern Paris have been as fun as they have been informative. Bertrand Boute's friendship and occasional linguistic assistance have been of great value to me. I am extremely fortunate to have colleagues at Cambridge whom I count as my friends; their academic example and the warmth of their support have been very important to me, and I would like to thank in particular Emma Gilby, Michael Moriarty, Tim Chesters, Ian James, Bill Burgwinkle, Emma Wilson, Mark Darlow, John Leigh, Jenny Mander, Angela Leighton, and Subha Mukherji. Heidi Ellison thought nothing of traveling from Paris to Cambridge just to come to a concert of street songs, and that is typical of the generosity of her friendship. Adam Merton, Jacob Baldwin, and Tashiana Marday helped make the illustrations look a whole lot better in this book. Those at Penn State University Press, including the series editor Mark Smith, editor in chief Kendra Boileau, editorial assistant Alex Vose, copyeditor Lori Rider, production coordinator Brian Beer, and the original readers of the book, have been exemplary in their approachability, professionalism, and efficiency. Marian Aird was very efficient and professional in compiling the index. Finally, I would like to thank Alexander Mohabeer for being there for me.

Author's Note

A large number of songs and texts quoted in this book remain in manuscript form or exist only in early editions. Except where there are modern editions from which I quote, and where the spelling has been modernized, I have kept the original (often idiosyncratic) spelling. Unless stated otherwise, all translations from the French are my own. The transcribed text of thousands of songs and performances of a range of songs by the period instrument group Badinage can be found on the Parisian Soundscapes website: http://www.parisiansoundscapes.org.

Early versions of a very small part of chapters 1 and 2 appeared in "Striking the Air: Early Modern Parisian Sound Worlds," in "Soundings and Soundscapes," ed. Sarah Kay and François Noudelmann, special issue, *Paragraph* 41, no. 1 (2018): 42–51.

Introduction

The inspiration for this book came from a chance encounter with one four-line song, hidden within an eighteenth-century manuscript collection of thousands of songs, poems, and satirical pieces from the seventeenth and eighteenth centuries (fig. 1). Although the two names mentioned in the song, Chausson and Guitaut, were unfamiliar to me at the time, the sense of injustice expressed in the piece was too intriguing not to explore further.

On the eighteenth-century manuscript of the song, no musical notation accompanies the text, but the name of the melody to which it should be sung, "Réveillez-vous, belle endormie," appears alongside the title. This song was in all probability not intended for publication or preservation but was destined for, at the most, a few performances before being forgotten. The person or people who had written it down had either happened to hear it in passing or been instructed to take note of it. Otherwise, it would have been lost.

Although the words themselves were the initial source of my interest, the idea that this was a song to be performed and heard by others began to take on particular importance in my reconsideration of assumptions I had tended to make, without necessarily even articulating those assumptions: namely, that the sounds heard in Paris at that time were off-limits precisely because they could not be recovered in the same way that a printed book could be perused and interpreted. Indeed, once I started working with a professional group of musicians with performances of many street songs from the time,[1]

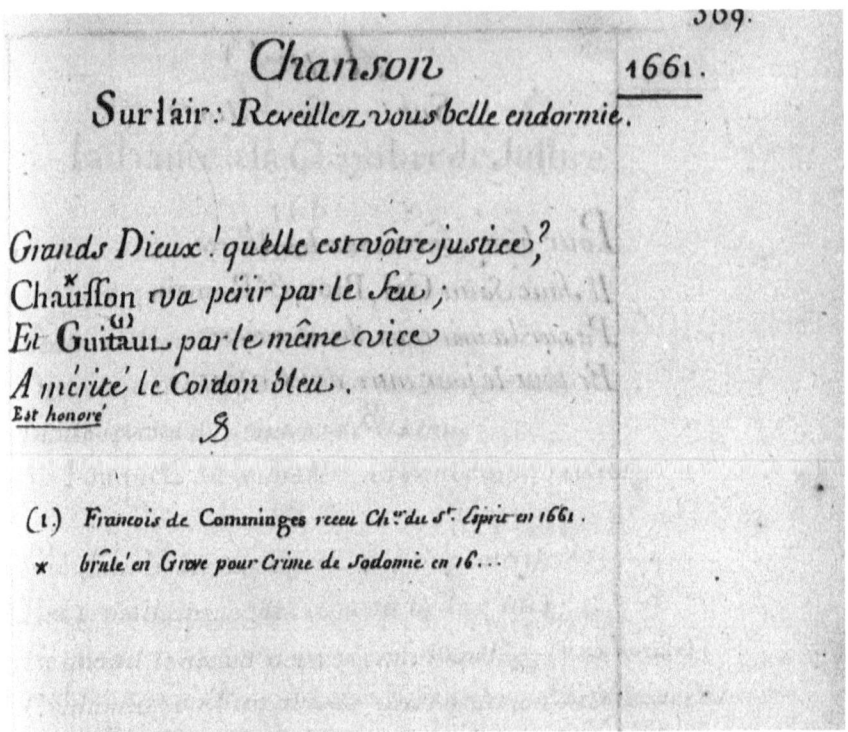

Fig. 1 Manuscript detail from *Chansonnier Maurepas*, vol. 23, fol. 369. Photo: BnF.

the experience of hearing the song, as arranged by Jonathan Rees, helped shape and change my initial interpretation of the song, as will be shown in part 2 of this book.

The transience and orality of this song, and the opportunity that my chance discovery of it gave me to examine its content and track down its melody, brought to mind the many other pieces that must have been performed on the streets of Paris and thereafter disappeared, undocumented and unpreserved for future generations. Furthermore, not only songs but also many other sounds from earlier ages have inevitably remained unrecorded. The seeming irrecoverability of such sounds might explain why, until relatively recently, scholars in the arts and humanities have tended to ignore or neglect the auditory past and have concentrated instead on the easily salvageable—printed books, paintings, prints, sculptures, monuments, buildings—or only on those aspects of music for which printed scores are readily available.[2]

Given that the short song I had uncovered dated from 1661, a crucial year in the history of the French *ancien régime*, when Louis XIV declared himself absolute ruler, I began to wonder how a predominantly sonic reading of such an interesting age might help us both to reconsider and to cast potentially new light on a time that is usually described in overwhelmingly visual terms. It therefore became evident that a wider consideration of sound in seventeenth-century Paris in the first part of the book would most usefully precede the extraordinary facts and circumstances surrounding the Chausson/Guitaut song in the second part.

Part 1 of this study, titled "The Power of Sound," therefore offers a broad social, cultural, and historical context to the primacy of sound in early modern Paris. Chapter 1, "The Sounds of Paris," concerns recent sonic theories, as applied to the early modern period, and to representations of sound in the city at the time by poets, writers, and visitors: often sounds are represented as invasive, dissonant, and dangerous, no more so than in the vicinity of the Pont Neuf, which became indelibly associated with noise and disorder. Examination of its function as the first truly communal entertainment space will lead to an analysis of the origins, practice, and purpose of songs performed on the bridge. The link between the compilation of songs and the control and policing of them brings out a theme that will recur throughout the book: crime and the attempted suppression of crime.

In chapter 2, titled "Singers and Listeners," attention is drawn to the singers who performed songs on the Pont Neuf and to those people who came to listen to the songs, with a detailed case study provided of one singer and one listener from the time. Philippot, known as "Le Savoyard," is both typical and atypical of street singers from the early modern period: like many other singers, he was disabled, but he was also almost unique in the fact that songs written and performed by him were published during his lifetime. These songs (and the engravings of Philippot that exist) will highlight the location where they were performed and give important clues as to how they were sung and with which musical instruments they were accompanied. Philippot constantly draws attention to his blindness and invites listeners to enter his sound world. As a listener, the immensely cultivated and aristocratic marquise de Sévigné might not seem the most obvious example of an ear-witness to street songs, but her correspondence brings out the coexistence of the literate and nonliterate in such songs and shows the many ways in which these pieces were consumed by all classes of people.

Chapter 3, "*Informé de tout*: Sound and Power, 1661–1662," revolves around the time of Louis XIV's appropriation of absolute control following the death of Cardinal Mazarin. As monarch, Louis is usually associated with visual spectacle, but in this chapter his relationship to sound in particular will be explored, with the theme of Louis as listener to his subjects, to preachers, to musical entertainment, and to songs about himself taking center stage. Three events in which sound or competing voices play a significant part will be discussed: the Lenten sermons preached at the Louvre by the great churchman Jacques-Bénigne Bossuet in early 1662, the lavish entertainment staged by Nicolas Fouquet at Vaux-le-Vicomte in August 1661, and the arrest and trial of Fouquet, from 1661 to 1664.

The broader brushstrokes of part 1 are replaced in part 2, "Chausson's Song," by detailed examination of the four-line song that was performed on the cusp of 1661 and 1662, the very time that Louis was asserting his authority. Chapter 4, "The Death and Afterlife of Jacques Chausson," retraces the circumstances and sound world of Chausson's death (and that of his companion Jacques Paulmier) on 29 December 1661 through analysis of trial and interrogation transcripts, manuals for confessors, street songs, and poems. The impact of Chausson's execution (for sodomy) on a number of poets, writers, and song composers in subsequent years demonstrates the sense of outrage at the unequal treatment meted out to sodomites from different strata of society. The poet Claude Le Petit, who himself was burned at the scaffold less than a year after Chausson's death, proves to be a particularly eloquent and combative supporter of Chausson's cause, depicting him as not only subversive of normative practices but also courageous and heroic. Such was the impact of Chausson's death that sodomites began to be referred to as "chaussons."

Chapter 5, "Guitaut, Condé, and the *Cordon bleu*," will map the very different fate of Guillaume de Comminges-Pechpeyrou, comte de Guitaut. His elevation at the end of December 1661 by Louis XIV to the rank of Chevalier de l'Ordre du Saint-Esprit, which came at the request of his master and (if the song is to be believed) lover le Grand Condé, will act as the chapter's starting point. Not only will Guitaut's past as a page boy in various aristocratic households be examined, but also the systems of patronage and circles of male favorites associated with Condé will be explored. An unpublished series of letters from Condé to Guitaut uncovers fascinating details of their relationship and brings out a strong awareness in the two men of the disparity between what can be written on paper and what can be expressed verbally in person. Guitaut's later friendship with the marquise de Sévigné gives added insight into the relationship between the two men.

Chapter 6, "Different Worlds," concerns the seemingly diverse worlds in which Chausson and Guitaut lived, but it will also reveal extraordinary overlaps between the two men's lives. The question of whether Condé would have been aware of the four-line song will be raised in connection to his knowledge of the Pont Neuf song culture. Finally, three names are mentioned and debated as possible authors of the song, leading to some intriguing conclusions.

This book does not try or claim to act as a chronological survey of all possible sound worlds from the seventeenth century; rather, it aims to encourage readers to acknowledge and embrace an aural dimension that has all too often been suppressed or forgotten and to offer a sense of the possibilities offered by sound studies in recovering and rediscovering the past.

Although Chausson's song will be the piece that both drives and dominates this book, many other songs, voices, and sounds will function as aural accompaniments to each chapter. It is striking how many of the writers, political figures, and personalities that we will encounter over the course of this book interact with each other on many levels, their voices performing an intricate counterpoint to both major political events and seemingly transitory moments. By learning to listen to early modern Paris, it is hoped that we can move beyond our overreliance on the visual and better appreciate the complexity and fascination of a vibrant oral culture.

PART I

THE POWER
OF SOUND

CHAPTER 1

The Sounds of Paris

When examining the life of a city from three or four centuries ago, it seems almost axiomatic that one's attention will be drawn immediately to whatever is still accessible to the modern eye. The easy availability of books and images of monuments, buildings, paintings, sculptures, engravings, and prints to future generations has given the visual inevitable priority over the auditory. Where the ear is concerned, however, before the advent of recording technology in the twentieth century, once a sound was made it disappeared immediately and remained unrecorded for posterity. Musical notation has allowed for certain kinds of music from the period to be performed, but the diverse sounds that were part of daily life would seem to be unrecoverable. In other words, there appears to exist a disparity between the permanent, material nature of the visual and the fleeting, transitory, intangible quality of what is heard.

Yet to pass over the role played by sound in premodern times would both underestimate the real significance of the transient and ignore an essential component of what makes up the premodern world and the people who inhabited that world. Often it is precisely the very evanescence of a sound that makes it all the more memorable or intense, such as the beauty of a musical phrase heard live, a remembered conversation, or even the silence of a shared moment.[1] Brandon Labelle vividly sums up the different kinds of information that even a brief sound can produce: "The seemingly innocent trajectory of sound as it moves from its source and toward a listener, without forgetting all the surfaces, bodies, and other sounds it brushes against, is a story imparting a great deal of information fully charged with geographic, social, psychological, and emotional energy. My feeling is that an entire history and culture can be found within a single sound."[2] Recent scholarship in the thriving area of sound studies has made an attempt to move away from using terminology derived overwhelmingly from visual culture (with expressions such as "soundscapes" and "sound mark") by emphasizing the distinctive qualities of sound.[3] Other thinkers, such as Jean-Luc Nancy, have questioned the dominance of visuality in phenomenological philosophy.[4] In his short work *À l'écoute* (*Listening*), which explores the relationship between sound, bodily sense, and self, he specifically rejects reflection on the presence of sound in visual terms (with expressions such as "en vue de" [in view of] or "vis-à-vis"); instead, he considers "présence au sens d'un 'en présence de'" (presence in the sense of an "in the presence of"). "It is an 'in the presence of' that does not let itself be objectified or projected outward. That is why it is first of all presence in the sense of a *present* that is not a being (at least not in the intransitive, stable, consistent sense of the word), but rather a *coming* and a *passing*, an *extending* and a *penetrating*. Sound essentially comes and expands, or is deferred and transferred."[5] Such protean qualities lead Nancy to consider the way in which sound opens up its own space, a space that is "omnidimensional and transversate through all spaces."[6]

The penetrative nature of sound is exemplified by the difficulty one has in suppressing or ignoring noise as opposed to the relative ease with which one can block out the sight of something simply by closing one's eyes (when awake or asleep). As the historical and cultural geographer George Revill puts it, "The substantially passive receptivity of hearing and its 365-degree field of reception ensure that sounds encompass us while at the same time seeming to reverberate deep inside our heads. Thus sound brings us into intimate contact with activities, actions and events that lie well outside the reach of other senses, behind us, round the corner or over the next hill."[7]

Although a sound may occasionally be intensified by the sight of what is creating that sound, it is not reliant on the other senses for it to be heard. Moreover, whereas the view of a building or a street or even a landscape will be identical or similar from day to day, the sounds surrounding them are rarely exactly the same.

Brandon Labelle's thesis that sound can be used as a model for thinking and experiencing what he calls "the contemporary condition"[8] perhaps exposes the assumption that sounds from the distant past cannot be recaptured in the way that current sounds can. However, I would argue that the story enclosed within sound is possibly even more highly charged in the seventeenth century than it is in the present time, for, as I hope to show, the impossibility of recording sounds prior to the twentieth century meant that they carried even greater urgency and possible danger to those who were unable to capture or silence them.[9] Labelle's notion of sound as "promiscuous" is enormously suggestive in this regard,[10] for even if a sound can have an immediate effect on one listener or several listeners, it cannot be fully contained, defying conventional modes of representation and mediation;[11] as soon as it belongs to us, it is no longer with us.

So many ordinary and extraordinary events in history are defined by sound and noise that it seems perverse for subsequent scholarly research to have all but ignored their significance. Jacques Attali makes the interesting point that Western scholarship has over the ages been misguided in trying to understand the world through sight rather than hearing, arguing that the world has always listened to itself: "Our scientific research has always desired to monitor, measure, abstract, and castrate meaning, forgetting that life is full of noise and that death alone is silent: work noise, celebratory noise, noises of daily life and of nature; noise bought, sold, imposed, prohibited; noise of revolt, revolution, rage, despair."[12] Many such noises, as heard in the urban setting of Paris during the seventeenth and eighteenth centuries, will be the story of this book, for the early modern city was filled with sounds that could be disturbing, comforting, seductive, repellent, received in very different ways by different listeners, but always sounds that were, as Niall Atkinson writes with reference to Renaissance Florence, "burdened with meaning."[13]

The lack of any scientific instruments that could have recorded noise and acoustic levels in early modern Paris means that it is impossible to reproduce the actual sounds that were heard on the street at the time. Our best way of recapturing, however imperfectly, those sounds must be through the (mostly written) accounts of people from the time. However, such depictions of sounds that have been heard are themselves fraught with difficulty. For a start, a seventeenth- or eighteenth-century ear would have been attuned to and accustomed to very different sounds from those perceived by the modern ear; noises in the background that might have been so familiar to an early modern listener as to be unworthy of mention would very probably sound extraordinary to a modern listener, and vice versa. Moreover, those chroniclers of sound from a number of centuries ago would come to their descriptions weighed down with the baggage of their own prejudices and preconceptions. Inevitably, the kind of people writing down their impressions would have been more likely to come from the educated classes and so might have depicted such sounds as the street cries of peddlers either in an overly idealistic way or simply as a nuisance.[14] It is therefore with these notes of caution in mind that we might most productively explore representations of sound and noise from the time while at the same time embracing the wealth of aural detail that gives us the opportunity to listen in to the sonic spaces of the city.

Roland Barthes's oft-quoted opening sentence to his brief essay "Écoute" (usually translated as "Listening" but more accurately rendered as the imperative "Listen!"),[15] "*Hearing* is a physiological phenomenon; *listening* is a psychological act,"[16] can act as a helpful starting point to our examination of the sounds of early modern Paris. Hearing amounts to an unconscious, passive awareness of the sounds that surround us: as James Batcho puts it, "In this mode, the soundscape of the world is uneventful and unworthy of noticing."[17] Listening, on the other hand, involves the conscious, active processing of even the most seemingly uneventful of sounds. In many ways, we will come across early modern poets and writers finding meaning in, and applying their own prejudices to, the daily noises that many of the people inhabiting that sound world would not find remarkable. Our task will be to listen to, rather than hear, the extraordinary range of sounds that emanate from this world, where the smallest four-line song can be found to have as much meaning as the grandest, most overwhelming of sounds.

Almost all contemporary accounts of early modern Paris remain as alert to the sounds as to the sights of a city in transformation. Arlette Farge's observation about eighteenth-century Paris that "one heard the city before seeing it, as people noted at the time" holds true for the seventeenth century also.[18] At the beginning of his Satire VI, titled "Les Embarras de Paris" (first published in 1666 but likely to have been written a few years earlier),[19] the poet and critic Nicolas Boileau gives a vivid description of a city assailed by noise:

> Qui frappe l'air, bon Dieu! de ces lugubres cris?
> Est-ce donc pour veiller qu'on se couche à Paris?[20]
>
> (Good Lord! Who is striking the air with these lugubrious cries? /
> Do we go to bed in Paris in order to stay awake?)

Significantly, all the sounds that the poet hears as he tries to settle down for the night are from outside, and out of sight. Even though he may require visual memory to recognize the noises, he is disturbed by them because they are outside his field of vision and beyond his immediate control, unlike indoor noise, which comes from fewer sources and can more easily be silenced.[21] Here we find what Nancy calls the "property of penetration and ubiquity" of sound.[22] After complaining about the sound made by cats, rats, and mice, the poet continues with a list of all the noises that prevent him from sleeping:

> Tout conspire à la fois à troubler mon repos,
> Et je me plains ici du moindre de mes maux:
> Car à peine les coqs, commençant leur ramage,
> Auront des cris aigus frappé le voisinage
> Qu'un affreux serrurier, laborieux Vulcain,
> Qu'éveillera bientôt l'ardente soif du gain,
> Avec un fer maudit, qu'à grand bruit il apprête,
> De cent coups de marteau me va fendre la tête.
> J'entends déjà partout les charrettes courir,
> Les maçons travailler, les boutiques s'ouvrir:
> Tandis que dans les airs mille cloches émues
> D'un funèbre concert font retentir les nues;
> Et, se mêlant au bruit de la grêle et des vents,
> Pour honorer les morts font mourir les vivans.[23]

(Everything conspires all at once to trouble my restfulness, / And I complain here only of the least of my woes; / For hardly will the cocks have started to crow / With their shrill cries shaking the neighborhood, / Before a grim locksmith, like a laborious Vulcan, / That the ardent thirst for profit will soon awake, / With cursèd iron prepares noisily / To split open my head with a hundred hammer blows. / Everywhere I hear already wagons trundling, / Masons working, shops opening, / While at the same time a thousand agitated church bells / Make the clouds echo with a funereal concert of sound; / And, mingling with the noise of hail and winds, / Make those alive die while the bells honor the dead.)

The piece continues with the poet venturing outdoors and finding that "c'est encor pis vingt fois en quittant la maison" (it's twenty times worse when leaving the house),[24] as he encounters the noise made by crowds of people (including swearing lackeys), clattering carriages, barking dogs, mooing cows, mules with bells around their necks, and the indistinct cries of passersby.[25]

Even allowing for Boileau's poetic license to stray from the realms of documentary realism,[26] this evocation of an early modern city assailed on all sides by sounds is one shared by numerous other commentators from the time. The thinness of the walls of houses, especially belonging to the poor, meant that street noises would penetrate interior spaces without any difficulty; by the same token, shouts, curses, and laughter from within houses or rooms flowed out onto staircases and the street, making it easy, as Arlette Farge has argued in reference to the eighteenth century, for rumors about people's personal lives to circulate rapidly.[27]

The reference in the Boileau satire to a thousand bells ringing was in reality not as far-fetched as it might seem, as bells were rung not only to summon the faithful to every kind of Mass and to weddings and funerals but also to mark the passing of time, with bells sounding the Angelus at the beginning and end of every day, and with workers and their employers measuring time by yet further bells that signaled each hour (and even quarter and half hours). Writing in the mid-eighteenth century, Rémi Carré even attests to bells being rung during thunderstorms "in order to calm or deflect them."[28]

Often reliant on stereotypical images of the contrast between rural quiet and urban clamor, the depictions of Paris bring to the fore the notion of a completely disordered world, one that is socially structured and very clearly linked to social class.[29] Peter Denney, writing about the late eighteenth century in England, uses the helpful term "plebeian noise," for in almost all cases written depictions of noise and disorder are created by literate and distinctly nonplebeian writers about the noises made largely by working-class urban dwellers.[30]

Thus, as Claude Louis Berthod (also spelled Berthaud) writes in the preface to the 1654 edition of his work *La Ville de Paris* (first published two years earlier), he is interested in presenting to his provincial reader not the visual magnificence of the city but rather "la confusion et le desordre" (its confusion and disorder).[31] The poet Claude Le Petit, whom we shall encounter again later in this book, satirizes the world of the Parisian food markets (Les Halles) in his work *Paris Ridicule* (Ridiculous Paris, first published in 1668 but written before 1662, the year of the poet's death) through his association of overwhelming sounds with the notion of total disarray:

Fut-il jamais clameurs pareilles?
Si le Ciel n'a pitié de moy,

Je deviendray sourd, par ma foy,
En despit de mes deux oreilles:
Chacun parle et nul ne respond,
Chacun se mesle et se confond,
Tout marche, tout tourne, tout vire.
Après cela, Père Eternel,
Qui ne croira, dans cet Empire,
Le mouvement perpetuel?³²

(Was there ever such perpetual clamor? / Unless Heaven takes pity on me, / Believe me, I will become deaf, / In spite of my two ears: / Everybody talks and nobody replies, / Everybody gets into a jumble and confusion, / Everything walks, turns, wheels around. / After that, Eternal Father, / Who in this Empire will not believe in / Perpetual motion?)

Such mayhem is only exacerbated later in the same piece, in a section titled "Embarras de la confusion de Paris" (Perplexity from the confusion of Paris), where the poet exclaims:

De tous costez, on me dit *Gare*!
Et je ne sçay duquel tourner:
Dans cet horrible tintamarre,
On n'entendroit pas Dieu tonner.³³

(On every side, people say *Watch out*! to me, / And I do not know which way to turn: / In this awful jangling, / You could not even hear a thunderclap.)

The diverse cries of street sellers or tradespeople, known as *Cris de Paris* (Cries of Paris), which had been characteristic of Paris life since medieval times and had been represented in musical form by composers such as Clément Janequin in the sixteenth century,³⁴ formed an integral part of the cacophony associated with this early modern urban sound world. These workers were invariably depicted textually and pictorially as character types, and the cries of their trades were often described as disruptive and raucous.³⁵ When she finds herself in the countryside, for example, the marquise de Sévigné is able to write, "Un bruit des oiseaux [...] nous a paru bien plus joli que les vilains cris des rues de Paris" (The noise made by birds . . . seemed much more pleasant to us than the base street cries of Paris).[36] No observer of Paris during this time is more alert to such sounds than the eighteenth-century moralist and reformer Louis-Sébastien Mercier, who depicts the noises emitted by "le petit peuple" (the common people) in largely negative terms:

> Le petit peuple est naturellement braillard à l'excès; il pousse sa voix avec une discordance choquante. On entend de tous côtés des cris rauques, aigus, sourds. *Voilà le maquereau qui n'est pas mort; il arrive! Il arrive! Des harengs qui glacent, des harengs nouveaux! Pommes cuites au four! Il brûle, il brûle! Ce sont des gâteaux froids. Voilà le plaisir des dames! Voilà le plaisir. C'est du croquet. A la barque, à la barque, à l'écailler! Ce sont des huîtres. Portugal, Portugal!* Ce sont des oranges.
>
> Joignez à ces cris les clameurs confuses des frippiers ambulans, des vendeurs de parasols, de vieille ferraille, des porteurs-d'eau. Les hommes ont des cris de femmes, et les femmes des cris d'hommes. C'est un glapissement perpétuel; et l'on ne sauroit peindre le ton et l'accent de cette pitoyable criaillerie, lorsque toutes ces voix réunies viennent à se croiser dans un carrefour.[37]

(The common people are by nature excessively braying: they sound their voices with shocking discord. On all sides harsh, piercing, dull voices can be heard. *Here's mackerel not yet dead; it's arriving! It's arriving! Frozen herring, new herring! Apples cooked in the oven! It is burning hot! It is burning hot! Here are cold cakes! Here's women's pleasure! Here's pleasure!* This is a dainty morsel. *All aboard, all aboard, come to the fish scaler!* These are oysters. *Portugal! Portugal!* These are oranges. Join with these cries the confused clamor of wandering clothes-menders, parasol vendors, old iron, water carriers. Men have the cries of women, and women the cries of men. There is a perpetual bawling, and it is hard to depict the tone and accent of this pitiable babbling, when all these voices come together at a crossroads.)

Often the most discordant sounds were heard when street cries clashed with the different kinds of music played in street fairs, such as the Foire Saint-Germain (which took place over a period of three to five weeks around the Easter festival) and the Foire Saint-Laurent (which generally lasted from early August to late September). The writer Paul Scarron's *Foire Saint-Germain*, first published in 1654, provides a vivid depiction of such sounds:

> Ces Cochers ont beau se haster,
> Ils ont beau crier, gare, gare,
> Ils sont contraints de s'arrester,
> Dans la presse rien ne démare,
> Le bruit des penetrans sifflets,
> Des flustes et des flageolets,
> Des cornets, hautsbois et muzettes,
> Des Vendeurs et des Acheteurs,
> Se mesle à celuy des Sauteurs,
> Et des Tabourins à sonnettes,
> Des joüeurs de Marionnettes,
> Que le peuple croit enchanteurs.[38]

(These coachmen make haste in vain, / They cry in vain, look out, look out, / They are forced to stop, / In the throng nothing gets going, / The noise of penetrating whistles, / Of flutes and pipes, / Of cornets, oboes, and bagpipes, / Of vendors and purchasers, / Mingles with the noise of acrobats, / And drums with bells, / And Puppeteers, / Whom the people think are magicians.)

François Colletet's evocation of the Foire Saint-Laurent a few years later gives a similar impression of overwhelming noise as flutes and drums vie for attention:

> N'as-tu point déja les oreilles
> Aussi pleines que des bouteilles,
> Du bruit que font tant de chifflets?
> Donne une paire de soufflets
> A ces fripons qui t'étourdissent,
> Il semble que tes mains languissent,
> Romps leurs flûtes et leurs tambours
> Qui nous vont rendre presque sourds,
> Et puis tourne deçà ta veuë.[39]

(Don't you already have ears / As full as bottles, / From the noise made by so many whistles? Administer a pair of clouts / To these rascals who make you giddy, / Your hands seem to droop, / Snatch their flutes and drums / Which are going to make us almost deaf, / And then turn away your gaze.)

It should not be forgotten that the (often negative) emphasis on deafening and dissonant urban sounds that we have witnessed in these portrayals of Parisian daily life was useful for the primarily satirical or moralistic purposes of such writers. However, for visitors to Paris, such as the English physician Martin Lister, who wrote an account of his stay in Paris during 1698, noises such as the reverberating sounds of coaches being driven through the narrow streets are described in rather more harmonious terms: "It must needs be said, the streets are very narrow, and the Passengers a-foot no ways secured from the hurry and danger of Coaches, which always pass the Streets with an air of haste; and a full trot upon broad flat Stones, betwixt high and large resounding Houses, makes a sort of Musick which should seem very agreeable to the *Parisians*."[40]

Pont Neuf: Making Noise

One Parisian space in the early modern period is defined above all by noise and disorder: the Pont Neuf. We will be revisiting this crucial location at several junctures over the course of this book. An engraving titled "L'Embaras [*sic*] de Paris" (Confusion of Paris) from around 1700 by Nicolas Guérard (fig. 2) appears to give sound equal prominence to sight in the depiction of chaotic scenes on the Pont Neuf at that time.

The picture shows a melee of horses, sheep, and women and men of all classes, including people selling their wares, a wide variety of carriages, store holders, actors, singers, drummers, and no doubt other musicians. The accompanying six-line verse, with its entreaty to keep ears open, gives even more emphasis to the sounds of a busy thoroughfare:

> Pour marcher dans Paris ayés les yeux alertes,
> Tenez de tous côtez vos oreilles ouvertes,
> Pour n'être pas heurté culbutté ou blessé,
> Car si vous n'écoutez parmy le tintamarre
> Garre garre la bas Garre rengez vous garre
> Ou du haut ou du bas vous serez écrasé.

Fig. 2   Nicolas Guérard, "L'Embaras [sic] de Paris." Photo: BnF.

(In order to walk in Paris, keep your eyes alert, / Keep your ears open to all sides, / So as not to be knocked over, overturned, or injured, / Because if you do not hear in the middle of the jangling / Look out, look out down there, get out of the way, look out, / You will be crushed from above or below.)

Such disarray and dissonance might at first seem emblematic of a disordered old world, but in fact the unruly crowds and carriages testify to the bridge's widespread popularity at the time, considered by all to be a magnificent example of modern engineering. The diarist John Evelyn writes at length on what he calls "this stately bridge," not only marveling at the impressiveness of its construction but also dwelling on "the confluence of the people and multitude of coaches passing every moment over the bridge," with the added sonic contribution of the Samaritaine hydraulic water pump (located at the foot of one of the bridge's arches). The Samaritaine included a carillon that sounded the hours and even played a variety of tunes, contributing greatly to the bridge's very different sound worlds, as duly noted by Evelyn:[41] "Above, is a very rare dial of several motions,

Fig. 3   Eighteenth-century engraving of the Samaritaine water pump. Photo: Adam Merton.

with a chime, etc. The water is conveyed by huge wheels, pumps, and engines from the river beneath."⁴² Providing water to the Louvre and the Tuileries, the Samaritaine (fig. 3), named after a sculpture on the facade representing Christ and the Samaritan woman at Jacob's well, taken from the Gospel of John, chapter 4, was a major piece of civil engineering and, like the bridge itself, the object of admiration by locals and visitors alike. The chiming clock and bells, which sounded at regular intervals, punctuated and gave rhythm to people's lives, providing what Alain Corbin describes in a different context—nineteenth-century bells—as "the temporal architecture of life, the habitus."⁴³

In *How Paris Became Paris: The Invention of the Modern City*, Joan DeJean makes the compelling argument that various construction projects during the reigns of Henri IV and Louis XIV were even more influential in reshaping Paris than Haussmann's nineteenth-century overhaul of the city. Among the most innovative building schemes, DeJean singles out the Place Royale (now the Place des Vosges), which was the first purpose-built public recreational space in any European capital, and the Pont Neuf. The Pont Neuf was completed in 1606 and inaugurated by Henri IV in 1607. Constructed out of stone instead of wood, paved throughout, and measuring nearly one thousand feet in length and seventy-five feet in width, it was the first bridge to cross the Seine in a single span. And it completely revolutionized the way that Parisians moved about and viewed their city. Unlike older bridges that had houses built on them, such as the earlier version of the Pont au Change and the Pont Notre-Dame, and a later bridge such as the Pont Marie, the Pont Neuf allowed pedestrians and carriages the opportunity to move across the bridge, linking the Right and Left Banks. Moreover, the provision of wide, raised pavements enabled pedestrians to enjoy views of the river, away from the bustle of vehicles. For the first time, aristocrats discovered the pleasures of being on foot, and the Pont Neuf became indelibly linked with such an activity, to the extent that the marquise de Sévigné urges her daughter traveling in Provence, "Ne faites point le Pont-Neuf" (Don't do a Pont Neuf),[44] but to go on horseback or in a litter instead. DeJean has shown the ways in which the bridge was a "great social leveler,"[45] with people of all classes rubbing shoulders. This close proximity of men and women from different classes on the Pont Neuf will in ways both direct and indirect punctuate the discussion of the following chapters.

The bridge also performed the function of being the city's first truly communal entertainment space, with actors performing on makeshift stages, singers presenting the latest songs, puppeteers, organ-grinders, and newssheets and song sheets (which became known as *ponts-neufs*) being sold. Boileau, in *L'Art poétique* (The poetic art, 1674), his influential treatise on different genres of writing written in conscious imitation of the ancient Roman poet Horace, evokes his ideal playwright, who "plaît par la raison seule" (pleases through reason alone). Any writer or performer who prefers to indulge in morally dubious or salacious subject matter should go, he suggests, "sur deux tréteaux monté, / Amusant le pont Neuf de ses sornettes fades, / Aux laquais assemblés jouer ses mascarades" (on two table stands / Entertaining the Pont Neuf with unsavory tales / And acting out his masquerades to the assembled lackeys).[46]

Over the course of the seventeenth century, to quote DeJean, "whenever a major event transpired in seventeenth-century Paris, it either took place on the Pont Neuf or was first talked about on the Pont Neuf."[47] As Mercier, writing in the eighteenth century, shows, the Pont Neuf became the most important meeting point for the widest variety of people in Paris:

Le Pont-Neuf est dans la ville ce que le cœur est dans le corps humain, le centre du mouvement et de la circulation. Le flux et le reflux des habitans et des étrangers frappent tellement ce passage, que, pour rencontrer les personnes qu'on cherche, il suffit de s'y promener une heure chaque jour.[48]

(The Pont-Neuf is to the city what the heart is to the human body, the center of movement and circulation. The ebb and flow of inhabitants and foreigners so block this passage that, if you want to encounter people that you are searching for, you need to walk there for one hour every day.)

With the convergence of book stalls, shops, street sellers, quacks, tooth pullers, performers of all kinds, and the many pedestrians, the Pont Neuf was overrun with people, both rich and poor. Germain Brice, author of perhaps the first guidebook to Paris, *Description nouvelle de ce qu'il y a de plus intéressant et de plus remarquable dans la ville de Paris* (1684), notes that the feature of the bridge that most astonishes visitors to the city is "la presse continuelle qui se trouve incessamment sur ce Pont" (the constant throng to be found at all times on this bridge).[49] Inevitably, therefore, such an assortment of people attracted thieves and criminals, perhaps most vividly described by Berthod in a section of his *La Ville de Paris en vers burlesques* titled "Les Filouteries du Pont-Neuf" (The crimes of the Pont Neuf):

> Vous, rendez-vous de Charlatans,
> De Filoux, de passe-volans,
> Pont Neuf, ordinaire theatre
> De Vendeurs d'onguent et d'emplastre,
> Sejour des Arracheurs de dents,
> Des Fripiers, Libraires, Pedans,
> Des Chanteurs de chansons nouvelles,
> D'Entremetteurs de Damoiselles,
> De Coupe-bourses, d'Argotiers,
> De Maistres de sales mestiers,
> D'Operateurs et de Chimiques,
> Et de Medecins spagiriques,
> De fins joüeurs de gobelets,
> De ceux qui rendent des poulets.[50]

(You, meeting place of quacks, / Thieves, false soldiers, / Pont Neuf, common theatre / Of vendors of ointments and plasters, / Abode of tooth pullers, / Of clothes vendors, booksellers, pedants, / Singers of new songs, / Pimps of young ladies, / Cut-purses, wranglers, / Masters of filthy trades, / Quack-salvers and chemists, / And alchemist doctors, / Impostors, / Deliverers of love letters.)

The term "filou," which initially had the precise sense of someone who stole cloaks and was directly associated with the Pont Neuf, came to have the more general meaning of a thief or crooked character.[51] Indeed, with fabric and cloth worth a great deal of money, cloaks were the most commonly stolen commodity on the Pont Neuf, especially at night. For example, the Anglo-Welsh historian James Howell, while visiting Paris during 1620, writes that "there is never a night passeth but some robbing or murder is committed in this town, so that it is not safe to go late anywhere, specially about the Pont-Neuf," before recounting how a secretary of state, accompanied by his valet on the bridge after dark, had encountered two armed robbers, who "unmantled him of a new plush cloak."[52] The Scottish traveler William Lithgow similarly describes Paris in the early years of the seventeenth century as "a tumultuous place, a nocturnal den of theeves, and a confused multitude."[53]

The inclusion above by Berthod of "Des Chanteurs de chansons nouvelles" (singers of new songs) among the list of charlatans and pimps that are to be seen and heard on the Pont Neuf might seem to be out of place, but in fact the singing of songs in public was considered a crime and was officially prohibited. The dangers of performing songs in public had been signaled in rulings such as the "Règlement general pour la Police de Paris" (General ruling by the Paris police) of 30 March 1635 in which it was stated, "Sont faites défenses [. . .] à Chanteurs de Chansons de s'arrester en aucun lieu, et faire assemblée du peuple" (Singers of songs are forbidden from lingering and assembling people in any location), with the suggested punishment "de prison, et du foüet" (of prison and a whipping).[54] Given the reality that songs and singers proliferated in the city at the time, it is probable that these rulings were intended as deterrents and that the recommended punishments were not carried out frequently. However, the act of performing before a crowd on the Pont Neuf was nonetheless suffused with danger, and retribution remained a constant possibility. Certainly those in authority remained sufficiently concerned that large audiences on the bridge might hear a variety of potentially seditious songs and so would have spies ("mouchards") placed on the bridge and in the streets to listen to the songs in order to report those deemed to be harmful, either on a political or a moral level.[55] Indeed, one letter, written on 17 January 1703 by Jérôme Phélypeaux, comte de Pontchartrain, who was secretary of the state of the navy and the king's chamber, to Jean Phélypeaux, "Intendant de Paris," writes of the arrest of certain singers and peddlers of songs: "Les chanteurs du Pont-Neuf et les colporteurs chantent depuis quelque temps, et distribuent par la ville, des chansons infâmes; quelques-uns ont esté arrestez" (The singers of Pont Neuf and the sheet peddlers have been singing for some time, and distributing disgraceful songs; some of them have been arrested).[56] From 1667 onward (after Louis XIV appointed his first lieutenant general of police), all song texts were supposed to be read and approved by the police.

During times of unrest, such as the civil insurrections (the Frondes) during the middle years of the seventeenth century, the latest news was conveyed through politically motivated documents and songs known as the "mazarinades."[57] The nineteenth-century dramatist and librettist Eugène Scribe, in his *Discours de réception à l'Académie française* of 28 January 1836, highlights the important role played by song during the years that absolute royal authority asserted itself:

> En France et sous nos rois, la chanson fut longtemps la seule opposition possible. On définissait le gouvernement d'alors une monarchie absolue tempérée par des chansons; et c'était là en effet le seul contrepoids, la seule résistance aux empiètements de l'autorité.[58]
>
> (In France and under the reign of our kings, song was for a long time the only possible way of opposition. The government of the time was defined as an absolute monarchy tempered by songs, and that was in effect the only counterweight, the only form of resistance to the encroachment of authority.)

Similarly, during the Revolution, at the same time that republican repression was severely curtailing printed outputs, song production soared.[59] Such proliferation of songs does not mean that these forms of opposition were readily accepted by those in authority; rather, they were far more effective means of protest, because of both the high number of songs being produced and the difficulty of tracking them down.[60]

Bruce Smith's argument about early modern English ballads and the political implications of the use of voice and acoustic space holds true when considering street songs: "As voice projects the singer into the acoustic space around him, as the singer takes her place in a speech community, so the ballad ranges outward to grasp authority figures and draw them by force into the singer's song."[61] At moments of political crisis, or, as we will see in chapter 3, when one prominent personality (Nicolas Fouquet) was placed on trial, all those authority figures involved become subsumed into individual songs where political conventions or orthodoxies are questioned or thrown into doubt.

A large majority of the songs to be found in manuscript collections have little or no overt political purpose, concentrating more on (often salacious) gossip circulating at the time. The Pont Neuf as the locus of both buying song sheets containing such gossip and hearing them performed seems crucial here. As a bridge between different sides of the city, with the Seine flowing beneath, the Pont Neuf encapsulates both the transience of the songs that were sung and the movement between different worlds that forms so much of their subject matter. Moreover, the social and gender mixing that the bridge enabled was ideally suited to the way that gossip functions, for gossip can just as easily be about valets and servants as it can be about the rich and famous, and the performance of songs on the Pont Neuf makes such gossip available to and consumed by all. Although these songs might not have had the dangerous impact of overtly political pieces, their often amused or tolerant tone toward sexual or moral excesses made them objects of suspicion to religious authorities and members of the governing elite, who often found themselves ridiculed in the songs.

Despite some songs seeming not to be political, we should not forget the political implications of any sound world. As Sarah Kay and François Noudelmann have argued, "The political dimensions of a soundscape are manifest in how it reflects and determines relationships between individuals and groups and how it intersects with gender, race and class, with an urban or rural setting. A soundscape is thus a means to comprehend the social economy in which we live and the sonic ecology of our existence."[62] We will discover many such intersections during the course of this book.

The combination of the dubious morality and the orality of songs was furthermore considered by theorists of good taste and *galanterie* in the early modern period to be particularly troubling. In diplomat and courtier François de Callières's 1692 treatise devoted to *raillerie* (translated by Cotgrave in his dictionary as "jesting"),⁶³ *Des bons mots et des bons contes*, instances of wordplay are considered distasteful, precisely because "l'oreille a plus de part que l'esprit à leur découverte" (the ear plays a greater part than the mind in decoding them).⁶⁴ The fact that the sound of the joke has primary impact, without the restraining effect of reason (and good taste) being able to intervene, makes it particularly unsettling for those who are unable to prevent the sound from being emitted and heard. When later in the treatise Callières moves to an examination of song as the origin of French *raillerie*, it is the orality of word and music in conjunction with each other that is signaled as especially poisonous:

> Les François sont les inventeurs d'une autre maniere d'exercer leurs railleries, en laquelle ils excellent sur toutes les autres nations, c'est en ces chansons plaisantes et malignes qui courent frequemment, et dont les Auteurs sont d'ordinaire inconnus, elles ne sont presque jamais produites par les Poëtes de profession, ce sont des gens de la Cour, de la ville, ou des troupes qui étant en débauche et plus échauffés par le vin que par l'amour du prochain, les font d'ordinaire à table et le verre à la main, ce sont aussi quelquefois des Dames peu charitables, qui font contre d'autres Dames ou contre des hommes qui leur auront déplû, de ces chansons ingenieuses et plaisantes, dont le venin est d'autant plus dangereux, qu'étant animé par l'harmonie du chant et de la Poësie, il s'insinuë agréablement en flatant l'oreille des Auditeurs et la malignité qui regne parmi les hommes, et que ces sortes de chansons s'apprennent avec beaucoup de facilité, et ne s'oublient pas si facilement.⁶⁵

> (The French have invented a different way of making jests, in which they excel over all other nations, and that is found in the jovial and malicious songs that frequently make the rounds; the authors of these songs are usually unknown, and the songs are hardly ever written by professional poets but rather by people from Court or town, or by troops in a state of debauchery more fired up by wine than by love for one's neighbor, usually performing them at table with glass in hand; sometimes they are written by ladies of a rather uncharitable disposition who create them in order to oppose other ladies or men who have displeased them; they compose ingenious and jovial songs, whose venom is all the more dangerous, being animated by

the harmony and poetry of song; the venom insinuates itself pleasantly, all the while flattering the listener's ear with a maliciousness that reigns among men; these kinds of song are very easily learned and not so easily forgotten.)

The idea expressed by Callières at the end of this passage, that songs flatter the listener's ear in such a way as to be both easily learnable and unforgettable, reveals the specific power inherent in songs that made authorities so keen to try to suppress them: not only did their orality and the anonymity of their creators make it difficult to control their dissemination, but also their very memorability meant that performers and listeners alike were able to retain their scurrilous content without there being documentary proof available to those attempting to police them.[66]

Other measures needed to be taken by authorities to try to stem the spread of what Callières called "venin" (venom).

Sound Control: *The Chansonnier Maurepas*

During the eighteenth century in France, numerous anthologies of songs were assembled, mainly for the purpose of private performance. Perhaps the most interesting and in some ways atypical collection is the multivolume *Chansonnier Maurepas*, which would seem to have been created principally for historical, documentary, or anecdotal reasons. Largely comprising satirical, subversive, or bawdy songs, vaudevilles, and poems from the seventeenth and first half of the eighteenth centuries, the Maurepas songbooks do not on the whole contain any musical notation, but each song is usually accompanied by the title of a popular tune of the day. People performing or listening to the songs would have easily recognized the melody and could have adapted a wide range of different texts to a smaller number of well-known tunes.[67]

Initially compiled, put into chronological order, annotated, and bound in separate volumes by the royal genealogist Pierre Clairambault (1651–1740), the songbooks were later augmented with eighteenth-century texts and recopied in an admirably clear hand under the supervision of the comte de Maurepas, Jean-Frédéric Phélypeaux (1701–81), who was an administrator and military strategist under Louis XV and minister of state under Louis XVI until his death, and who encapsulated, according to Émile Raunié, "the facetious and biting spirit of the age."[68] It was the comte de Maurepas's father, Jérôme Phélypeaux, whose 1703 letter about the arrest of singers and peddlers we have just seen. Clairambault's notes are often extensive and display both erudition (derived from memoirs and histories of the time, which he had read assiduously) and a vivid awareness of the veracity or inaccuracy of gossip contained within the songs (gained from acquaintance with and anecdotal knowledge of people evoked in the songs). Although precise dates are sometimes left blank, clearly with the expectation of being filled in at a later stage, his detailed knowledge of battles and historical events helps explain even the most obscure pieces.

The vast majority of the songs contained in the volumes are anonymous, and, given their often scandalous content, their authors would very probably have remained unnamed even at the time the songs were first performed. Indeed, many songs explicitly draw attention to the fact that nobody knows who wrote them, thereby in some ways exonerating the singers from blame over their content and protecting their creators from being identified.[69]

One of the origins of the songbooks compiled by Clairambault and Maurepas underlines the need for the songwriters to preserve their anonymity. The first lieutenant generals of police (appointed by Louis XIV) in Paris, Gabriel-Nicolas de la Reynie (who remained in the role from 1667 to 1697) and Marc René d'Argenson (in the post from 1697 to 1718), noted down in their *gazetins* (bulletins) those songs sung in the streets that were deemed to be potentially subversive or provocative. Many of the songs were copied from these police bulletins by Clairambault.[70] As Clairambault began collecting scurrilous songs in the years before the establishment of the police lieutenancy general, it would indicate that such songs were already being monitored and written down for surveillance purposes.

The very notion of what constituted a crime is questioned in a number of the songs that were being collected by the authorities. One song, dating from 1650, exposes the very different standards applied to court and town:

> Ce qu'on nomme un crime à Paris,
> En Cour n'est que bagatelle;
> Les favoris y sont permis;
> Ce qu'on nomme un crime à Paris,
> En Cour si l'on se fait maris
> Jamais on n'epouse pucelle.
> Ce qu'on nomme un crime à Paris,
> En Cour n'est que bagatelle.[71]

(What is called a crime in Paris, / Is but a trifle in Court; / Favorites are allowed there; / What is called a crime in Paris, / If in Court you become a husband, / Never marry a virgin. / What is called a crime in Paris, / Is but a trifle in Court.)

While some songs helped serve as evidence in trials against those thought to have dissident or criminal tendencies, others remain useful to subsequent students of the period, for they are able either to provide invaluable information on events that have left no written trace or to give very different perspectives on crimes from those recorded in official transcripts.[72] Certainly, the legalistic terminology of interrogations usually gives little idea of the lives or personalities of those involved. Although songs often satirize and give a distorted idea of their subjects, the relative infrequency of moral condemnation in the songs allows for a more empathetic sense of the people depicted, as we will see in the second part of this book.

But before that, a brief examination is needed of the kinds of people who performed and listened to songs in early modern Paris, which will be the subject of the next chapter.

CHAPTER 2

Singers and Listeners

The way in which song exists in and supports a socially mixed space will be further developed in this chapter through the case studies of one singer, who felt more at home among the paupers gathered at the foot of the statue of Henri IV on the Pont Neuf, and one listener, who, though highly born, showed an eagerness to listen to the songs being performed on the bridge and elsewhere.

It is true to say that certain people made a (usually class-based) distinction between those songs sung in the streets or on the Pont Neuf and those songs performed in other settings. The Furetière dictionary, for example, which was first published in 1690, associates a particular kind of song with the common people, calling it "Petite piece de vers qu'on met en air pour chanter, et qui se chante par le peuple" (Small piece of verse that is put to a melody in order to sing, and which is sung by the people). The dictionary even gives a definition for "Vaudevilles ou chansons du Pont-neuf" as "les *chansons* communes qui se chantent parmi le peuple avec grande facilité et sans art" (common songs sung by the people with great facility and without artfulness).

Yet, as will be shown in this chapter, such seemingly clear-cut distinctions found in dictionary definitions and in the prejudices displayed, usually by upper-class listeners, are more complex than they might at first appear. Songs circulated from court to street and street to court, with sound enabling and even promoting the multidirectional movement of identities.

Singing but Not Seeing: Philippot Le Savoyard

With the dangers and severe regulations associated with singing songs on the Pont Neuf, we must ask who, exactly, was brave or foolhardy enough to perform such scurrilous songs at the time. Boileau devotes part of Chant II of his *Art poétique* to singers and songs, and, while warning that certain irreligious songs "conduisent tristement le plaisant à la Grève"[1] (lead the joker sadly to the scaffold—he is referring here to the execution in 1662 of the poet Claude Le Petit, whom we shall meet again later in this book), he evokes the French tradition of the itinerant street singer:

> Le Français, né malin, forma le vaudeville,
> Agréable Indiscret, qui, conduit par le chant,
> Passe de bouche en bouche et s'accroît en marchant.[2]

> (The French, born mischievous, created vaudeville, / Indiscreet and agreeable people, who, led by song, / Pass from mouth to mouth, gathering pace as they walk.)

In a section of his *Tableau de Paris*, titled "Chanteurs publics" (Public singers), Mercier gives a characteristically lively account of the different kinds of singer to be found within a few paces of each other, those who "lamentent de saints cantiques" (wail holy hymns), selling fragments of holy cloth (*scapulaires*) on the side, and those who "débitent des chansons gaillardes" (distribute bawdy songs). When it comes to which of the two kinds of singer is more popular, there is no contest:

> La chanson joyeuse fait déserter l'auditoire du vendeur de scapulaires; il reste seul sur son escabelle, montrant en vain avec sa baguette les cornes du démon tentateur, l'ennemi du genre humain. Chacun oublie le salut qu'il promet, pour courir à la chanson damnable. Le chanteur des réprouvés annonce le vin, la bonne chere et l'amour, célebre les attraits de Margot; et la piece de deux sols qui balançoit entre le cantique et le vaudeville, hélas! va tomber dans la poche du chantre mondain.[3]

> (The joyful song makes those listening to the vendor of holy cloth desert him; he remains alone on his low stool, pointing out in vain

with his stick the horns of a tempting demon, enemy of the human race. Everybody forgets the salvation that he is promising in order to run across to hear the condemnable song. The singer of the damned heralds wine, good living, and love, celebrating the attractions of Margot; and the two-sol piece that was balancing between the hymn and the vaudeville is going to fall, alas, into the worldly singer's pocket.)

Inevitably, the names of the vast majority of the singers and musicians have disappeared through both the necessity at the time to remain anonymous and the subsequent lack of surviving manuscript evidence.[4] However, many interesting details about the lives of these singers can be gleaned from various written and pictorial sources. Although the most famous singers from the time were male, we know not only that both women and men composed songs[5] but also that singing on the Pont Neuf was not a uniquely male privilege. Tallemant des Réaux, the writer and inveterate collector of anecdotes, for example, recounts how the poet Marc Maillet "alla trouver une femme qui chantoit sur le Pont-Neuf" (went to find a woman who sang on the Pont Neuf).[6] In the eighteenth century, a female singer known as Fanchon was reputed to have bought a house with the money earned from her singing.[7] Most singers lived on the margins of society, selling pamphlets with the words to the songs on them, rather like peddlers selling their wares.[8] Many of them were disabled, which suggests that their exclusion from mainstream employment forced them to earn a living through their music. The Pont Neuf, while being an attraction for all classes of people, seemed to embrace those who were marginalized by society and give them the means to live independently.

Of the names that are still known, nothing or little remains of their musical output. Engravings of street singers and musicians were included in a book published by Jacques Lagniet in Paris in 1663, but most appear to be character types with names such as Louis Organiste des Carrefours, Le Superius (a soprano), Le Contratenor, and Orlande de Lassus (supposedly a derisory nickname for a mediocre singer).[9] Other named singers include Charles Minard, who specialized in salacious songs; the Coachman of M. de Verthamont, who still wore the livery of his former master and who reportedly survived by committing crimes on the Pont Neuf at night while singing there by day; and, in the mid-eighteenth century, the hurdy-gurdy player Michel Leclerc, who performed execution songs on the nearby Place

Fig. 4
Gérard Audran, "Guillaume de Limoge." Photo © Musée Carnavalet / Roger-Viollet.

de Grève, some of which were believed to have been commissioned by the police, who wanted the crowds to listen to appropriately moralizing songs about soon-to-be-executed criminals.[10]

One singer who caught the attention of both musicians and artists was Guillaume de Limoges, known as Le Gaillard Boiteux (the Cheerful Lame Man, named as such because of his physical disabilities), who used to perform on the Pont Neuf. François Couperin (a court composer) was content to write a harpsichord piece titled "Le Gaillard Boiteux," published in 1722 but probably written in the final decade of the seventeenth century, showing how people attached to the royal court were aware of and in many cases heard the music of street performers. The piece is to be played "dans le goût burlesque" (in the burlesque style) and would appear to be a musical portrait of the singer.[11] An engraving by the celebrated engraver Gérard Audran (fig. 4) depicts him perched on the parapet of the Pont Neuf, his crutches beneath him, holding song sheets in his left hand, and with printed pamphlets poking out of a bag beside him. His right hand points toward the musical notes in his left hand rather than to the printed words in the bag, drawing attention to the sound world that he creates and to his primacy as a musician rather than simply a pamphleteer.

The verse accompanying the engraving testifies to his fame:

Voicy le Portrait et l'Eloge
De ce chantre fameux
Nommé Guillaume de Limoge
Autrement le gaillard Boiteux.

(Here is the Portrait and hymn of praise / Of the famous singer / Named Guillaume de Limoge / Otherwise known as the Cheerful Lame Man.)

However, of all the fabled figures to populate the Pont Neuf in the seventeenth century, one singer-songwriter (labeled "chantre" by historian of song Patrice Coirault)[12] above all caught the imagination of writers and engravers alike: the blind singer Philippot Le Savoyard.[13] The title of "Savoyard" does not necessarily mean that he actually came from the Savoy region, as the term became widely used simply to describe an itinerant worker or performer.[14] It is very possible that Philippot used the title "Savoyard" as a way of identifying himself, just as Guillaume de Limoges embraced his nickname of "Le Gaillard Boiteux"; in so doing, they form part of a tradition like the commedia dell'arte (so popular in seventeenth-century France) where actors would be known by their characters' names, such as Harlequin or Scaramouche.[15]

The element that sets Philippot apart from most of his contemporaries and underlines his fame in Paris is that two volumes of songs, composed by him and by others and (according to his claim) sung by him alone, were published by the printer-publisher Jean Promé and subsequently by his widow, whose shop was situated near the Pont Neuf[16] and whose attachment to oral culture is further evident from the edition she published of the *Cris de Paris*.[17] The renown of these editions of Philippot's songs (and the second 1656 edition in particular) can be seen in Boileau's ironic assertion in his Satire IX, where, in satirizing his own pretensions to literary immortality, the poet imagines his own writings ending up "demi-rongés" (half-gnawed), on the "rebords du pont-Neuf" (edges of the Pont Neuf),[18] and addresses himself:

Le bel honneur pour vous, en voyant vos ouvrages
Occuper le loisir des laquais et des pages,
Et souvent dans un coin renvoyés à l'écart
Servir de second tome aux airs du Savoyard![19]

(What a great honor it is for you, while seeing your works / Take up the leisure time of lackeys and page boys, / And often thrown aside in a corner / Being used as the second volume of the Savoyard's songs!)

In a later edition of the same satire from 1701, Boileau even refers to Philippot as "fameux chantre du Pont-Neuf dont on chante encore les chansons" (famous singer on the Pont Neuf whose songs are still sung).[20]

The majority of Philippot's published output varies little from what one finds in many song collections of the time:[21] most are drinking songs (with Philippot invoking himself in one piece: "Sus, Savoyard d'un ton divin, / De Bacchus chante icy la gloire" [Savoyard, know how with a divine tone / To sing here to the honor of Bacchus])[22] or bawdy ballads ("chansons gaillardes"). A few songs celebrate military exploits, including a propaganda piece in praise of the general who would become known as le Grand Condé ("Chanson amoureuse à la louange de Monseigneur le duc d'Anguien" [Love song in praise of the duke of Enghien])[23] and whom we will meet again in the second part of this book. However, as John Romey has analyzed,[24] other songs are set to traditional dance tunes and are based on courtly love songs (*airs de cour*). One of the published songs, "Cruel tyran de mes désirs" (Cruel tyrant of my desires), for example, is mentioned as having been danced "au ballet de Monsieur Cardinal,"[25] which almost certainly would have been from a ballet staged for Cardinal Richelieu in 1623 or 1624, during the reign of Louis XIII. The original air was composed by Louis's superintendent of music, Antoine Boësset, and, as Romey argues, "suggests that tunes from aristocratic productions circulated in the streets long after their original performance."[26] Philippot's own manipulation of the original text is interesting, as, apart from retaining the first line and parts of the refrain (perhaps doing so in order to signal the tune that might have been familiar to his audience), he composes his own words around the theme of unrequited love.[27] It is evident, therefore, that a street performer such as Philippot was happy to use and exploit popular music emanating from the court, in addition to using popular tunes that circulated around the Pont Neuf.

Fig. 5   Jacques Lagniet, "L'Apollon de la Grève." Photo: BnF.

Given that so few named singers from the period left published works, it is perhaps tempting to use Philippot's songs as a template for understanding exactly what was being sung on the Pont Neuf by known figures during the seventeenth and eighteenth centuries, and it is indeed likely that these printed songs formed part of Philippot's repertoire. However, it should be remembered that such published pieces would have had to be judged permissible by the royal censor, and any politically sensitive or overly licentious material that Philippot may have sung would not have been included. Of the songs that do appear in the editions, some mention food shortages, but usually in the context of money being used for drink instead of food.[28]

Some songs give an idea of the musical instruments that might have been used to accompany singers on the Pont Neuf. Philippot himself is depicted in one engraving (fig. 5) with a violin in his hand and with a woman beside him playing the bagpipes.

In his songs he refers to different words for bagpipes, "musette" and "chevry."[29] We are drawn into the sound world of Philippot and his fellow musicians in this engraving. Not only Philippot but also his two male companions have their mouths open, with words flowing from each of the two helpers' mouths, the one on the left proclaiming that "Mon Maistre, il n'y a plus d'Enfant à nostre âge" (My master, we are no longer children at our age)—perhaps referring to the fact that usually Philippot was assisted by children—and the man on the right (whose text is upside down) commenting, appropriately, about this "monde à l'envers" (upside-down world).

He is happy also to poke fun at another singer known as Orlande de Lassus, all the while depicting the sounds of life on the street:

> Qu'enten-je dans la ruë
> Est-ce un charivary,
> Si musique bouruë
> Me rend ton chevry,
> Qu'on chasse, qu'on taille
> Chantons sur le dessus,
> Bernans cette canaille
> Et l'envoyons la sus
> Voir Orlande de Lossus [sic].[30]

(What do I hear in the street? / Is it a foul noise, / If extravagant music / Gives me back your bagpipes / That are chased away and cut adrift, / Let's sing the treble part, / Deriding these rogues / And let's send them on / To see Orlande de Lassus.)

The commerce of songs, newssheets, and poems that formed such an essential part of life on the Pont Neuf is also evoked in a song about rhymed verse ("bouts rimés"):

> Debiteurs de nouvelles,
> De chansons et sonnets:
> Vous n'avez plus accez

Aux plus chastes et cruelles,
Si vous n'y apportez
Des bouts, des bouts, etc.³¹

(Distributors of news, / Songs and sonnets: / You no longer have access / To the most chaste and cruel of women / Unless you bring / Some rhymed verse.)

Philippot's blindness brings to the fore the primacy of the Pont Neuf sound world over its visuality. Philippot himself, far from underplaying his condition, draws attention to it, all the while emphasizing the aurality of his songs. This practice of making his disability a central feature of his artistic output is one shared by other writers of the time, notably the poet Denis Sanguin de Saint-Pavin, who was even able to assert that physical disability made him superior in many respects.³² In one song in particular, titled "Courante nouvelle, à la louange du Savoyard" (New courante in praise of the Savoyard), Philippot the singer-songwriter shows a supreme confidence in his capacities (the first-person pronoun "je" dominates the song), trumpeting the observation that his renown is in no way hampered by his blindness. The dissolute life that he advocates serves as some kind of counterexample, for he claims not to want to offer advice that should be followed but at the same time asks his listeners to imprint his dictum of "il faut rire, chanter et boire" (You must laugh, sing, and drink)—all three elements of which do not rely on sight in order to enjoy them, with the first two stressing the aural—onto their memories:

Je suis ce fameux Savoyart
Qui par l'adresse de mon art
Surmonte la melancolie:
Je ne suis jamais content
Qu'alors qu'en bonne compagnie
Je trouve à bien passer mon temps.

Malgré la perte de mes yeux,
Mon nom éclatte en divers lieux,
Sous ce titre d'incomparable.
Si je passe pour debauché,
Je n'en suis pas moins estimable,
Moins heureux ny moins recherché.

Je ne veux donner des advis
Qui soient dignes d'être suivis,
Gravez-les dans vostre memoire.
Messieurs, c'est que pour vivre heureux
Il faut rire, chanter et boire
Parmy les debats amoureux.

Quand j'ay pratiqué mon conseil,
Je suis dispos, frais et vermeil,
Je coule heureusement ma vie,
Je frequente les cabarets,
Les plaisirs de la comedie,
Les jeux, la dance et les balets.

N'oubliez pas le Savoyard,
Avec ses chansons dissolües.
S'il n'eust pas esté si paillard,
Il n'auroit pas perdu la veuë.[33]

(I am the famous Savoyard / Who through the skill of my art / Overcomes melancholy: / I am only ever happy / When in good company.

Despite the loss of my eyes, / My name is well known in different places, / Under the title "Incomparable." / If I seem like a dissolute person, / I am no less estimable, happy, or searched for.

I do not want to give advice / That is worthy of being followed, / Carve this into your memories, / Gentlemen, that in order to live a happy life, / You must laugh, sing, and drink / In the midst of lovers' tiffs.

Whenever I have carried out my advice, / I am lusty, fresh, and ruddy, / I happily let my life run its course, / I frequent bars, / The pleasures of the theater, / Games, dance, and ballet.

Do not forget the Savoyard, / With his dissolute songs. / If he hadn't been such a rascal, / He wouldn't have lost his sight.)

In the final stanza above, the singer would seem to suggest (as he does elsewhere) that his sexual and alcoholic excesses (Cotgrave defines "paillard" as "a lecher, wencher, whoremunger, whore-hunter; also, a knave, rascall, varlet, scoundrell, filthie fellow") have led to his blindness. In other words, the song appears to end with a moralizing warning to others who might wish to lead a similar life of moral turpitude. Yet if we consider the stanza more closely, especially within the context of the song as a whole, which twice equates such an existence with happiness ("c'est pour vivre heureux" and "je coule heureusement ma vie"), his blindness is embraced as a necessary and joyous sacrifice for both his name ("N'oubliez pas le Savoyard") and his "chansons dissolües" to endure in the public memory.

In addition to calling himself "ce fameux Savoyart" in the song just quoted, Philippot begins another much longer self-portrait ("Air Nouveau du Savoyard") in militaristically grandiose terms:

> Je suis l'illustre Savoyard,
> Des chantres le grand capitaine,
> Ie ne meine pas mon soldat,
> Mais c'est mon soldat qui me meine.[34]

> (I am the illustrious Savoyard, / The great captain of singers, / I do not lead my soldier, / Instead it is my soldier who leads me.)

The singer's reference to a soldier leading him rather than the other way around immediately punctures any pomposity attached to imagery of military prowess (which runs throughout the song) while at the same time signaling to his listeners the reality that he is blind and requires a helper to guide him. The blind musician accompanied by a child guide was a recognizable type in seventeenth-century France. In *Histoire Comique de Francion* (1623), for example, the author, Charles Sorel, uses remarkably similar language to Philippot's description when he describes a "vielleux" (a player of the "vielle," described by Cotgrave as "a rude, or harsh-sounding Instrument of Musicke, usually played on by base Fidlers, and blind men"), who exclaims: "pardonnez moy, [. . .] je ne vay que là où l'on meine: mon pauvre luminaire est esteint" (Forgive me, . . . I only go where I am led: my poor candle is snuffed out), before adding:

> J'appelle ainsi un petit garçon qui me conduit, [. . .] parce qu'il me dit ce qu'il voit dans la ruë, et je le reçois en mon imagination, comme si je le voyois aussi.[35]

Fig. 6
Jacques Lagniet, "Le Savoyard." Photo: BnF.

(For this purpose, I call on a little boy who guides me, . . . because he tells me what he sees in the street, and I receive it in my imagination, as if I could see it also.)

Later in the "Air nouveau du Savoyard," Philippot compares himself to Homer, "ce Chantre divin" (that divine Singer) whose blindness, like the Savoyard's own, he attributes to having drunk too much wine.[36] He resorts also to mythology, calling himself "l'Orphée du Pont-Neuf" (Orpheus of the Pont Neuf), pointing out "les Bestes que j'attire" (the Beasts that I attract).[37] This same reference heads another engraving of him (fig. 6), where he is depicted as being flanked by a child helper. The child holds a sheet containing words, no doubt for sale to listeners. Interestingly, Philippot holds his hand to his mouth. I would argue that, contrary to the initial impression that he is imposing silence on himself, he is in fact drawing attention to the body part that enables him to ply his trade. Unlike his nonseeing eyes, his mouth functions fully as the conduit through which his singing voice passes. In other words, orality rather than visuality is emphasized.

In contrast to the more generalized pieces about wine, women, and song that dominate his published collection and that, according to him, were performed for the pleasure of his listeners, here Philippot the singer places himself at the forefront of his creativity:

> I'ay chanté Bachus et l'Amour
> Car ie voy que chacun les ayme.
> Maintenant ie veux à mon tour,
> Devant vous me chanter moy-mesme.[38]

(I have sung of Bacchus and Love, / For I see that everybody loves them. / Now I want to take my turn, / By singing about myself in front of you.)

Not only at several junctures in the song does he reiterate the reality of his sightlessness, but also he draws the audience into his own sound world through the refrain, with the repeated use of the verb "écouter" and evocation of his own songs:

> Accourez filles et garçons
> Escoutez bien notre musique,
> L'esprit le plus melancolique
> Se rejouyt à mes chansons.[39]

(Come running, girls and boys, / Come and hear our music, / Even the most melancholy of spirits / Rejoices in my songs.)

Moreover, Philippot's sense of self is inextricably connected to place, in particular the Pont Neuf, at the foot of the statue of Henri IV, and to the ruffians (mischievously referred to as Henri's courtiers) who share that space with him daily. "Les enfans de la Gibeciere" may well be the children who assisted him, holding out a large purse (Cotgrave translates "gibbeciere" as "pouch" or "bag") for donations or money from the purchase of song sheets by those who came to listen to his songs:

> Les courtisans du grand Henry,
> Les enfans de la gibeciere
> Me tiennent pour son favory
> Et m'en font tous le pied derriere.⁴⁰
>
> (The great Henri's courtiers, / The children of the purse, / Hold me as their favorite, / And all give me a kick up the backside.)

Philippot gives a list of all those on the bridge near him who, he claims, sing the praise of his songs: "nos voisins les Operateurs" (defined by Cotgrave as "a Quack-salver, cheater, Imposter"), tooth pullers ("arracheurs de dents," whom he calls "menteurs"),⁴¹ and even "l'honneste homme en passant chemin" (the civilized man passing by).⁴² The murky world of criminality is never far behind, and, just as we might be invited to doubt the honesty of these cheats and liars who perform their own theatrical acts near him, his insistence that "N'ayez peur chantant devant vous / Que vostre bourse soit coupée" (Have no fear as I sing before you / That your purse might be cut)⁴³ might reasonably be taken with a large dose of salt. As everybody knew, thieves were always lurking on the Pont Neuf, and a moment's loss of concentration could lead to one's purse or cloak being removed.

The economic necessity for Philippot of singing and selling his songs is accentuated in the final quatrain of the song, where, once again, hearing, as opposed to sight, is given particular emphasis:

> Accourez filles et garçons,
> Venez ouyr nostre musique
> Et que chacun de vous se pique
> De bien achepter mes chansons.⁴⁴
>
> (Come running girls and boys, / Come listen to our music, / And may each of you be so interested / As to buy my songs.)

Much of Philippot's self-depiction in his published songs is supported by an extraordinary account by Charles Coypeau (1605–1677), who took the name of Sieur d'Assoucy, or, as he usually spelled it, Dassoucy, in his *Avantures burlesques*, first published in 1677. Dassoucy devotes an entire chapter to his encounter with the blind singer. Having grown up in Paris, when he used to skip school lessons to watch the puppeteers and organ-grinders on the Pont Neuf, Dassoucy became a musician and composer, traveling widely, including to Italy, where he learned to play the theorbo, a musical instrument that was little known in France at the time. He became court composer to Louis XIII in the 1630s and was even commissioned by Pierre Corneille to write the music for his machine play *Andromède* in 1650. During the 1640s Dassoucy became attached to a group of freethinkers (*libertins*), including Gassendi, Chapelle, Cyrano de Bergerac, Tristan l'Hermite, Saint-Amant, and Scarron, and he came into contact with Molière on several occasions.[45]

It is probably during his travels between 1655 and 1665 that Dassoucy met Philippot. In his *Avantures burlesques*, he, like many of his *libertin* friends in their prose narratives, plays the role of what Joan DeJean calls "the myth of the writer larger than life": as she continues, "they dramatize themselves and forge their own destinies, arranging and shaping occurrences in a literary way, according to literary models," in the end making "reality imitate the fictional."[46] The chapter devoted to his encounter with Philippot (which takes place somewhere along the river Saône, near Lyon) seems to play with this overlap between reality and fiction. Indeed, Dassoucy chooses terminology that appears to emanate directly from the images used by Philippot about himself in his songs. Yet the amount of documentary detail in this chapter about Philippot's appearance, blindness, and songs gives the sense that reality predominates, in complete contrast to the following chapter, when a charging bear suddenly interrupts proceedings and Philippot (who has now become a character type, simply labeled "l'Aveugle") becomes involved in a drunken dispute with a pedant over a shoulder of mutton.

Dassoucy describes his first encounter with Philippot (whom he calls "ce personnage enluminé" [this enlightened character]) while he is playing the theorbo:

> J'attiray un auditeur qui fera bien voir le progrés que j'ai fait dans l'empire des Muses, puisque celuy qui attiroit plus de bestes en un jour qu'Orphée n'en eust attiré en dix ans, me reconnut pour son Apollon et son maistre. Celuy-cy estoit un homme qui avoit beaucoup de sujet de se plaindre de la nature, qui ne luy avoit pas accordé, comme au reste des animaux, la faculté de discerner les objets, puisque, faute d'une paire d'yeux, il estoit contraint d'en prendre à louage du tiers et du quart, et de laisser conduire comme la plupart des Grands, qui ne voyent le plus souvent que par les yeux d'autruy.[47]

(I attracted a listener who will have seen the progress I have made in the dominion of the Muses, since the person who attracted more beasts in a day than Orpheus attracted in ten years recognized me as his Apollo and master. He was a man who had much to complain against nature, which had not given to him, unlike the rest of animals, the faculty of discerning objects, since, lacking a pair of eyes, he was obliged to take his sight from others, and to be led like most great people, who only see for the most part through the eyes of others.)

Dassoucy's account not only tallies with information found in the published songs but also gives a vivid idea of Philippot's life in Paris as a singer and of the sound world of the area around the Pont Neuf, not least the fact that his child guides also performed songs with him. In the *Avantures*, Philippot introduces himself by comparing himself (as he does in the "Air nouveau du Savoyard") to Homer, whom he again calls "ce Chantre divin" (that divine Singer),[48] before adding that he, too, is "Poëte et Chantre fameux" (a famous Poet and Singer):

> Mais un Chantre doué d'une voix si éclatante et si forte, que, pourveu que j'aye pris seulement deux doigts d'eau de vie, si je chantois sur le Quay des Augustins, le Roy m'entendroit des fenestres de son Louvre. Cela dit, sans attendre d'estre prié, il tira de sa poche un petit livre couvert de papier bleu, et, l'ayant donné à un jeune garçon qui luy servoit de guide, ils unirent tous deux leurs voix, et tous deux, le chapeau sur l'oreille, ils chanterent ces agreables chansons.[49]

(But I am a Singer endowed with such a loud and strong voice that, provided I have drunk only a little brandy, if I were singing on the Quai des Augustins, the King would hear me from the windows of his Louvre. That said, without waiting to be asked, he pulled a little book covered in blue paper from his pocket, and after giving it to a young boy who was acting as his guide, they sang together, and, wearing their hats, both sang these enjoyable songs.)

Although the Savoyard's published output contains only joyous or bawdy pieces, it is likely that his performed songs contained greater variety, certainly if Dassoucy's tale is to be taken seriously. In the *Avantures*, for example, when Philippot sings a sad song about a shoemaker who cut his throat in response to his wife's infidelity, Dassoucy is unable to prevent himself from weeping.[50]

When Philippot finally introduces himself by name to Dassoucy, he identifies himself firmly through his preferred Parisian location beside the statue of Henri IV and the Samaritaine water pump on the Pont Neuf, even though the two men within the narrative are conversing by the river Saône:

> Je m'appelle, dit-il, Philippot, à vostre service, autrement le Savoyard, et, si vous passez jamais sur le Pont-neuf, c'est sur les degrez de ce pont que vous verrez mon Parnasse; le Cheval de bronze est mon Pegaze, et la Samaritaine la fontaine de mon Helicon.[51]

> (My name, he said, is Philippot, at your service, otherwise called the Savoyard, and, if ever you come onto the Pont Neuf, you will see my Parnassus on the steps of the bridge; the bronze Horse is my Pegasus, and the Samaritaine water pump is my Fountain of Helicon.)

Philippot's gift to Dassoucy of a book of his songs (probably one of the published versions) may explain the equivalence of the *libertin* writer's representation of Philippot's spoken words and the singer's self-description in his published book. However, when Dassoucy offers a collection of his own songs in return, he is astonished to be rebuffed by Philippot, who tells him, "Non, Monsieur, gardez vos belles chansons pour les oreilles des Princes et le cabinet des Roys" (No, sir, keep your beautiful songs for the ears of princes and the chamber of kings).[52]

Philippot is clearly proud of the autonomy of the street singer's craft, and, even if he claims that his father used to sing songs written by Louis XIII's court composers, Pierre Guedron and Antoine Boësset, he is clearly distancing himself from current tastes in the royal court (incarnated by composers such as Michel Lambert and the up-and-coming Jean-Baptiste Lully) and is staking out his own musical ground.[53] While he is content to appropriate popular courtly tunes and even images more associated with the French court (with his self-description as Orpheus or Apollo and his reference to the paupers gathered at the foot of the statue of Henri IV as "courtiers"), I would argue also that in shunning the royal court he deliberately situates himself away from conventional systems of authority. The sound world of street singers, vendors, tooth pullers, charlatans, thieves, and passersby is the milieu that he embraces and calls his own.

Witnessing Song: The Marquise de Sévigné

We have already seen from Philippot's published works that those who enjoyed his songs or came to listen to him on the Pont Neuf came from diverse backgrounds. The area where he performed, beside the statue of Henri IV, was the favored spot for paupers to congregate, as various seventeenth-century depictions of the bridge show,[54] so they, too, would have heard songs by him and the many other singers who performed within earshot of the statue.

Inevitably, owing to the high rate of illiteracy,[55] the response of paupers to the sounds of the Pont Neuf remains unrecorded. However, detailed consideration of one much more highly born listener, Marie de Rabutin-Chantal, marquise de Sévigné, can help us gain a more vivid idea of the ways in which song permeated individual lives in early modern France. Sévigné herself was an accomplished singer, described by her cousin Bussy-Rabutin as having "l'oreille encore juste" (still a good ear) and "la voix agréable" (an agreeable voice).[56] With her eye and ear for telling detail and her desire to give a vibrant depiction of Parisian daily life to her daughter, Françoise-Marguerite, comtesse de Grignan (herself described in one song as knowing how to "chanter, danser divinement" [sing and dance divinely]),[57] who was living in Provence, or to other correspondents, such as Bussy-Rabutin, who were away from the city, Sévigné's voluminous correspondence affords later readers the opportunity to listen to the sounds of Paris as she hears them.[58]

Although the written correspondence of a figure such as Sévigné might appear not to have any intrinsic connection with sound worlds, Sévigné herself compares her letters at various junctures to spoken conversations.[59] Moreover, as I have discussed elsewhere, personal letters were often mediated by public performances; silent reading only became common practice in the eighteenth century, and Sévigné often imagines her daughter reading her letters aloud both to herself and to a wider audience of family and friends.[60]

At first glance, Sévigné might seem unrepresentative of the wider populace who would have witnessed or performed songs on the street or in taverns: much of the urgency, desperation, and outright bawdiness of certain songs would in all probability have elicited a very different reaction from her, as a privileged and highly literate aristocrat, than from an illiterate or socially less fortunate listener.

We have already seen at the beginning of this chapter ways in which certain people and dictionary definitions tried to make clear class distinctions between street songs and other forms of song. This kind of categorization would appear also to be evident when Sévigné quotes two songs in a letter to Bussy-Rabutin, who himself was well known as the author of many satirical songs,[61] imploring him not to write any songs about her, as "je les entends dans les rues" (I hear them in the streets [24 November 1678, 2:636]). His response, that "l'un est bon pour nous, et l'autre pour le Pont-Neuf" (one is good for us, the other for the Pont Neuf [27 November 1678, 2:637]), would suggest a similar prejudice.

Yet Sévigné's choice to cite the two songs together, coupled with the very clear enthusiasm that she shows for the Pont Neuf and her acknowledgment that she hears songs in the street, indicates that it would surely be ill judged to make such clear-cut class distinctions when analyzing song. She jokingly ascribes her love of song to her "vertus populaires" (popular virtues [30 October 1680, 3:50]), but the reality that song in all its manifestations plays such an integral part in Sévigné's correspondence shows the extent to which it permeated different levels of society.[62] Allusions to the Pont Neuf that punctuate her letters often act as a metaphorical bridge between mother and daughter. On 6 April 1672, for example, no doubt referring to songs she has been sending to Madame de Grignan, she starts a letter with the words, "Recevez la visite du Pont-Neuf, votre ancien ami; puisque vous ne voulez pas le venir voir, il va vous rendre ses devoirs" (Receive a visit from the Pont Neuf, your old friend; since you do not wish to come and see him, he is going to pay you his dues [1:470]), and she finishes it by playfully retracting her offer: "Je ne vous envoie plus le Pont-Neuf; c'est à vous à le venir voir" (I am no longer sending you the Pont Neuf; it is up to you to come see him [474]). Such personification of the bridge is extended in another letter to portray it as a generator or even composer of songs: citing one of the many songs circulating in Paris that commemorated the recent disastrous (for the French) siege of Philippsburg,[63] Sévigné states, "Le Pont-Neuf a fait ce couplet" (The Pont Neuf wrote this couplet [18 September 1676, 2:401]). As early as 1649, during the time of the Fronde, Sévigné was aware of the most popular form of song sung on the bridge at the time, the *triolet*, writing to her friend Pierre Lenet, "Vous faites des triolets comme celui qui les a inventés" (You write triolets like the person who invented them [20 March 1649, 1:12]). The songs performed and sold on the Pont Neuf are not used by Sévigné solely for her own and others' entertainment; they can also serve a useful purpose, such as when she is keeping her friend Pomponne informed of the trial of their mutual friend Nicolas Fouquet (who will feature prominently in the next chapter): "Dès qu'il y aura des vers du Pont-Neuf et autres, je vous les enverrai fort bien" (As soon as there are verses from the Pont Neuf and other news, I will certainly send them to you [26 December 1664, 1:81]), she explains, underlining the urgency and efficacy of obtaining news from songs rather than official accounts. It also suggests that either she learned songs by heart in order to communicate them by letter or she engaged in the transactional commerce of the Pont Neuf by buying the sheets containing the words from the singers and their helpers.

Although many of the songs emanating from the Pont Neuf might be associated with vulgarity and coarseness, Sévigné delights in the ways in which the songs often intrude or cross over into different, more rarefied worlds. As deeply committed a Catholic as she was, she enjoys in particular those episodes where salacious songs impinge on the daily routines of the church. One story that Sévigné recounts on 20 March 1671 involves the Jansenist preacher Joseph Desmares, who thought that he had been given an edict from the newly appointed archbishop of Paris, François Harlay de Champvallon, to read out in the pulpit, only to find halfway through that it was a song that we know to have been sung elsewhere that year, set to the tune "O filii et filiae,"[64] mocking the archbishop's womanizing ways:

> On donna l'autre jour au P. Desmares un billet en montant en chaire. Il le lut avec ses lunettes. C'était:
> > De par Monseigneur de Paris,
> > On déclare à tous les maris
> > Que leurs femmes on baisera,
> >> Alleluia!
>
> Il en lut plus de la moitié; on pensa mourir de rire. Il y a des gens de bonne humeur, comme vous voyez. (1:193–94)

(The other day, Father Desmares was given a note just as he was climbing into the pulpit. He read it with his glasses. It was: *Signed by Monsignor of Paris, / It is declared to all husbands / That their wives will be fucked, / Alleluia!* He read out more than a half of it, and we thought we would die from laughing. There are people with a very good sense of humor, as you see.)

Similarly, Sévigné exclaims that she and her son Charles "avons ri aux larmes" (laughed until we cried [12 January 1676, 2:221]) at her daughter's tale of a young girl who told her confessor in church that she had been singing a "chanson gaillarde" (bawdy song), only to be asked by the priest to sing it aloud there and then. As Charles adds in Sévigné's letter, "Elle avait autant d'envie d'avoir l'absolution que le bon père de savoir la chanson, et apparemment ils se contentèrent tous deux" (She wished to receive absolution as greatly as the good father wanted to know the song, and apparently they were both happy [2:223]). Given this love of mischief, we know better than to take Sévigné at face value when she reports that a young man who "fait des chansons avec une facilité surprenante [. . .] craignait d'offenser mes chastes oreilles" (writes songs with an amazing facility . . . feared offending my chaste ears [24 June 1676, 2:327]).

As can already be seen, far from being scandalized by earthy songs, Sévigné tends to delight in their subversive potential. Thus, when her friend Segrais shows her his collection of the notoriously libertine baron de Blot's songs (sixteen years after the latter's death), she is able to inform her daughter that they "ont le diable au corps, mais je n'ai jamais tant vu d'esprit" (have the devil about them, but I have never seen so much wit [6 May 1671, 1:242]).[65] Even in her account of the days leading to the execution of serial killer Catherine Deshayes, known as la Voisin, which demonstrates how closely songs, and especially drinking songs, were associated with debauchery in the public consciousness, Sévigné displays a ghoulish fascination but never moral outrage. Writing immediately after la Voisin was burned at the stake ("ses cendres sont en l'air présentement" [her ashes are right this moment in the air]), Sévigné describes how la Voisin drank large quantities of wine before singing twenty drinking songs:

> On lui en fit honte, et on lui dit qu'elle ferait bien mieux de penser à Dieu, et de chanter un *Ave maris stella* ou un *Salve* que toutes ces chansons; elle chanta l'un et l'autre en ridicule. Elle mangea le soir et dormit. Le mercredi se passa de même en confrontations et débauches et chansons; elle ne voulut point de confesseur. (23 February 1680, 2:846)

(They tried to make her ashamed, telling her that she would do well to think of God and to sing an *Ave maris stella* or a *Salve* rather than all those kinds of songs; she sang each one in a parodic way. She ate in the evening and slept. Wednesday passed by similarly with confrontation and debauchery and songs; she did not want a confessor.)

All moral condemnation here is assigned to an unspecified "on," presumably la Voisin's jailers and those who sentenced her to death, but Sévigné refrains from offering judgmental observations of her own.

Another characteristic of street songs at the time was the coexistence of what one might call higher and lower culture. Although the majority of songs were set to popular tunes, from the latter part of the seventeenth century onward, the latest arias being sung on the stage in Paris were imitated and parodied on the Pont Neuf, thereby allowing both those unable to afford opera tickets the opportunity to hear the latest arias by a composer such as Lully and those like Sévigné, who had been able to be present, to hear the music again in a different form.[66]

Writing in 1704, the magistrate and musicographer Jean-Laurent Le Cerf de La Viéville gives a colorful account of the popularity of different kinds of music within all sectors of society. Far from being entirely dismissive of those songs that started life on the Pont Neuf, he claims that, while the worst examples never leave the Pont Neuf, others that have "des tons agreables" (agreeable tonality) are heard throughout the country and have real merit: "Vous pourrez observer néanmoins qu'en fait d'airs de pur Pont-neuf, ceux qui gagnent le fond de nos Provinces, sont ceux qui ont quelque harmonie ou quelque vivacité" (You will observe nonetheless that out of the tunes that are pure Pont Neuf in origin, those that gain favor in the furthest reaches of our provinces are those that have some kind of harmony or vivacity).[67] He then describes how by the same token operatic arias (and street versions of such music) have come to be appreciated by a wide range of classes:

> Ces airs de l'Opera et du grand monde, qui ont décendu jusqu'au petit peuple, ont de nécessité passé par la bouche de tous les gens respectables, desquels ils portent avec eux l'aprobation, par ce cercle qu'ils ont assurément fait. Lorsque j'entendois, par exemple, l'air d'Amadis,
>
> Amour que veux-tu de moi, etc.
>
> chanté par toutes les Cuisinieres de France, j'avois droit de penser que cét air étoit déja sûr d'avoir eu l'aprobation de tous les gens de France d'un rang entre la Princesse et la Cuisiniere: que cét air avoit parcouru tous ces rangs-là, pour en venir au plus bas, et avoit emporté l'estime et le suffrage de tout ce peuple de qualité, de tous les Connoisseurs, de tous les Sçavans, de ce nombre immense de personnes distinguées, par la bouche desquelles il avoit passé: et remarquant qu'il sçavoit

toucher la Cuisiniere, comme il avoit sçû toucher la Princesse, qu'il plaisoit également au sçavant et à l'ignorant, aux esprits du premier ordre et du dernier: je concluois qu'il devoit être bien beau, bien dans la nature, bien plein d'une expression vraye, pour avoir remué tant de divers cœurs, et flatté tant d'oreilles différentes.[68]

(Those melodies from the Opera and from the upper echelons of society, which have been disseminated down as far as the common people, have of necessity been passed by word of mouth from all respectable people, and these melodies gain approval wherever people go, having formed their own circles. When, for example, I would hear Amadis's aria, *Love, what do you want from me,* etc., sung by all the women cooks in France, I was justified in thinking that this aria had the approval of all the people of France ranked between princess and cook; that this aria had done the rounds through all these ranks in order to reach the lowest level, and had gained the esteem and favor of all these highly ranked people, of all connoisseurs, of all scholars, indeed of all such distinguished people, passed on by word of mouth. After noticing how the aria was able to move the cook just as much as it had moved the princess, that it pleased both wise and ignorant equally, minds of the highest and lowest order, I concluded that, in order for it to have moved so many diverse hearts and to have flattered so many different ears, it must be very beautiful, both in nature and in true expression.)

Sévigné herself responds with enthusiasm to a parody of Lully's opera *Psyché*, which was still to receive its premiere, and was clearly new to the comtesse de Grignan, living far away from Paris:

D'Hacqueville vous a envoyé une assez plaisante chanson sur M. de Longueville. C'est à l'imitation d'un certain récit de ballet que vous ne connaissez point, et que je vous ai dit qui était le plus beau du monde. Je le sais, et je le chante bien. (20 March 1671, 1:193)

(D'Hacqueville has sent you a rather enjoyable song on M. de Longueville. It is in imitation of a certain ballet tune that you do not know and that I have told you is the most beautiful in the world. I know it and sing it well.)

It is likely also that Sévigné's daughter was aware that she and her husband, who himself was an accomplished musician,[69] appeared as characters in parodies of other Lully operas (possibly written by members of her family), as the *Chansonnier Maurepas* shows on a number of occasions.[70] Some of these parodies would have been performed within aristocratic and salon circles, but there were also many street songs, set to Lully's melodies, being circulated and performed. Indeed, Évrard Titon du Tillet, in his collection of anecdotes about famous people of the time, *Le Parnasse françois* (1732), reports that Lully was said to have been charmed to hear his melodies, set to different words, performed on the Pont Neuf, and he was even known to have stepped down from his carriage to inform the singer and violinist of the correct tempi.[71]

Quite apart from the ease with which Sévigné moves between different worlds through her love of song, her detailed commentary on the way in which both the knowledge and performance of them permeates daily life gives us valuable clues of how songs were used by individuals and families in the early modern period. Normally Sévigné quotes from or sends the latest songs circulating at the time, often on the most topical or scurrilous subjects, but there is some evidence that she occasionally composed songs herself to entertain her correspondents, such as the occasion when she and her son write to the comtesse de Grignan, "Nous fîmes des chansons, que nous vous envoyons. L'estime que nous avons de votre prose ne nous empêche point de vous faire part de nos vers" (We composed some songs that we are sending you. The respect that we have for your prose does not prevent us from letting you experience our verse [1 July 1671, 1:285]). Moreover, if her comments to her friend Gilles Ménage, who had sent her a *canzonetta*, are to be believed, she had the ability to compose her own tunes: "Je tâche de l'ajuster sur quelqu'un de tous les airs que j'ai jamais sus; et n'y trouvant bien mes mesures, je pense que j'entreprendrai d'y en faire un tout neuf, tant j'ai d'envie de la chanter" (I am trying to set it to a single tune of all the ones I have ever known, and, because I cannot find the right modulation, I think that I will attempt to compose a completely new tune, such is my desire to sing it [12 September 1656, 1:39]).

Another of her cousins, Philippe-Emmanuel Coulanges, who, like her, lived on the Place Royale (now the Place des Vosges) in Paris, took a similarly keen interest in the songs being sung around Paris. On one occasion, he writes to Sévigné of "mille chansons qui courent, toutes plus méchantes et plus plaisantes les unes que les autres" (a thousand songs doing the rounds, each more wicked and enjoyable than the last) on a single topical issue (14 March

1696, 3:1149); on another occasion, he refers to the new vogue among young courtiers at the end of the seventeenth century for not only singing but also dancing to the latest songs (3 February 1696, 3:1140). Moreover, Coulanges was himself a prolific songwriter, one of the relatively few named authors of songs from the time. Inevitably, therefore, Sévigné frequently quotes from Coulanges's *chansons*, many of which could be termed salon-inspired pieces, but which, like most of the songs circulating at the time, are largely set to popular tunes of the day. One such song, for example, on the marriages of family relatives, is set to the melody known as "La Joconde" and is quoted by Sévigné in a letter to her friend Guitaut (whom we shall meet later in this book).[72] His works are marked by a cheerfulness that coheres with Sévigné's description of him as "toujours aimé, toujours estimé, toujours portant la joie et le plaisir avec [lui]" (always well liked, always respected, always carrying joy and pleasure with him wherever he goes [8 January 1690, 3:802]), and they usually celebrate the frivolity of the moment without having the memorability or mischievous charm of many other songs from the time. Even though he published a collection of songs in 1694, followed by an expanded edition in 1698, their subsequent neglect is not entirely unjustified. Sévigné herself, who often shows herself to be a receptive literary critic, tends to enjoy Coulanges's work not for any profundity but for its "gaieté" (30 October 1680, 3:51). When, for example, she sees a collection of the songs in manuscript, she exclaims that it is "la plus plaisante chose du monde" (the most pleasant thing in the world [6 March 1680, 2:860]).

However, the Coulanges songs are representative of an important function of song in the households of the time: communality. Songs were sent between family members not simply to be admired or read silently but to be shared and sung. Knowing the popular tune to which the words were set was therefore crucial, and on the rare occasion that Sévigné is not familiar with a melody, she remarks that this has hampered her performance of it (14 February 1680, 2:834). Just as she often imagines her daughter reading out her letters aloud, so, too, does she anticipate the performance of songs that she sends to her daughter's family, almost always associating them with shared laughter. Thus, at a moment of despondency, she writes, "Si je n'avais point le cœur triste, je vous enverrais de jolies chansons; M. de Grignan les chanterait comme un ange" (If my heart were not so sad, I would send you pretty songs; M. de Grignan would sing them like an angel [23 May 1672, 1:518]). Even in the final years of her life, when she spent much time with her daughter, she was able to communicate to Coulanges that "nous avons chanté et rechanté vos chansons" (we have sung and resung your songs [14 October 1694, 3:1063]).

It is evident that Sévigné had a keen ear for the latest tunes. Many of the songs that she mentions in her letters correspond to songs from the same year found in the *Chansonnier Maurepas*, and, where she quotes only the words, the *Chansonnier* often provides the name of the tune that she would have sung or heard. The slight changes of wording from version to version testify to the likelihood that the songs would have been heard and memorized as often as they would have been read and copied. Indeed, Sévigné's comment in a letter to Bussy-Rabutin that "on m'a appris une chanson qui m'a fait rire" (I was taught a song that made me laugh [24 November 1678, 2:635]) indicates that she learned the words orally. It is also possible that different versions would have been performed, depending on who was listening: for example, in the same letter Sévigné quotes another song in which the purported speaker is the duchesse de la Ferté talking about her husband:

> Que la Ferté ne m'aime pas,
> Qu'il soit traître comme Judas,
> Qu'il s'enivre comme Silène,
> Qu'il soit cocu, battu, content,
> Qu'il soit fils d'un grand capitaine,
> Tout cela m'est indifférent. (24 November 1678, 2:636)

(That la Ferté does not love me, / That he is a Judas-like traitor, / That he becomes drunk like Silenus, / That he is a cuckold, beaten up, happy, / That he is the son of a great captain, / All of this is indifferent to me.)

From the almost identical song in the *Chansonnier Maurepas* (4:502), we find that it was indeed sung to a very popular tune of the day ("La Rochelle"), as mentioned by Sévigné herself (2:635), but also that the fourth line is noticeably bawdier in the Maurepas version—"Qu'il baise derriere ou devant" (That he fucked in the front and in the rear)—alluding to la Ferté's sexual proclivities. Whether Sévigné herself composed a more refined line for Bussy to read or she heard a version that the singer might have thought was more appropriate to someone of her standing, the protean nature of various versions shows how songs could be readily adapted to changing circumstances, fashions, performances, and listeners.

For all Sévigné's erudition and breadth of reading, the sound of song plays a constant part in her correspondence. As alert as she remains to the latest melodies heard on the Pont Neuf, song also becomes enscribed in her longer-term memory: indeed, one *chanson* containing the words "on ne rit pas toujours" (we don't always laugh) that she quotes to her daughter in 1671 (1:359) is evoked again in one of her final letters from 1695 (3:1126).

Although Philippot and Sévigné represent just two case studies among the host of singers and listeners in seventeenth-century France, it will have become clear how multifaceted the sound worlds of Paris were at that time and how alert people were to the sound of songs surrounding them. While Philippot and Sévigné belonged to very different strata of society, with each making distinctions between music of the street and music in aristocratic circles, both were happy to enjoy and make use of the sounds from worlds to which they did not seemingly belong. Philippot, as we saw earlier, was reported to have boasted that his loud singing voice on the Pont Neuf could be heard by the king in the Louvre, and it is to the Louvre and the royal court that we shall now turn.

The next chapter will focus on the role played by sound and song at a time when Sévigné's correspondence was just beginning to act as a crucial eye- and ear-witness to political change, a time when Louis XIV endeavored to assert absolute political and cultural control.

CHAPTER 3

Informé de tout
Sound and Power, 1661–1662

The songs enjoyed by listeners such as Sévigné and performed by singers such as Philippot bring to the fore sound worlds that would have been an integral part of Parisians' daily experience at the time. When it came to times of momentous change, the songs almost always offered alternative commentaries to official accounts, and, as is evident from Sévigné's correspondence, people of all classes would rush to the Pont Neuf to listen in to these counternarratives.

One short period that has long been considered of great historical significance is also the time that will dominate the second part of this book: 1661–62. It marks the moment of Louis XIV's assumption of full power at the age of twenty-three after the death (on 9 March 1661) of his deeply unpopular first minister, Cardinal Jules Mazarin.

Of the many books that have been devoted to Louis and the importance of 1661 in particular, all have focused on the ways in which the Sun King presented and stage-managed his reign through primarily visual means.[1] The role played by sound and song, on the other hand, has been less well documented. What would normally be heard rather than seen? What would be expressed orally rather than on paper? This chapter will cover key moments from 1661 and 1662 as heard in church, law courts, theatrical performance, reported conversations, and the streets. In all of them, the oral predominates over or is of equal importance to what is written or seen.

Mazarin's Death

With the exception of the time he had spent in exile during the civil unrest known as the Fronde (1648–53), Mazarin had overseen all affairs of state on behalf of the Regent Anne of Austria (widow of Louis XIII) and her son Louis XIV since 1643. Deeply unpopular for much of that time, Mazarin even had his name applied to the subversive pamphlets, songs, and libels that circulated during his time in office, known as *mazarinades*. The Pont Neuf was the major location for both the distribution of the printed leaflets and the performance of the many scurrilous songs that variously pilloried his and Anne's national origins (he was of Italian heritage, she Spanish), questioned his sexual tastes (at times depicting him as a sodomite and at others as Anne's lover, and even in some cases claiming him to be Louis XIV's real father), satirized his avarice, and disseminated the general perception that he was mismanaging government of the state and stripping the nation's coffers bare for his own enrichment.

After Mazarin's death, the king's cousin, Anne-Marie, duchesse de Montpensier, better known as la Grande Mademoiselle, recounts in her memoirs that "le cardinal ne fut pas trop regretté" (the cardinal was not greatly mourned),[2] even by those closest to him. Rather more dutifully, Loret reports in the *Muze historique* on 2 April 1661 that

> Lundi, le cœur de l'Éminence
> Avec grand ordre et grand silence,
> De Vincenne, en solennité,
> Fut aux Théatins transporté.[3]

(On Monday his Eminence's heart / With great orderliness and silence, / Was solemnly transported / From Vincennes to the Convent of the Théatins.)

However, any such respectful official silence would very probably have been drowned out, as Mazarin's heart made its way across the Pont Neuf from the

Right to the Left Bank of the Seine on its way to the Couvent des Théatins, by the many songs that were sung celebrating his demise. As the abbé de Choisy commented, Mazarin's death "fit plaisir au petit peuple" (gave pleasure to the common people).[4] The *Chansonnier Maurepas* includes many pieces that were, if anything, even more vituperative about Mazarin after his death than during the Fronde. One song, set to the popular tune "Les Rochellois" (a jaunty melody more suggestive of dancing on the cardinal's grave than reflecting grief at his death)[5] makes reference to the same heart that was being transported to its final resting place but in far less awed terms than those of the deferential Loret:

> Icy dessous gist Mazarin,
> Qui plus adroit que Tabarin,
> Par ses ruses dupa la France;
> Il eut éternisé son sort,
> Si par finesse ou par finance,
> Il avoit pû duper la mort.
>
> Enfin s'il est vray ce qu'on dit,
> L'Avarice eut tant de crédit
> Dessus son cœur insatiable,
> Qu'afin d'acquérir plus de bien,
> S'il n'eut donné son ame au Diable,
> Il n'auroit jamais donné rien.[6]

(Here lies Mazarin / Who, wilier than Tabarin, / Duped France through his ruses; / He would have made his fate eternal, / If through cunning or finance, / He had been able to dupe death.

Finally it is true what they say, / Avarice had so much credit / Upon his insatiable heart, / That in order to acquire more wealth, / If he had not given his soul to the Devil, / He would never have given away anything.)

Another piece, sung to the same melody, makes the point that Mazarin's life, rather than his death, should have been mourned.[7] Moreover, the popular practice of writing parodic epitaphs after famous people's deaths was given particularly free rein on the passing of the cardinal, not least in one scathing two-line epitaph:

Cy gist la Cardinal; Je suis fâché passant,
Qu'au lieu de ce cy gist tu ne vois pas cy pendant.⁸

(Here lies the Cardinal; I am angry in passing by, / That instead of "here lies" you do not see "here hangs.")

Louis XIV as Listener: The Preacher's Voice

Louis had up to 1661 shown far more interest in the diversions and dalliances provided by court life than in the minutiae involved in governing France. As the abbé de Choisy remarked, "Les plaisirs venaient de toutes parts pour endormir sa vertu" (Pleasures coming from all sides managed to put his virtue to sleep).⁹ It therefore came as a surprise to all, not least his own mother,¹⁰ when Louis announced that he was taking personal control of all state matters. According to Secretary of State Brienne, Louis summoned a number of princes, dukes, and secretaries of state "pour leur faire entendre de sa propre bouche qu'il avoit pris la résolution de gouverner lui-même son État sans s'en reposer que de ses propres soins (ce furent ses termes)" (to make them hear from his own mouth that he had resolved to govern the state himself without relying on anything other than his own diligence [these were his terms]).¹¹ Louis's requirement of his audience to witness the words spoken by him shows the authority and significance that the monarch attached to the oral communication of his resolve as opposed to a published edict or a letter communicating the news. Far from becoming bored with the details, as people had predicted, Louis (for all his continuing enjoyment of courtly pleasures) devoted several hours a day to the study and application of political rule, and he maintained this rigorous approach until his death in 1715.

Although Louis was concerned with presenting a visual spectacle of himself as the perfect monarch from 1661 onward, he was also preoccupied with sound on a number of levels, not least in the summoning of his courtiers to hear his declaration of absolute power. We have already seen in chapter 1 how he dispatched police and spies to listen in to ordinary conversations on the street and to note down any songs being performed in public that might be deemed subversive. Over the course of his reign, he made other attempts to control the sound world of Paris, such as licensing town criers to publicize royal edicts or announce criminal convictions. One Paris town crier, Charles Canto, was officially enshrined in his post for more than twenty-five years from the time that Mazarin was first minister and through the time that Louis assumed absolute power, and he was normally accompanied by at least three trumpeters to give him additional sonic support.[12]

In his memoirs, begun in 1661 and in all probability cowritten with the help of a number of secretaries, historiographers, and ministers, ostensibly for the instruction of Louis's son, born on 1 November of that year, the monarch portrays himself as the only person able to maintain silence while listening to all the sounds that surround him: as he describes himself, he is "informé de tout; écoutant mes moindres sujets" (informed about everything; listening to my lowliest subjects).[13] Saint-Simon supports this perception, mentioning that "il était né sage, modéré, secret, maître de ses mouvements et de sa langue" (he was born wise, moderate, secret, master of his movements and of his tongue).[14] Louis's seeming objectivity in listening to his subjects is necessarily compromised by the knowledge that his courtiers would have had of the person to whom they were talking, which inevitably would have made them shape their words accordingly. The dangers of being swayed by others' praise are indeed signaled by Louis in his memoirs, where he exhorts his son to "croire votre propre cœur plus que leurs louanges" (believe your own heart more than their praise).[15]

Such advice was rarely made by others to the king directly, but the one space in which he would have heard guidance of this kind was in church, and the most prominent French court preacher he listened to at the time was the eminent theologian Jacques-Bénigne Bossuet. Bossuet is rightly remembered for his brilliant funeral orations of the major political and royal figures of the day, but the other sermons that he preached also demonstrate his rhetorical panache and theological profundity, not least those sermons delivered at the Louvre chapel (located in the Oratory on the Rue Saint-Honoré and serving as the official royal chapel since 1623) before the royal family during Lent in the early months of 1662. Even though the queen mother had heard Bossuet preach before, these sermons were the first given by him in the presence of Louis himself.

Pulpit oratory of the time came from a rich European rhetorical tradition that was very different from judicial or forensic oratory. Unlike in a law court, where a jurist's speech seeks to produce an act by a juror or judge, the preacher or predicator is, in Richard Lockwood's words, "focused on defining who the listener is."[16] Moreover, sermons had an aesthetic priority that gave prominence to the shape of the speech and of the words themselves. As Peter Bayley has argued, pulpit oratory has a triple interest: "It is a valid autonomous art form, a guide to understanding some of the conventions of taste in a period, and a gauge of changing prose styles."[17] I would argue that there is a fourth interest, and that is in the need to consider these sermons as they were originally intended, to be heard rather than read.

Bossuet was a fervent believer in the divine right of kings, but this did not prevent him from either giving Louis his opinion on how those in power should lead their lives or criticizing the pursuits of pleasure enjoyed by the royal court and by the young king in particular. Among the Lenten sermons given by him that year, most prominent is that devoted to the duties of kings, in which he proclaims that "tous les crimes publics et scandaleux doivent être le juste objet de l'indignation du prince" (all public and scandalous crimes ought to be the rightful object of the king's indignation),[18] with the additional instruction that all princes "doivent élever, défendre, favoriser la vertu" (must promote, defend, and favor virtue).[19]

Another sermon in which he addresses Louis directly, the "Sermon sur la Prédication Évangélique" (Sermon on Evangelical Preaching), delivered on 26 February 1662, is remarkable for the prominence that Bossuet gives to the sense of hearing. Unlike other sermons in which sight alone or in conjunction with hearing is highlighted,[20] here Bossuet starts with the biblical citation, "L'homme ne vit pas seulement de pain, mais il vit de toute parole qui sort de la bouche de Dieu" (Man shall not live by bread alone, but by every word that proceedeth out of the mouth of God [Matt. 4:4]) and applies it to both the time of year (Lent) and the (to him) dissolute age in which he is living. He begins the sermon with a provocation, invoking not the concept of sound but rather that of silence: "C'est une chose surprenante que ce silence de Dieu parmi les désordres du genre humain" (The silence of God in the midst of the disorders of the human race is a surprising thing).[21] The idea that in all aspects of everyday life God is ignored and scorned brings Bossuet to his notion of a silent divinity. Yet when he begins the second paragraph of his homily with "Je me trompe" (I am mistaken), one could just as easily substitute the sense of his own error with "Je vous trompe" (I am deceiving you), as the opening words are clearly a deliberate ploy to destabilize his listeners. God's voice, according to the preacher, is in fact there to be heard and heeded:

> Je me trompe, Chrétiens, il ne se tait pas; et sa bonté, ses bienfaits, son silence même est une voix publique qui invite tous les pécheurs à se reconnaître. Mais, comme nos cœurs endurcis sont sourds à de

tels propos, il fait résonner une voix plus claire, une voix nette et intelligible, qui nous appelle à la pénitence. Il ne parle pas pour nous juger, mais il parle pour nous avertir; et c'est cette parole d'avertissement qui retentit en ce temps dans toutes les chaires.[22]

(I am mistaken, Christians, he does not remain silent, and his goodness, his good deeds, even his silence are a public voice that invites all sinners to recognize themselves. But, as our hardened hearts are deaf to such discourse, he allows a clearer voice, a precise and intelligible voice, to resonate, calling us to penitence. He does not speak in order to judge, but he speaks in order to warn us, and it is this word of warning that resounds presently from all pulpits.)

The image of a reverberating voice would surely have been replicated by the preacher's own voice resonating within the wide spaces of the Louvre chapel in the Oratory, a church with a single nave that allows for good acoustics and was especially conducive to the audibility of preachers' voices in the seventeenth century.[23] Interesting work has been done in re-creating, or rather reimagining, the sound world of sermons from the time. Eugène Green, the film director and expert in declamation and pronunciation of the seventeenth century, has recorded Bossuet's Sermon on Death in a church that was completed in the seventeenth century, the Notre-Dame Church in Arques-la-Bataille (Normandy). The sermon is delivered in pronunciation deemed to be close to that of early modern France, and the echo of the preacher's voice within a genuinely seventeenth-century edifice gives us a better idea of how Bossuet's voice might have sounded.[24] Green makes the useful point that great church orators of the day would often improvise on the text that they would have written in advance, adding that "c'est un aspect du genre qui le rapprochait de la musique" (it is an aspect of the genre that brought it close to music).[25] Green does not try to replicate the other sounds that would undoubtedly have been heard (such as the noise of the congregation and bells chiming at regular intervals), but recent digital recreations of the sounds of early modern preaching in London give a vivid idea of the kinds of sound that Bossuet's voice would have had to rise above when delivering his sermons.[26]

Bossuet clearly had confidence in the authority of the preacher's voice: as Anne Régent-Susini explains with reference to Bossuet, "The preacher's voice and the voice given to God himself overlap."[27] In this sermon devoted to preaching, Bossuet makes just such a conflation as he rails against the sins of the world and the sins of the court in particular:

> Venez donc écouter attentivement la défense de la vérité, dans la bouche des prédicateurs; venez recevoir par leur ministère la parole de Jésus-Christ condamnant le monde et ses vices, et ses coutumes, et ses maximes antichrétiennes: car, comme dit saint Jean Chrysostome, Dieu nous ayant ordonné deux choses, d'écouter et d'accomplir sa sainte parole, quand aura le courage de la pratiquer celui qui n'a pas la patience de l'entendre? quand lui ouvrira-t-il son cœur, s'il lui ferme jusqu'à ses oreilles? quand lui donnera-t-il sa volonté, s'il lui refuse même son attention?[28]

> (Come and listen attentively to the defense of the truth through the mouths of preachers; come and receive through their ministry the word of Christ condemning the world and its vices, customs, and anti-Christian maxims: for, as Saint John of the Cross said, because God has ordered us to do two things, to listen and to carry out his holy word, when will he who does not have the patience to hear it have the courage to put it into practice? When will he open his heart to it, if he closes his ears to it? When will he bend his will to it if he refuses even to pay it any attention?)

The questions posed at the end of this extract about those who close their ears to Christ's words are surely directed also at the members of the court present at that time listening to the preacher himself. Blocking one's ears to the truths of the church is an option that Bossuet refuses to countenance. Later in the sermon, he brings to the fore again the vividness of the moment, quoting from another section of the gospel of Matthew (13:13), in order to compare those who are listening with attention and those who are not:

> La presse est dans les églises durant cette sainte quarantaine; plusieurs prêtent l'oreille attentivement; mais qu'il y en a, dit le Fils de Dieu, qui en voyant ne voient pas, et en écoutant n'écoutent pas![29]

> (The churches are full during this holy time of Lent; several people lend their ears attentively; but there are those, says the Son of God, who while seeing see not and while hearing hear not!)

Just as Bossuet the preacher might not be receiving the full attention that he feels he deserves, so, too, does he consider the figure of Christ as one who "n'est plus écouté, ou il est écouté si négligemment, qu'on donnerait plus d'attention aux discours les plus inutiles" (is no longer listened to, or is listened to so negligently that more attention is paid to the most useless of discourses).[30]

Bossuet reiterates over the course of the sermon that the truth need not be heard outwardly through sounds that are "distincts et articulés" (distinct and clear) but can be found instead "dans les consciences" (in our consciences).[31] As he emphasizes toward the end of the sermon, "La véritable prédication se fait dans le cœur" (True preaching takes place in the heart).[32]

The sermon concludes with an evocation by Bossuet of the actual space in which he is preaching and a prayer to find the right words to speak in front of the king, for he considers it a thing of joy to "annoncer votre Évangile à ce grand monarque" (announce your Gospel to this great monarch).[33] And it is that monarch, God's representative on earth according to Bossuet, who is addressed directly at the end as the ideal person to listen to Christian truth: "Sire, c'est Dieu qui doit parler dans cette chaire" (Sir, it is God who must speak in this pulpit).[34]

Even if Bossuet's rhetoric failed to transform the king into a model of piety, Louis's mistress of the time, Louise de la Vallière, was suitably disturbed by the preacher's words to flee to a convent in Chaillot, only for Louis to pursue her and persuade her to return to court.[35] After Louise finally entered the Carmelite convent in the Faubourg Saint-Jacques in 1674, long after she had been usurped in Louis's affections by the marquise de Montespan, she was able to hear Bossuet's voice once more when he preached the sermon on her solemn profession in the presence of the queen. Having made her decision to leave the diversions and trappings of courtly life behind, Louise is told by Bossuet that, now that her spiritual transformation is effected, words are no longer necessary: "Je n'ai pas besoin de parler," he tells her, "les choses parlent assez d'elles-mêmes" (I do not need to speak, things speak enough about themselves).[36]

Bossuet's reputation as a remarkable and memorable orator was assured for many more years. His final funeral oration, given on 10 March 1687, for the king's cousin le Grand Condé, Louis de Bourbon, who will play a major part in the second half of this book, ends with an affecting reminder of the preacher's voice. We are left with an evocation of sound, albeit a fading one: "Je réserve au troupeau que je dois nourrir de la parole de vie les restes d'une voix qui tombe, et d'une ardeur qui s'éteint" (I reserve for my flock, whom I must feed with the word of life, the remnants of a voice that falls and an ardor that is petering out).[37]

Vaux-le-Vicomte, 17 August 1661

At the same time that Louis's divinely ordained status was being affirmed by Bossuet at the Louvre, the monarch set about asserting his power on a more temporal level. He was resolute in his wish to demonstrate to his subjects a break with the pattern of government that had persisted under the cardinals Richelieu and Mazarin. One spectacular event that took place just a few months before Bossuet's Louvre sermons was to prove emblematic of this change, and it was an event in which sound played an essential role.

On 17 August 1661, the king along with his brother Philippe (known as Monsieur); Philippe's wife, Henriette d'Angleterre (Madame); the Queen Mother; and an entourage including the prince de Condé made their way from Fontainebleau to Nicolas Fouquet's extravagant castle and estate at Vaux-le-Vicomte to attend an event staged by Fouquet in honor of the king and attended by six thousand guests. The royal party was invited to rest in the château (designed by Louis le Vau and with interior decor by the painter Charles Le Brun) and to wander through the gardens created by André Le Nôtre. As the superintendent of finance under Mazarin, Fouquet had had designs on being named the king's new first minister after the cardinal's death, and he thought that Louis would be suitably impressed by the magnificent display put on for his benefit. However, Fouquet's fate, it would seem, had already been sealed,[38] and such a show of opulence only hardened Louis's resolve (aided by the connivance of Fouquet's rival, Jean-Baptiste Colbert) against him.

For the event at Vaux-le-Vicomte, other witnesses wrote with awe about the spectacle that had been prepared by Fouquet, most notably Jean de La Fontaine, André Félibien, and Jean Loret (in the gazette *La Muze historique*), all three of whom had themselves received Fouquet's generous support and were unaware of their patron's impending disgrace. Although the 17 August event is usually described in primarily visual terms, Fouquet clearly wished the entertainment to appeal to all the senses. As La Fontaine, describing the evening in both verse and prose to his friend François de Maucroix a few days later (22 August), writes, "Tous les sens furent enchantés" (All the senses were enchanted),[39] with Félibien also mentioning how the darkness of night helped "surprendre les sens" (surprise the senses).[40] While the castle, firework displays, fountains, and theatrical entertainment might have appealed to the eyes, the lavish banquet (created by François Vatel) and sumptuous gardens would have enticed the senses of taste, smell, and touch.

Félibien gives a succinct summary of the entertainments on offer. At first glance, the repetition of "on voit" would seem to accentuate the visual over the other senses, but closer examination shows that "voir" here masks the involvement, both direct and indirect, of all the senses:

> Si vous vous faites réflexion sur toutes ces choses, vous trouverez que tout ce qu'on a écrit de fabuleux dans les romans n'égale point cette vérité: on se promène entre deux murs d'eau, on marche sous une voûte de feu, les rochers s'ouvrent, les arbres se fendent et la terre marche: on voit des danses, des ballets, des mascarades et des comédies. On voit des fleurs, on voit des batailles, on voit la nuit et le jour en même temps, on entend la plus douce harmonie du monde; on mange de toutes sortes de viandes et l'on boit des vins les plus exquis.[41]

> (If you reflect upon all these things, you will find that all the fables contained in romances are nothing compared to this truth: we wander between two walls of water, we walk under a vault of fire, rocks open up, trees are riven in two, and the earth walks: we see dance, ballet, masques, and theatrical plays. We see flowers, battles, night and day at the same time, we hear the sweetest harmony in the world; we eat all kinds of meat and drink the most exquisite wines.)

The power of sound would seem to have assailed the guests with particular force, and it was a force that was not unambiguously positive. On the less threatening side, Félibien notes that the fountains made "un agréable murmure" (an agreeable murmuring) and that the waterfalls "faisaient un si grand et si beau bruit, que chacun jurait que c'était le trône de Neptune" (made such a great and beautiful noise that everybody swore that it was Neptune's throne).[42] Moreover, while the king dined, "les vingt-quatre violons faisaient retentir tous les lieux d'alentour de leur charmante harmonie" (the king's twenty-four violins made all the surrounding places resonate with their charming harmony),[43] with music composed by Jean-Baptiste Lully, who that year was appointed as master of the king's music. Yet both Félibien and la Fontaine describe the way in which the fireworks depicted a raging battle: the former writes that "la prodigieuse quantité de boîtes, de pétards et de fusées rendait l'air aussi clair que le jour, et le bruit des uns et des autres mêlé à celui des tambours et des trompettes représentait fort bien une grande et furieuse bataille" (the prodigious quantity of rockets, squibs, and fireworks made the air as light as day, and the noise made by all of them mingled with that made by the drums and trumpets gave a very impressive representation of a great and furious battle),[44] and in the following passage from La Fontaine's letter, the noise is described in one rhyming couplet as both "épouvantable" (terrifying) and "agréable" (agreeable), with only the reassuring presence of the king managing to calm "la peur":

> Parmi ce spectacle si rare,
> Figure-toi le tintamarre,
> Le fracas, et les sifflements,
> Qu'on entendait à tous moments.
> De ces colonnes embrasées
> Il renaissait d'autres fusées,
> Ou d'autres formes de pétard,
> Ou quelque autre effet de cet art
> Et l'on voyait régner la guerre
> Entre ces enfants du tonnerre.
> L'un contre l'autre combattant,
> Voltigeant et pirouettant,
> Faisait un bruit épouvantable,
> C'est-à-dire un bruit agréable.
> Figure-toi que les Échos
> N'ont pas un moment de repos,
> Et que le chœur des Néréides
> S'enfuit sous ses grottes humides.
> De ce bruit Neptune étonné
> Eût craint de se voir détrôné,
> Si le monarque de la France
> N'eût rassuré par sa présence
> Ce dieu des moites tribunaux,
> Qui crut que les dieux infernaux
> Venaient donner des sérénades
> A quelques-unes des Naïades.
> Enfin, la peur l'ayant quitté,
> Il salua Sa Majesté.[45]

(In the middle of such a rare spectacle, / Imagine the jangling, / The din, and the whistling, / That could be heard at every moment. / Out of the burning columns, / Yet more fireworks were reborn, / Or other kinds of squib, / Or some other effect of this art, / And war could be seen to reign / Between these children of thunder. / One fighting against the other, / Tumbling and pirouetting, / Made a terrifying noise, / That is to say, a very agreeable noise. / Imagine how the echoes / Had no time to rest, / And the chorus of Nereids flee into their damp grottoes. / From this noise astonished Neptune / Would have feared seeing himself dethroned / Were it not for the French monarch / Who reassured him by his presence, / And this God of watery seats of justice / Who thought that the infernal gods / Were coming to serenade / Some of the Naiads. / Finally, his fear having left him, / Neptune greeted His Majesty.)

Even if Louis's presence placated the fear that followed such noise, it did not prevent what La Fontaine calls "la catastrophe de ce fracas" (the catastrophe of this din): two horses that took fright "à cause du feu et du bruit" (because of the fire and the noise) were killed by plunging into a deep ditch. The poet's words, "Je ne croyais pas que cette relation dût avoir une fin si tragique et si pitoyable" (I did not think that this account would have such a tragic and pitiable end), on one level indicate the dangers associated with noise, distinctly at odds with the celebratory tone of the occasion, but on another level seem strangely prophetic of the imminent disgrace and ruin of the man who had created this feast of the senses: Nicolas Fouquet.

It is evident that Fouquet's opulence and political ambitions were not the only aspects that provoked Louis's anger: seizing cultural as well as political control was fundamental to the king's (and Colbert's) plans.[46] The entertainment at Vaux-le-Vicomte overtly presented Fouquet, who between 1654 and 1661 was already known to be the most significant literary and artistic patron in the land,[47] as a rival protector of writers and artists. Only two years earlier, the dominant playwright of the age, Pierre Corneille, had dedicated his new play *Œdipe* to Fouquet, praising the *surintendant* for his support of "gens d'esprit" (people of spirit) and, in what might have seemed like an affront to Louis's cultural ambitions, adding that "sa bonté s'est étendue jusqu'à ressusciter les Muses ensevelies dans un long silence" (his goodness has extended so far as to resuscitate the Muses who have been buried in a long silence).[48] In other words, as Corneille implies,

Fouquet was giving a voice to writers who previously had not been granted the opportunity by other patrons.

One of the centerpieces of the evening was the staging of Molière's *Les Fâcheux*. Having already hosted a performance of Molière's *L'École des maris* (The School for Husbands) in the presence of Monsieur (who was the official patron of the dramatist's troupe) just a few weeks earlier at Vaux-le-Vicomte, Fouquet was here displaying a newly commissioned—and experimental—work by the playwright. If Molière is to be believed, *Les Fâcheux* had been "conçue, faite, apprise, et représentée en quinze jours" (conceived, written, learned, and staged within fifteen days).[49] The episodic nature of the drama, about a young man, Éraste (played by La Grange), whose attempts to meet his lover are thwarted by encounters with a succession of *fâcheux*—old bores (many of whom were performed by Molière himself)[50]—may reflect the hastiness of the enterprise, but as the editors of the Pléiade edition of Moliere's theater, Georges Forestier and Claude Bourqui, note, it marks also "the occasion of a completely original mingling of danced and spoken theatre, which paved the way for a mixed genre which Molière and Lully were to make their speciality":[51] Molière and Lully were in effect combining their talents to create the first *comédie-ballet*, a genre they were to develop considerably in later works, most notably *Le Bourgeois Gentilhomme* (The Bourgeois Gentleman). Not only do ballets conclude each of the three acts in *Les Fâcheux*, but also songs are sung within the play itself, not least by the *fâcheux* Lysandre in the first act who, as the stage directions indicate, "chante, parle et danse tout ensemble" (sings, speaks, and dances all at once),[52] and refers to Lully directly as "Baptiste le très cher" (the very dear Baptiste [I.3, p. 162]).

In the prologue to *Les Fâcheux*, written by Fouquet's secretary Paul Pellisson and recited by Madeleine Béjart in the guise of a nymph emerging from a seashell (which itself inspired a street song),[53] Louis is hailed as "le plus grand Roi du Monde" (the greatest king in the world [line 1]), the only person able to "Agir incessamment, tout voir, et tout entendre" (act constantly, see and hear everything [14]) and to unleash "ce nouveau Théâtre" (this new theater [24]) by making the statues walk and the trees speak (17–18). Given the knowing references made throughout to the king's presence at Vaux-le-Vicomte and to the theatrical and musical circumstances of that evening of 17 August, Molière's text, albeit within a primarily comic context, alludes to another benefactor. The *fâcheux* Caritidès, played by Molière, tells Éraste that "auprès de notre Roi, vous serez mon Mécène" (beside our king, you will be my patron [III.2, p. 664]), and, even though the term "mécène" is here used with the specific sense of "mediator,"[54] it is perhaps telling that this line was omitted from later performances of the play, after Fouquet's arrest.[55] Caritidès reads aloud his written request (known as a *placet*) that he would like to have conveyed to the monarch. This submission of a *placet* was very much a current issue that the audience would have known about: Louis, as he explains in his *Mémoires*, had given "à tous mes sujets sans distinction, la liberté de s'adresser à moi à toutes heures, de vive voix et par placets" (to all my subjects, without distinction, the freedom to address me at any hour, both in person and through petitions), resulting in, he admits, "un très grand nombre" (a very great number) of such requests.[56] The bore Caratidès's *placet* contains a lengthy and pedantic complaint about the poor use of urban signage, concluding with the request that the king create, "pour le bien de son État, et la gloire de son Empire, une Charge de Contrôleur, Intendant, Correcteur, Réviseur, et Restaurateur général desdites inscriptions" (for the good of his State and the honor of his Empire, a post of Controller, Superintendent, Corrector, Reviser, and general Restorer of said signages [183]). It is surely not too far-fetched to imagine Molière (who would not have been aware of Fouquet's imminent disgrace, already decided by Louis and Colbert) playfully referring here to the title most closely associated with Fouquet, *surintendant*, and to his benefactor's political and cultural ambitions. Most of the audience able to hear Molière himself reciting these words would no doubt have chuckled at the evocation of the host of the evening's entertainment, but it is unlikely that Louis would have appreciated such a reminder of his minister's pretensions.

Fouquet's arrest two weeks later marked to a large extent the end of the complex networks of clientelism and patronage that had prevailed throughout the seventeenth century (described in the title of one collection of essays on the subject as the golden age of patronage).[57] As Craig Moyes puts it, "It was upon the ruins of Fouquet's success that Colbert would build the *representational* absolutism of Louis XIV."[58] Even though individual cultural patrons still existed in the later years of the seventeenth century, 1661 marks the moment when Colbert, as the sole keeper of the state's purse, centralized a system of remunerating writers, musicians, and artists with the precise expectation that they participate in the collective glorification of the king.[59]

The Arrest and Trial of Fouquet: Competing Voices

As Louis left Vaux-le-Vicomte in the early hours of the morning to the accompaniment of another sound, that of the "tambours,"[60] Fouquet may have had little inkling of the fate that had already been prepared for him, but by the time he was summoned to attend the king and his entourage (including the two greatest military leaders of the time, le Grand Condé and Turenne) in Nantes at the beginning of September, he seemed to be wavering between hope of preferment and fear of arrest. As ever, in the world of courtly intrigue, the most information that could be gleaned was through hearsay and secretive conversations, for the greater part words spoken rather than committed to paper; we should not forget that one of the most common French words for "rumor" was "bruit," which was the same word used for "noise." Similarly, a host of other terms denoting gossip and rumor, such as "babiller" (babble), "caqueter" (prattle), "causer" (chatter), and "murmurer" (murmur), relate to sounds that are heard rather than words that are written down.[61]

Fouquet's confidant, Jean Hérault, known as M. de Gourville, writes in his memoirs that, just before his departure for Nantes, Fouquet

> me demanda ce que l'on disait à son sujet, et comment on croyait qu'il était avec le Roi. Je lui répondis que les uns disaient qu'il allait être déclaré premier ministre, et les autres qu'il y avait une grande cabale contre lui pour le perdre.[62]
>
> (asked me what was being said about him, and on what terms it was believed he was with the king. I replied to him that some said that he was going to be announced as first minister and others that there was a great plot against him with the aim of bringing him down.)

Another friend, Louis-Henri de Loménie, comte de Brienne, known as le Jeune Brienne, reports in his memoirs that when in Nantes Fouquet also asked what was being spoken about in the king's entourage, de Brienne's reply, "Que vous allez être arrêté" (That you are going to be arrested), was met with the response, "C'est Colbert qui sera arrêté, et non moi" (Colbert is the one who will be arrested, not me).[63]

Fouquet was wrong. On 5 September 1661, he, and not Colbert, was arrested in Nantes on the king's orders by the comte d'Artagnan (best known today as one of the Three Musketeers). As Colbert had provided detailed plans for the suggested arrest of Fouquet to Cardinal Mazarin as far back as 21 December 1659 (including the place, circumstances, and even name of the arresting officer), it is evident who was behind the 1661 arrest.[64] Fouquet's papers were seized (first in Nantes itself, then in all his other properties), a number of his subordinates (including Pellisson,[65] who had penned the Prologue to Molière's Les Fâcheux) were arrested, and troops were immediately sent to secure Belle-Isle, the island on the south coast of Brittany that Fouquet had purchased in 1658. The discovery of a document (written a few years earlier) hidden behind a mirror in his château at Saint-Mandé, in which Fouquet detailed plans for an armed assault and for fortifying Belle-Isle in the event of his arrest, only hardened Louis's resolve against him. In fact, Fouquet's concealed paper was concerned with mobilizing familial networks to defend himself against Mazarin should the cardinal turn against him (something Mazarin had done with other ministers) and not against the monarch, but it became easier for Louis and Colbert to include the severe charge of *lèse-majesté* against the disgraced minister.[66]

Fouquet's trial was officially set in motion in November 1661 by a "Commission" (officially a proclamation by the king) naming those appointed to the *chambre de justice* and detailing the "abus et malversations, crimes et délits" (abuses and misdemeanors, crimes and offenses) ostensibly committed against the state ever since 1635 by people "de quelque qualité et condition qu'ils soient" (of whatever status or birth they may be).[67] Colbert's decision not to name Fouquet individually at this point and to appear to be launching a general investigation into financial malpractice may well have contributed to the extreme slowness of the whole process.[68] Of the twenty-eight judges who were appointed, eleven came from the Paris courts, eight from the royal administration, and nine from a range of provincial parlements. Colbert was actively involved in the vetting of candidates of both judges and officers of the court, taking care to avoid those who might be overly favorable to Fouquet.[69] Before his arrest, Fouquet (thinking that he was in line to become first minister) had been persuaded by the king to sell his charge of *procureur général* at the Parlement of Paris, thus preventing him from taking up his right to be tried by his fellow parlementaires.[70]

Although Colbert did not appear in the chamber, he remained in the wings, choreographing as far as he could the attacks against his rival. In Daniel Dessert's words, Colbert "meticulously constructed all the workings of the machine that was destined to bring him down."[71] Evidently there were many who felt that Colbert's words in the king's ear had been instrumental in bringing his rival to justice. The sentiments uttered by Bossuet in the same set of Lenten sermons considered earlier in this chapter could easily be interpreted as a direct criticism of Colbert at the very time that the trial was in its early stages, with Fouquet's "crime" being considered of less seriousness than Colbert's attempts to prompt the monarch. "Infecter les oreilles du Prince, ha! c'est un crime plus grand que d'empoisonner les fontaines publiques, et plus grand sans comparaison que de voler les trésors publics" (Infecting the ears of the prince, ha! It is a greater crime than poisoning the public fountains, and greater beyond compare than stealing public treasures),[72] declared Bossuet from the Louvre pulpit.

A core group of people who were loyal to Colbert played a prominent role in the trial and contributed to the strong sense that the cards were stacked against Fouquet from the outset. Pierre Séguier, the chancellor of France, who had a long history of hostile relations with Fouquet,[73] headed the chamber; Colbert's maternal uncle, Henri Pussort, was one of the most partisan and prominent members of the Paris judges; Louis Berryer, who had no legal background, played a significant role in the proceedings and reported back to Colbert during the trial; and Joseph Foucault, who had been actively involved in the gathering and suppression of a number of Fouquet's papers, was appointed as *greffier*, the court clerk. Olivier Lefèvre d'Ormesson and Jacques le Cormier de Sainte-Hélène were the two *rapporteurs* at the trial, appointed by the royal council and initially viewed with suspicion by the Fouquet family, who suspected that both men would be biased. The *rapporteur* was a judge who reviewed all the evidence accumulated in a trial and reported on all the various legal discussions, arguments, and points of law to the other judges; for a trial such as this one, which was so complex and detailed, the role of the *rapporteur* was crucial in clarifying and verifying evidence and legal procedure (under the aegis of the *procureur du roi*). While d'Ormesson showed an extraordinary independence in exercising his functions (he seemed impervious to pressure from the king and Colbert), Sainte-Hélène, who had ties to Colbert, remained closely aligned to the royal prosecutors.[74]

The chamber convened for the first time in a grand opening ceremony at the seat of the high courts in Paris, the Palais de Justice, on 3 December 1661, where Séguier, Guillaume de Lamoignon (the *premier président* of the Parlement of Paris), and the newly appointed *procureur général* Denis Talon (a former colleague of Fouquet on the royal bench at the parlement) gave long speeches to a large audience consisting mainly of people from society circles. With Fouquet incarcerated in Vincennes prison from late December and not initially required to appear in person, all proceedings would take place in the Palais de Justice until June 1663, when Fouquet was moved to the Bastille and the court relocated to the nearby Arsenal. Soon after, Talon was replaced as prosecutor by another protégé of Colbert, Guy Chamillart.

The significance of the location of the Palais de Justice, immediately adjoining the Pont Neuf, cannot be overstated when considering Parisian sound worlds of the time. Not only did the singing of songs and the sale of polemical newssheets on the Pont Neuf act as a running commentary and gauge of opinion on the trial, but also many participants in the legal proceedings would have found it impossible to ignore the songs as they made their way to and from the Palais. As Tom Hamilton has written of the last years of the sixteenth and early years of the seventeenth centuries, the Palais itself was "the center of the Parisian commerce and information exchange," its courtyard filled with stalls (selling books and prints in particular) and peddlers.[75] The great hall nearby was another important selling space, with the more established booksellers located there. We know also that actors and singers performed in the Place Dauphine, immediately in front of the Palais de Justice. Even though there were strict rules about what *colporteurs* were allowed to sell and where they could be stationed, it is likely that these directives were often flouted,[76] and songs may well have been performed and purchased near the palace itself, even though the presence of armed guards in the immediate environs would have made access less easy.

Before and during the early stages of the trial, the general attitude toward Fouquet in the street seems to have been largely negative. Fouquet himself was well aware of the jeers and hostile songs of crowds as he was transferred in early December 1661 from prison in the Château d'Angers to confinement in the Château d'Amboise, and then again at the end of the month from Amboise to Vincennes.[77] One anonymous sonnet, titled "La France à la Chambre de Justice 1661" (France in the Chamber of Justice 1661), for example, gives the advice, "Si Fouquet est coupable, avance son supplice" (If Fouquet is guilty, bring his punishment forward).[78] Yet as the trial progressed, the mobilization of Fouquet's friends, including La Fontaine and even Pellisson from his prison cell, in circulating various pamphlets in his defense enabled people outside the courtroom to have a more nuanced knowledge of the facts, a more favorable impression of Fouquet himself, and an awareness of Colbert's seemingly malign influence on proceedings. One quatrain (found in the *Chansonnier Maurepas* and dated 1662) compares Fouquet the squirrel (his family's coat of arms bore a squirrel) to the lizard Michel le Tellier (Louis XIV's minister of state for war, responsible for overseeing Fouquet's incarceration) and the snake Colbert:

Le petit Escureuil est pour toujours en cage,
Le Lezar plus adroit, fait bien son personnage;
Mais le plus fin de tous est un vilain Serpent,
Qui s'abaissant, s'eleve et s'avance en rampant.[79]

(The little Squirrel is still in his cage, / The Lizard, more cunning, acts out his role well; / But the most skilled of all is a vile Serpent, / Who in prostrating himself, gets higher and advances himself while creeping along.)

There is no doubt that the content of songs that were being sung on the subject of the trial was known not only to the wider populace but also to both those participating in the chamber and those in power. D'Ormesson observes on 5 April 1664 how even the king was aware of what was being sung about him and Colbert:

L'on me dit que l'on avoit fait une chanson contre le roy, dont il estoit fort offensé, et offroit bien de l'argent à celuy qui luy en descouvriroit l'auteur, par laquelle on luy reprochoit qu'il n'aimoit que luy, opprimoit grands et petits et ne consideroit que Colbert. L'on en a fait aussy une fort sanglante contre M. le chancelier, sur son injustice, et qu'il veut estre juge de M. Fouquet pour le condamner.[80]

(I am told that a song was composed against the king, who was highly offended by it, and he offered a large amount of money to the person who could find out its author; in the song the king was accused of loving only himself and oppressing great and small alike and holding only Colbert in high esteem. A very bloody song was also composed against the chancellor, about his injustice and how he wants to be M. Fouquet's judge in order to condemn him.)

As much as he may have wished to restrain the voices and rumors that gradually became louder and more forceful in favor of Fouquet, the king's vain attempts to track down the authors of critical songs about him and Colbert show quite how intangible and widespread these sounds were. They managed to both inform the wider populace of Fouquet's plight and persuade people of the perceived injustice of those in power. For all Louis's tight control of his subjects, sounds and songs proved much more elusive and difficult to suppress.

The many conversations that were held about the trial (as reported in journals and letters from the time) formed further oral backdrop to the changing perception of Fouquet. Soon after the arrest in September 1661, Séguier received a letter from his secretary Saulger, informing him that "je vois bien du monde tous les jours qui me parle de la disgrâce de M. le Surintendant, mais c'est avec la plus grande joie du monde, dans les compagnies, et partout ailleurs" (I see many people every day who speak of the surintendant's disgrace, but they speak of it with the greatest joy, both in society and everywhere else).[81] Yet in the later stages of the trial, the marquise de Sévigné, whose fourteen surviving letters to Simon Arnauld de Pomponne present a vivid and moving account of the trial of their mutual friend, is at all times alert to what is being said about Fouquet outside the courtroom, and, even if she might be expected to report the positive descriptions of him, her comment in 1664 that "on parle fort à Paris de son admirable esprit et de sa fermeté" (they speak much in Paris of his admirable spirit and fortitude)[82] presents the impression that the wider public became more favorably inclined toward the former *surintendant* as the trial progressed.[83] Even relatives of the king, such as his cousin le Grand Condé, seem alert to the gossip on the street about Fouquet. As the trial neared its end, Condé wrote in a letter on 12 December 1664 that "on en parle fort diversement; lui [Fouquet] et tous ses parents paraissent dans une très grande sécurité, mais le reste du monde croit que son affaire ira mal" (everybody speaks about it in very different ways; Fouquet and all his relatives appear very secure, but everybody else believes that his case will end badly).[84]

Although the major sources on the trial itself inevitably come from written documents, we should not forget the orality that lies at the base of all the accounts. Sévigné, for example, deliberately evokes spoken conversations when discussing her written accounts with Pomponne: "Je n'ai pas moins de plaisir à vous entretenir que vous en avez à lire mes lettres" (I have no less pleasure in conversing with you as you have in reading my letters), she exclaims at the beginning of one letter (24 November 1664, 1:61). Moreover, her narrative derives not from direct experience of the trial (although she observed Fouquet leaving the court, she was never present within the chamber itself) but from discussions she held with her relative d'Ormesson. (Sévigné's uncle Philippe de Coulanges, who raised her, was married to d'Ormesson's sister.) D'Ormesson, for his part, despite his protests to the contrary, may have been influenced by Sévigné's conversations with him. In his journal from April 1664, he mentions an acquaintance suggesting to him "que Mme de Sévigné me gouvernoit en faveur de M. Fouquet contre le sentiment de mon père, et des sottises de cette force" (that Mme de Sévigné was directing me in Fouquet's favor against my father's wishes, and stupidities of that ilk).[85] Orality is always at the forefront of d'Ormesson's journal, as he relates the discussions held within and outside the courtroom. D'Ormesson's account is of particular interest, because we are able to witness an evolution in his attitude toward the accused man, especially as he began to uncover more and more irregularities in the legal process. Foucault the *greffier* also left a detailed, if more prosaic, account of all exchanges that took place in the chamber.[86]

Although from late 1661 to mid-1664 Fouquet did not appear in the chamber in person, the proceedings centered mainly on interviews conducted with the prisoner and involved the reading aloud of his many papers defending his position: Fouquet came from a legal background and was careful to use all his specialized knowledge in the presentation of his case. D'Ormesson's verbal exchanges with other participants, notably the hostile Foucault and Séguier, still make for vivid retelling, even when the factual details seem tedious. One incident from the days before Fouquet made his first appearance shows the lengths to which the chancellor Séguier attempted to silence d'Ormesson (aided by Foucault). Séguier tried to dominate the session by expounding on the *marc d'or* (a payment made to the king in exchange for titular offices of state), as described by d'Ormesson himself:

> Le mercredy 22 octobre, M. le chancelier commença par expliquer l'affaire du marc d'or et redire mille choses inutiles. Foucault estoit derrière moy, qui me disoit: "Ne dites mot." Enfin, je voulus parler d'un travail que j'avois fait pour expliquer cette affaire et faire voir la difficulté. M. le chancelier, persuadé que je ne puis jamais parler que contre le procureur général, ne voulut jamais le souffrir. Je le proposai trois fois exprès, et tousjours il l'empescha.[87]

> (On Wednesday, 22 October, the chancellor began explaining the business with the *marc d'or* and repeating a thousand useless things. Foucault was behind me, saying, "Don't say a word." Finally, I wanted to speak of work that I had done to explain this business and to show the difficulties involved. The chancellor, convinced that I can only ever speak against the public prosecutor, did not want to allow it at all. Three times I deliberately suggested it, and always he prevented it.)

The true drama of the trial came with Fouquet's appearance and the chance for those in the chamber to hear his voice directly. The eloquence of that voice was crucial not only in swaying those judges who were considering the death sentence (as was expected by Colbert and the king) but also in news of that eloquence being disseminated beyond the confines of the chamber to Fouquet's supporters and to the wider populace.

His exchanges with Séguier were closely followed, and his success in gaining the advantage over his adversary is commented on at several junctures by d'Ormesson and Sévigné. On 18 November, after one of Fouquet's first appearances, Sévigné notes that "il a parfaitement bien répondu" (he responded perfectly well) to detailed questions, adding that "s'il continue, ses interrogations lui seront bien avantageuses" (if he continues, his interrogations will work in his favor).[88] The following day, she mentions that Colbert himself is angry at "l'extrême approbation que l'on donne à tout ce que répond M. Foucquet" (the high level of approval that is shown for every response made by Fouquet), adding that "il [Colbert] craint qu'il [Fouquet] ne gagne des cœurs" (Colbert fears that Fouquet is winning over people's hearts).[89]

On the few occasions that he loses his rhetorical control, Sévigné signals the dangers he faces, such as when he showed his irritation on 21 November:

> Il s'est impatienté sur certaines objections qu'on lui faisait, et qui lui ont paru ridicules. Il l'a un peu trop témoigné, a répondu avec un air et une hauteur qui ont déplu. Il se corrigera, car cette manière n'est pas bonne.[90]

> (He became impatient over certain objections that were being made to him and which seemed ridiculous to him. He showed his impatience a little too much, and replied with an air and haughtiness that displeased people. He will correct himself, because this way of replying is not good.)

While d'Ormesson tends to report Fouquet's words in indirect speech, Sévigné relishes the dramatization of the exchanges, giving Fouquet a voice on the page by quoting or representing a number of his interventions through dialogue. On one occasion, late in the trial, she quotes him at length applying his considerable legal knowledge to a definition of "crime d'État" (of which he was accused): in specifying his own loyalty to the Crown, Fouquet succeeds in turning the accusation of such a crime onto Séguier himself, who had been opposed to the king during the Fronde a decade earlier, resulting in the chancellor's embarrassment and the barely suppressed laughter of the judges. "Toute la France a su et admiré cette réponse" (The whole of France knew about and admired this reply), she reports.[91] At all points, Sévigné registers her own reaction at different stages in the trial. As Michael Hawcroft writes, "The narration may be about Fouquet, but the reader perceives him through the trembling voice of the letter-writer."[92]

Fouquet for his part is unafraid to speak at length in his own defense, and Sévigné (no doubt having been informed by d'Ormesson) is keen to communicate the effect such speeches have on those people who are to decide his fate. One such person, Jacques Renard (or Regnard), an ordinary magistrate (*conseiller*) at the Parlement of Paris (and who had worked with Fouquet when the latter had been *procureur général* in the same chamber), is shown to have been particularly impressed by one such speech, as described by Sévigné:

> Notre cher et malheureux ami a parlé deux heures ce matin, mais si admirablement bien, que plusieurs n'ont pu s'empêcher de l'admirer. M. Renard entre autres a dit: "Il faut avouer que cet homme est incomparable. Il n'a jamais si bien parlé dans le Parlement; il se possède mieux qu'il n'a jamais fait."[93]

> (Our dear and unfortunate friend spoke for two hours this morning, but he spoke so admirably well that several people could not help themselves from admiring him. Renard among others said: "One must admit that this man is incomparable. He never spoke so well in parlement; he is much more self-possessed than he has ever been.")

Both d'Ormesson and Sévigné describe another time when the elderly and infirm Séguier dozes off during a particularly detailed speech by Fouquet. Sévigné even claims that her friend's muddling of some crucial dates might have compromised his case had the chancellor been awake to hear it.[94] They also voice their suspicions that Séguier is trying to curtail the length of interrogations. According to Sévigné, Séguier (whom she calls *Puis*) is at all times mindful of the wishes of Colbert (to whom she gives the nickname *Petit*):

> *Puis* a promis de ne faire parler l'accusé que le moins qu'il pourrait. On trouve qu'il dit trop bien. On voudrait donc l'interroger

légèrement, et ne pas aller sur tous les articles. Mais lui, il veut parler sur tout, et ne veut pas qu'on juge son procès sur des chefs sur quoi il n'aura pas dit ses raisons. *Puis* est toujours en crainte de déplaire à *Petit*. Il lui fit excuse l'autre jour de ce que M. Foucquet avait parlé trop longtemps, mais qu'il n'avait pas pu l'interrompre.[95]

(*Puis* has promised to allow the accused to speak as little as possible. Everybody finds that he speaks rather too well. They would therefore like to interrogate him lightly, without going back over all the details. But he wishes to speak about everything, and does not want his trial to be judged on principles about which he has not explained his reasons. *Puis* is always afraid of displeasing *Petit*. He apologized to him the other day because Fouquet spoke for too long a time, but he had been unable to interrupt him.)

This evocation of Colbert exerting influence from behind the scenes indicates the role played by the cacophony of offstage voices in the trial, some attempting to prompt or even threaten participants, others commenting on the proceedings: as Sévigné remarks in the latter stages of the trial, "Les menaces, les promesses, tout est en usage" (Threats, promises, everything is in play).[96] In his journal, d'Ormesson remains highly aware of what is being said elsewhere. In Séguier's case, for instance, he writes, "Ce que l'on dit, c'est que l'on est fort mal satisfait de luy à la cour, et que sa foiblesse augmente de jour en jour" (What they are saying is that those at court are very unsatisfied with him, and that his weakness becomes more and more apparent from day to day).[97] Yet he knows that the reliability of such talk needs always to be questioned, as he hears rumors about himself that suggest, wrongly, that he is as malleable as Séguier would seem to be: "J'appris d'une autre personne que l'on me faisoit discourir dans le monde, et qu'on disoit que je conclurois à la mort de M. Fouquet, pour me raccommoder à la cour" (I learned from another person that I was being talked about in society and that they said that I would end up opting for Fouquet's death, in order to find favor at court).[98] A little later, he also hears reports of the king saying that if d'Ormesson opted for the death penalty, "Fouquet est perdu" (Fouquet is lost).[99] It would have been difficult to avoid succumbing to the pressure of these powerful voices.

The sound of other people's voices is constantly in the background of the accounts of the trial. Sometimes those voices communicate a truth that is at odds with the official version of events; at other times, voices of power attempt to dictate the course of events, and at yet other times there are voices that move away from a truthful depiction of the trial. Those who listen rather than hear (if we are to return to Barthes's distinction between the passivity of hearing and the active processing of listening) need to analyze and think through these contradictory voices, eventually coming to a conclusion of their own, rather like the decisions that the different judges (who were going to perform the roles of both speaker and listener) were about to make.

Once d'Ormesson was ready to sum up the case and make his recommendation for sentencing, he took care to cut himself off from all external influences and from discussing the case any further. Sévigné makes it clear that, on leaving his company for the final time before the judgment, she lets him hear her voice even if he refrains from allowing her to listen to his viewpoint:

> M. d'Ormesson m'a priée de ne le plus voir que l'affaire ne soit jugée. Il est dans le conclave, et ne veut plus avoir de commerce avec le monde. Il affecte une grande réserve; il ne parle point, mais il écoute, et j'ai eu le plaisir, en lui disant adieu, de lui dire tout ce que je pense.[100]

> (M. d'Ormesson has asked not to see me again until after the trial is over. He is hidden away, and does not want any contact with the world. He shows himself to be very reserved; he does not speak but he listens, and I had the pleasure, in bidding him farewell, of telling him all my thoughts about the matter.)

First d'Ormesson (between 9 and 13 December) and then the other *rapporteur* Sainte-Hélène (on 15 and 16 December) spoke, each concluding with opposing suggestions for sentencing. After summing up, d'Ormesson recommended that Fouquet be saved from the death penalty but sent into exile instead. On Sunday the 14th, d'Ormesson attended Mass at Notre-Dame instead of his usual place of worship to avoid meeting people whom he knew and who knew him: "Car tout le monde tesmoigne tant de satisfaction de mon opinion, que j'ay cru fort à propos d'en éviter l'éclat" (As everybody is claiming to be so satisfied with my opinion, I thought it highly appropriate to avoid the glory).[101] Sévigné both corroborates d'Ormesson's modesty and praises above all his rhetorical skills and his ability to persuade his peers. If the judges were to vote for d'Ormesson's recommendation, this would in no small way be owing to his abilities as a speaker, moving away from the minutiae of written documents. As she informs Pomponne on the 17th,

> Je vous mandai samedi comme M. d'Ormesson avait rapporté l'affaire et opiné, mais je ne vous parlai point assez de l'estime extraordinaire qu'il s'est acquise par cette action. J'ai ouï dire à des gens du métier que c'est un chef-d'œuvre que ce qu'il a fait, pour s'être expliqué si nettement et avoir appuyé son avis sur des raisons si solides et si fortes; il y mêla de l'éloquence, et même de l'agrément. Enfin jamais homme de sa profession n'a eu une plus belle occasion de se faire paraître, et ne s'en est jamais mieux servi. S'il avait voulu ouvrir sa porte aux louanges, sa maison n'aurait pas désempli. Mais il a voulu être modeste; il s'est caché avec soin.[102]

(I told you on Saturday how M. d'Ormesson had reported on the trial and given his opinion, but I did not speak enough to you of the extraordinary respect that he has acquired through this action. I have heard people from the profession saying that he has created a masterpiece in explaining himself so clearly and basing his viewpoint on such solid and strong reasons; he has thrown eloquence, as well as enjoyment, into the mix. In the end, never has a man of his profession had a better opportunity to put himself on show, and never has such a man made better use of that opportunity. If he had wished to open his door to the praise, his house would not have been emptied of other people. But he wanted to remain modest; he has hidden himself away with care.)

By contrast, Sévigné is withering about Sainte-Hélène's lack of rhetorical skill as he summed up, mentioning how "il reprit toute l'affaire pauvrement et misérablement [. . .] lisant ce qu'il disait" (he went over the whole trial poorly and wretchedly, reading out what he had to say).[103] D'Ormesson is similarly critical of his colleague's way of "parlant languidement" (speaking languidly), noting also that the other judges appeared very dissatisfied with his performance.[104] Sainte-Hélène's recommendation was for Fouquet to be beheaded.

It now fell to each of the judges in the chamber to speak and to choose either d'Ormesson's or Sainte-Hélène's proposal. D'Ormesson noted the effectiveness of each man's rhetoric. Inevitably, he is particularly dismissive of most judges who opted for the death penalty, such as Noguès, who spoke "faiblement et misérablement" (weakly and wretchedly), or Hérault, who "a parlé peu et mal" (spoke little and badly), whereas he praises those who followed his recommendation, like La Toison (a councillor from Dijon), who spoke "fort bien, rapportant de belles citations de lois" (very well, making well-chosen quotation of laws),[105] or Roquesante, who "a parfaitement bien opiné" (argued perfectly well).[106] However, he maintains his fairness in praising Poncet for his "beaux termes" (beautiful words) even when the latter opts for the death sentence.[107]

When the final count of all judges was made, nine opted for a death sentence and thirteen for banishment. The eloquence of d'Ormesson had indeed been decisive. As the trial came to an end, d'Ormesson was able to reflect on the significance and effect of the proceedings on the whole of the nation, and he was keenly aware that the words spoken in the chamber extended to discussions far beyond the law courts: "Ainsy voilà ce grand procès fini, qui a esté l'entretien de toute la France du jour qu'il a commencé jusques au jour qu'il a esté terminé" (And so that is how this great trial has ended, a trial that has been the talk of the whole of France from the day it began up to the day that it ended).[108] The news of the verdict had immediately been passed on and had been received with joy, even by "les plus petites gens de boutique" (the lowliest shopworkers).[109]

A fortnight later, the wider conversation was still continuing, and it shows the extent to which people on the streets would have been able to hear strongly expressed sentiments excoriating the rich and powerful men who governed them. Set to memorable tunes, these songs had the power to be heard and remembered without needing to be read. One song that sets Fouquet's "innocence" against the "crime de ses ennemis" (crime of his enemies) proclaims that "toute l'Europe" (the whole of Europe) had been following the trial.[110] D'Ormesson's commentary on the number of songs appearing in the streets at that time shows the extent to which Fouquet's plight had affected people from all strata of society:

> La disposition des esprits sur cette affaire a paru, par la joye publique que les plus grands et les plus petits ont fait paroistre du salut de M. Fouquet, jusques à un tel excès qu'on ne le peut exprimer, tout le monde donnant des bénédictions aux juges qui l'ont sauvé, et à tous les autres des malédictions et toutes les marques de hayne et de mespris, les chansons contre eux commençant à paroistre; et je

suis surpris que, y ayant quinze jours passés que cette histoire est finie, le discours n'en finit point encore, et l'on en parle par toutes les compagnies comme le premier jour.[111]

(People's feelings on this matter have been made known, through the public joy that the greatest and the lowliest have shown at Fouquet's salvation, to such an extreme that it is impossible to express, with everybody giving their blessings to the judges who saved him, and curses and all the signs of hatred and contempt to all the others, with songs against them beginning to appear, and I am surprised that, fifteen days after the end of this tale, discussions about it have still not ended, and it is being spoken about in all kinds of company as if it were still the first day.)

The many songs about the trial that have survived confirm the comments made here. The judges who followed the wishes of Colbert and the king in suggesting the death sentence were targeted by name in several pieces. In one particularly scathing madrigal, it is suggested that these judges are the ones who should be hanged in Fouquet's place:

Le Cordeau de Fouquet est maintenant à vendre;
Mais nous avons Colbert, Chamillart, et Berrier,
Saint Helene, Pussort, Foucault, le Chancelier;
    Voila bien de quoy l'employer:
    Voila bien des Larrons a pendre;
    Voila bien des fous a lier.[112]

(Fouquet's rope is now for sale, / But we have Colbert, Chamillart, and Berrier, / Sainte-Hélène, Pussort, Foucault, the chancellor; / That is how to make good use of it: / Here are some felons to hang; / Here are some madmen to tie up.)

Another song, set to the popular tune "Laissez paître vos bêtes," excoriates the prosecutor Chamillart as a heartless man, full of fury, and accuses Sainte-Hélène of being solely interested in making his own fortune, while Pussort is depicted as having "beaucoup de langue / Et fort peu de Cerveau" (lots of talk / And very little brain).[113] By contrast, the same song ends with an evocation of d'Ormesson's courage:

> Ne finissons
> Point la chanson,
> Sans exalter ce d'Ormesson;
> Tant en renom
> Le bon dieu le bénisse
> Avec tous les gens de bien,
> Qui font bien la Justice,
> Et qui ne craignent rien.¹¹⁴

(Let us not finish / This song / Without exalting d'Ormesson; / So full of renown / May the good Lord bless him / Along with all goodly people / Who perform Justice well, / And who fear nothing.)

The general joy at the trial's outcome proved to be short-lived. The king, angry at the verdict, while not daring to risk public wrath by imposing the death sentence, used his powers to impose a much harsher sentence than that of exile: Fouquet was imprisoned for life in the cold and isolated royal fortress of Pignerol, situated in the Alps. In complete contrast to the jeers that had accompanied Fouquet's passage after his arrest, d'Ormesson writes of "tout le peuple luy donnant des bénédictions" (all the common people bestowing blessings on him) as he was taken away from the Bastille to make the journey to Pignerol.¹¹⁵ Fouquet died there in 1680, having spent the majority of the time in solitary confinement. Only in the final few years of his life was he allowed to exchange two letters a year with his wife. He was finally given permission to receive a visit from her and others in his family the year before his death.

D'Ormesson himself paid a heavy price for his resoluteness in not being swayed by the wishes of Colbert and the king during the trial, in direct contrast to those who had argued for sentencing Fouquet to death. After the death of his father, André d'Ormesson, in March 1665, it was expected that he would take up his father's seat as a councillor of state, but his attempts to lobby for the king's permission were pointedly ignored by Louis at court. In a direct snub, the seat was granted at the end of the year instead to his rival Henri Pussort (Colbert's uncle). Around the same time, d'Ormesson was relieved of his duties in the *chambre de justice*. The following year, his fellow (and rival) *rapporteur* in the trial, Sainte-Hélène, who had been all too easily swayed by those in the wings, was appointed as a councillor of state.¹¹⁶

At the moment of d'Ormesson's greatest triumph, he claims that he closed his door to those seeking to praise him. He was well aware of the irony that Fouquet, who had been regarded with "horreur" at the time of his imprisonment and whose execution was joyously anticipated at the beginning of his trial, was now "le sujet de la douleur et de la commisération publiques" (the subject of public sadness and commiseration). Indeed, d'Ormesson had perhaps the misplaced modesty but also the insight to recognize that "la véritable cause de l'applaudissement général" (the real cause of the general applause) was not so much praise of his own legal success as an expression of "la hayne que tout le monde a dans le cœur contre le gouvernement présent" (the hatred that everybody has in their hearts against the present government).[117]

Certainly, the songs and poems that circulated in the months and years following the trial point to an unease about those in power. One sonnet addressed to the king expresses the hope that "l'encens des flatteurs ne t'enteste jamais" (the incense of flatterers never makes you stubborn) and that "la verité seule aproche ton oreille" (truth alone comes to your ears).[118] Another sonnet, on Colbert, asserts that "vous ne méritez pas notre Surintendance" (you do not deserve to be our superintendent), unlike during the time of Fouquet when "on ne parloit en France, / Que de paix, que de rix, que de jeux, que d'amour" (in France people spoke only / Of peace, laughter, games, and love).[119]

Fouquet's disgrace, which came at the exact time the monarch was wishing to demonstrate his absolute control, instead raised questions on the street about the nature of that power and about Louis's choice of ministers and advisers. Jean-Christian Petitfils makes the point that, after Mazarin's death, the king needed an expiatory victim to atone for the financial misdemeanors of others.[120] The way in which Fouquet was treated during the trial and the very effective means used on the street to publicize his plight, on a primarily auditory level, brought to the fore the strong idea of Fouquet as victim in a trial that was perceived to be stage-managed by the ambitious Colbert. The fact that such manipulation was (temporarily) thwarted was even greater cause for the joy expressed at the trial's outcome. Louis, as we have seen, was well aware of what was being said and sung about him. It is telling that over the course of his long reign he never again risked public anger by reversing the judicial process in such an overt way. Voices on the street, both sung and spoken, did perhaps have an important part to play in the way that Louis conducted his reign.

Fouquet's popularity prior to his imprisonment and the deftness with which he pleaded his cause meant that it was not only those unattached to the royal court who took his side. We have seen already the fervent support offered by the marquise de Sévigné and her correspondent Pomponne. Others more closely connected to the reins of power were also sympathetic to his cause; for example, two figures who will play a prominent role in the second part of this book were involved on Fouquet's behalf. The king's cousin, the prince de Condé (known as le Grand Condé) and his favorite, Guitaut, were reported to have played an active role in offering encouragement and even trying to sway the judicial process. One month after the completion of the trial, d'Ormesson relates the story that Condé had sent Guitaut to one of the judges, La Toison, before the verdict. It is a story dominated by the power of the spoken word:

> L'on impute à M. le Prince l'avis de M. de la Toison; on dit qu'il luy envoya Guitaut et l'obligea de luy donner sa parole pour M. Fouquet. Je ne sçais si cette sollicitation est véritable; mais je sçais fort certainement d'une personne sûre, qui me l'a dit depuis le procès jugé, que, dès le voyage à Fontainebleau, M. le Prince avoit tesmoigné des sentiments très favorables pour M. Fouquet.[121]

> (M. de la Toison's viewpoint has been attributed to M. le Prince [Condé]; it is said that he sent Guitaut and obliged him to speak in favor of Fouquet. I do not know if this soliciting is true; but I know for certain from a reliable source, who told me that since the outcome of the trial, during a journey to Fontainebleau, M. le Prince revealed very favorable thoughts concerning Fouquet.)

In March 1665 Guitaut met d'Ormesson in the latter's home and assured him of Condé's support in his attempts to be accepted again by the king.[122] D'Ormesson continued to maintain cordial relations with Condé and writes in his journal that he was even received with great civility four years later at Condé's château in Chantilly.[123]

The figures that have been discussed in this chapter all come from the highest echelons of seventeenth-century French society. It might therefore justifiably be asked how and why such a privileged class might be affected by or at least reassessed through the sound worlds they inhabited.

The sumptuous festivities that Fouquet staged at Vaux-le-Vicomte before his arrest had relied as much on sound (music, recited lines, fireworks) as on sight in his misguided attempt to impress the king. Yet, as we observed, the descriptions of the event by those such as La Fontaine and Félibien hint at a darker side to the celebratory sounds, as the death of two horses taking fright at the noise was perceived to betoken an unexpectedly tragic end to the event and perhaps even was a presentiment of what was to come for the beneficent host that evening in August 1661.

As shown throughout part 1 of this book, the sound of song on the streets and particularly on the Pont Neuf proved a crucial counterbalance to the political, religious, and moral authorities in Paris at the time. Songs were accessible to and indeed accessed by people from all strata of society. Despite the attempts to curtail and censor song production, the ample opportunities for a song to be performed and heard at a given moment, without there necessarily being any documentary evidence, gave that piece an immediacy, freedom, and subversive potential that other, more permanent forms of art or writing could not achieve. Just as song could be used as propaganda to show the courage or steadfastness of military or political figures (and we will see an example of this in part 2), so, too, could it provide powerful counternarratives to those stories purveyed by the governing elite.

The major players in the Fouquet trial, from d'Ormesson right up to the king himself, were attuned to what was being sung about the events in the courtroom and about themselves, and they knew that such songs either reflected or had a bearing on the changing current of feeling expressed by the wider populace who called out as Fouquet's carriage passed by on the way to and from the trial. Even though the protagonists were almost exclusively highly born and educated, the extras in the drama were allowed a point of view and indeed a voice. Moreover, Fouquet relied above all on his verbal dexterity and quick-wittedness to defend himself in the chamber of justice and, crucially, to sway a majority of judges in his favor. Similarly, as d'Ormesson recognized, those judges who expressed themselves most skillfully during the summing-up process were generally those deemed to be most persuasive. In addition to the sound of singing and legal voices, the reported conversations of others about the trial (Colbert browbeating his allies, the king opining to his courtiers, others' discussion of Fouquet's and d'Ormesson's rhetorical successes in the chamber) had an effect on the outcome.

Another auditory forum in which the king's actions could openly be questioned was that of the church, where a preacher such as Bossuet (bringing motifs of hearing and sound to the center of his sermons) felt divinely ordained to address Louis directly, and not always uncritically. The primary impact of his preaching was through the immediacy of voice: most of Bossuet's sermons were not printed during his lifetime, and indeed they were not intended for publication; as Jean-Robert Armogathe argues, only through reading them aloud can their true authenticity be grasped.[124]

Examination of Louis XIV's reign in primarily visual terms, as has been the case with many studies of the monarch, can bring to the fore the ways in which Louis exploited his image as all-powerful ruler. There is certainly a clarity and fixity to be found in what is visible to all his courtiers and subjects, replicated in the many portraits, sculptures, engravings, and medals created in his honor. Even if, as cultural historian Peter Burke has done, the *revers de la médaille* of Louis's reign is explored,[125] it is still the visual impact of the reign that is highlighted. By contrast, as we observed in the first chapter, the intangibility, promiscuity, and omnidimensionality of sound can help give us a much more complex sense of a king who tried to control sound and yet was all too aware of the words that were being spoken, recited, and sung around him escaping his grasp. Sounds have the power to unsettle and even to triumph in unlikely circumstances—such as Fouquet's rhetorical success in the *chambre de justice*—but it should not be forgotten that sonic victories can be as transient as the sounds themselves that appear and disappear as soon as they are heard. After all, in Fouquet's case, Louis had the ultimate power to crush the court's verdict and impose a much harsher sentence. Similarly, even if Louise de la Vallière was so moved by a 1662 sermon to flee to a convent, Louis maintained the worldly strength to ignore Bossuet's exhortation for him to live a morally exemplary life.

While part 1 has been devoted to a wide range of sonic considerations (from literary representations of noise to songs, sermons, singers, speakers, and listeners), encapsulating diverse ranks of people, part 2 will revolve around one single four-line song performed on the cusp of 1661 and 1662, at the time of Louis's full assumption of power. And yet, as we will find, many of the ideas, themes, and sounds expressed thus far will come into particular focus through the sad song of the fate of Jacques Chausson.

PART II

CHAUSSON'S SONG

In this part of the book, we find ourselves moving from the wider pattern of sounds and song in early modern Paris (with the year 1661 featuring prominently) to one single four-line song that was first sung at the end of 1661. As in part 1, people from very different walks of life who nonetheless found themselves in very close proximity to each other will come to the fore. The singing of the song represents one key moment of sound, a sound that has led to the discovery of astonishing details about lives that have remained almost completely unknown until now and that might all too easily have been erased were it not for the brief mention of their names within a seemingly transitory and transient melody. We should not forget that the song would have had to compete with many of the sound worlds that were evoked in the first chapter of the book, perhaps even drowned out by the general hubbub of noise on the Pont Neuf. At times we will come into contact with other songs and sounds, and at other times those sounds will only be heard in the distance as we follow the trajectory of both privilege and prejudice.

CHAPTER 4

The Death and Afterlife of Jacques Chausson

Grands Dieux! Quelle est vôtre justice?
Chausson va périr par le feu;
Et Guitaut par le même vice
A mérité le Cordon bleu.[1]

(Great Gods! Where is your justice? / Chausson is about to die in the fire; / And Guitaut for the same vice / Has deserved the Cordon bleu.)

This song relates to a subject that is almost entirely absent from published literary texts of the period: homosexuality, or as it was called at that time, sodomy.[2]

The brevity of the song might initially make it all too easy for the reader to ignore or underestimate it; after all, there are few shorter poems among the many hundreds of often sexually explicit songs devoted to sodomy in the many volumes of the *Chansonnier Maurepas*. Even by reading the words alone, one might see the piece as a wry, even jocular reflection on the inequality of treatment of bourgeois and aristocratic people. The two men named in the song, Chausson and Guitaut, would seem to inhabit very different worlds.

Yet in actually hearing how the song might have sounded in performance, we gain a very different impression. Set to the popular tune "Réveillez-vous, belle endormie," our arrangement of the song (with two easily portable musical instruments, a single soprano recorder and a violin, accompanying the singer) brings out, I would suggest, a strong and profound sense of sadness and indignation, almost unique when compared to the many other, mostly lighthearted, songs about sodomites of the time. Jacques Chausson, a former customs officer, was about to be burned on the scaffold for sodomy (along with another man, Jacques Paulmier) at almost exactly the same time that Guillaume Pechpeyrou-Cominges, comte de Guitaut (1626–1685), favorite and reputed lover of the king's cousin Louis de Bourbon, prince de Condé, was being awarded one of the highest honors in the land, becoming a "Chevalier de l'Ordre du Saint-Esprit": the "cordon bleu" is the blue riband from which the Cross of the Holy Spirit hung.

The existence of more than one version of the song suggests that this song was performed not in just one place; a variety of people would have heard and performed it, changing the words slightly either through misremembering or perhaps wishing to highlight different elements. It also shows the ways in which the sound and words of song can move quickly and easily between different geographical locations, being heard and interpreted by different listeners. If the authorities tried to suppress or stop the performance of the song in one place, it could just as easily be performed elsewhere by the same singer or another singer who had memorized the words and melody, or even in the same location at a different time. Depending on the location and the audience, the performance style could shift, emphasizing different emotions, whether it be to display sadness, defiance, or even wit. The song (especially because of its brevity) is infinitely translatable.

The version that will be used in this book is that of the *Chansonnier Maurepas*, as it correctly dates the song from 1661 and is both more precise and functions more effectively with the song tune setting. Another version, found in manuscript form at the Chantilly library, is wrongly dated as 1651 and spells Guitaut's name incorrectly, but its slight variations give a different emphasis that is worth bearing in mind:

Grand Roy quelle est votre injustice
Chausson va perir par le feu
Et Goutaut pour le même vice
Est honnoré du Cordon bleu.[3]

(Great King how can you be so unjust? / Chausson is about to die in the fire / And Goutaut (Guitaut) for the same vice / Is honored with the Cordon bleu.)

By addressing the king here rather than the more general invocation of the gods in the first version, the singer's expression of frustration seems more explicitly directed at those in power. The song's tone would therefore appear to be one of resignation in the first version and anger in the second.

The case of Chausson is perhaps touching on its own accord, but it attained a significance that went beyond the mere fact of a sodomite being burned on the scaffold. In some respects the song is not unusual, as it follows a long tradition throughout early modern Europe of news about executions being communicated through song.[4] Writing in eighteenth-century Paris, Louis-Sébastien Mercier notes the rapidity with which songs would be composed and sung at the time of a significant event:

> Un parricide, un empoisonneur, un assassin, le lendemain, que dis-je, dès le jour même de leur supplice, enfantent des *complaintes* qui sont chantées dans tous les carrefours, et composées par les chanteurs du pont-neuf.[5]

> (A parricide, poisoner, killer, from the day after—what am I saying?—from the very day of their punishment, produce laments that are sung at all crossroads and are composed by the singers on the Pont Neuf.)

Mercier even remarks that the songs sung in the streets at such times contributed more to their renown than any printed literature would have done:

> Il y a encore les complaintes sur les pendus et les roués, que le peuple écoute la larme à l'œil, et qu'il achete avec empressement. Quand, par bonheur pour le poëte du Pont-Neuf, quelque personnage illustre monte sur l'échafaud, sa mort est rimée et chantée avec le violon. Ainsi à Paris tout est matiere à chanson; et quiconque, maréchal de France ou pendu, n'a pas été chansonné, a beau faire, il demeurera inconnu au peuple.[6]

> (There are still laments on people both hanged and broken on the wheel, which the common people listen to with a tear in the eye,

rushing to buy them. When, for the good fortune of the Pont Neuf poet, an illustrious persona mounts the scaffold, his death is turned into rhymes and sung along with a violin. In this way, everything in Paris is subject matter for a song, and whoever, whether it be a lord marshal or a simple hanged man, has not been put into a song, has acted in vain, for he will remain unknown to the people.)

Yet the invitation of the singer of the Chausson song to the listener to share a sense of outrage at Chausson's impending death is indeed less common, for the primary function of most execution ballads, in addition to announcing the killing of a criminal that had already occurred, was to attach moral condemnation of criminality to the execution.[7] The more traditional execution ballads, like so many of the street songs from the time, were set to familiar tunes, meaning that both listener and singer could share the experience and message carried within the song. As Una McIlvenna has argued, "Such sharing and participation helped to forge communal bonds, echoed in the communal and performative means by which each member of society was expected to participate in the punishment of criminals."[8] The Chausson execution ballad, by contrast, is being sung before the actual event and seems to be asking the listener to question both the punishment of this particular criminal and the unequal treatment of upper and lower echelons of society.[9]

One of the most remarkable aspects of the song is the strong sense of time in which it is rooted. The tenses emphasize the actuality of what is happening. While Guitaut's elevation by King Louis XIV to the Order of the Holy Spirit (l'Ordre du Saint-Esprit) has only just been announced (as brought out by the recent past of the passé composé in "a mérité"), the near future of Chausson's death ("va périr") locates singer and listener in the days or even hours leading up to his being executed. It is relatively rare to be able to date the songs precisely, but, given the fact that the announcement of the names of the new Knights of the Order was made on 3 December and Chausson's execution took place at the end of December 1661, we can know with a strong degree of certainty that the song was first sung during December, and probably near the end of the month, as both Chausson's execution and the actual ceremony for the investiture of the knights (1 January 1662) drew near. The court records show that Chausson was condemned to death at the Châtelet on 25 November, confirmed by the parlement on 29 December 1661, and, as was the case for capital punishment, was soon after burned on the scaffold.

Jurists' attitudes toward sodomy in the seventeenth century were often unflinching. Claude Le Brun de La Rochette (1560–1630), who practiced as a lawyer in the Beaujolais region and at the Parlement de Paris, lists masturbation, sex between man and man and between woman and woman, and bestiality under the term "Sodomie," calling it an "execrable crime" (terrible crime) and worthy of an array of divine punishments, such as plagues, wars, and famine.[10] The jurist Antoine Bruneau (1640–1720), who had moved from lowly roots in the Chevreuse area, south of Paris, to become a lawyer at the Parlement de Paris, is unequivocal in his description of the penalty for what he calls "une espece de luxure abominable" (a kind of abominable fleshliness): "La peine de la sodomie ne sçauroit être assez forte pour expier un crime qui fait rougir la nature, [. . .] de faire mourir l'agent et le patient par le feu qui les consomme, et les cendres jettées au vent" (The penalty for sodomy cannot be strong enough to expiate a crime that makes nature blush, . . . to put to death both the active and passive partners, with the fire consuming them and their ashes thrown to the wind).[11] Moreover, although certain jurists recommended that sodomites should be strangled or hanged before being burned on the scaffold, Bruneau makes the observation that ordinary judges had the right to order that they be burned alive, as was the case with Chausson. From the moment that a sodomite was arrested and accused, he was not allowed to write a valid will and testament, and he would have his assets seized. Women who "se corrompent l'une l'autre, sont appellées *fictrices et triballes* [sic]: c'est une espece de sodomie, pour raison de quoi elles sont punies" (corrupt each other are called *fictrices* and *tribades*: this is a kind of sodomy, for which reason they, too, are punished), but their punishment was much less severe, usually "deux ans de penitence" (two years of penitence).[12]

Legal texts and transcriptions from trials can provide invaluable evidence about the lives of people from classes about which there remains little written information. However, although such evidence might at first glance seem more reliable than that contained in a primarily oral form like a song, it is important to keep in mind the ways in which written documents can mislead or give a biased depiction of crimes or actions. As Carlo Ginzburg has argued about sixteenth-century witchcraft trials, such written sources "are doubly indirect for they are *written*, and written in general by individuals who were more or less openly attached to the dominant culture. This means that the thoughts, the beliefs, and the aspirations of the peasants and artisans of the past reach us (if and when they do) almost always through distorting viewpoints and intermediaries."[13]

A number of putatively legal documents give widely varying accounts of Chausson and Paulmier's interrogation (the "plumitif") and trial. These writings have largely been followed unquestioningly by the few scholars to consider them since the 1920 publication by Louis Perceau and Fernand Fleuret, under the pseudonym of Dr. Ludovico Hernandez, of legal transcripts concerned with early modern sodomy and bestiality trials.[14] Two texts relating to the two men's trial, both housed in the Archives Nationales in Paris, are from the seventeenth century and can confidently be claimed to be genuine: the "Arrêt" (AN X2A 324, 29 December 1661), in which Chausson's and Paulmier's sentences are announced, and the "plumitif du conseil de la Tournelle," a short interrogation of the two men in the parliamentary court (AN X2A 1027, 29 December 1661), and these will be discussed in this chapter. Although these are written documents, we should not forget their oral origins. Even if the scribe might follow a certain stylistic formula and place the interrogations in the moralizing context of those interviewing the prisoners, we are here at least able to read questions and answers as they were spoken and heard by both captives and captors.

Another of the trial texts, which includes much more detailed interrogation of other witnesses purported to have taken place at the Châtelet prison (published by Perceau and Fleuret from MS fr. 10969 at the Bibliothèque Nationale), dates from the eighteenth century, and very little is known of its provenance. The historian Alfred Soman, who concentrates on the transcripts of bestiality trials in the same manuscript, argues that they are very unlikely to be genuine, pointing out not only errors in dates and names of the accused but also numerous anachronisms in the use of legal terminology. He contends that the author of the manuscript took as a starting point a few basic facts (such as name, date, crime) of each case, but "tout le reste est plus ou moins imaginaire" (all the rest is more or less imaginary).[15] The specific facts and interrogation of witnesses in each case, including the Chausson trial, are, according to Soman, "[des] fantasmes rédigés sans doute pour la délectation privée de leur créateur" (fantasies no doubt written down for the private delectation of their creator).[16] Although Soman's warning about the validity of these accounts should be taken seriously, it is difficult to view them, as he does, as some form of private pornography, for, although the texts involve unusual sexual habits, at no point are they presented in an overtly salacious way. I would suggest that Soman's categorical refutation of these eighteenth-century "transcripts" could be nuanced: although we should view them with caution, it is surely possible that some further facts of the trial may have been remembered or recounted imperfectly, and rendered in eighteenth-century terminology. It is in any event interesting to see how the eighteenth century depicted or imagined a trial such as Chausson's from decades earlier, and it will be in this spirit that the dubious transcript (MS fr. 10969) will occasionally be evoked alongside the more reliable seventeenth-century documents. We can still place this eighteenth-century text into an oral context, as it contains at the very least an imagined spoken interrogation and exchange.

The interrogation of the two men by the "Parlement criminel" (X2A1027) includes a list of those present. The perceived severity of the crimes of which they were accused is perhaps reflected by the unusually large number of people who attended the session, led by two *présidents à mortier* (principal magistrates who chaired sittings of the court and who wore the *mortier*, a black velvet hat with two gold braid ribbons), named as Jean-Jacques de Mesmes (1640–1688) and François Le Coigneux de Bachaumont (1624–1702). The *rapporteur* (the judge who analyzed evidence and presented it to the court) is named as Ferrand, in all probability Michel Ferrand, who became a *conseiller* at the Parlement de Paris in 1607 and died in the elevated position of *doyen* of the Parlement in 1666. Each prisoner would have been placed in chains on the *sellette* (a stool) as they faced their questioners.

In reading about the Chausson/Paulmier trial, we should not forget, and perhaps we should even imagine, the sounds made by those sitting in the gallery, by jurists speaking to each other, and by the pauses, vocal emphases, and verbal eloquence of the leading participants in the trial.

As is common with criminal trials from the period, the names of both accused men are accompanied by their nicknames, probably in order for court registers to record the fact that frequently criminals were known by other names. Norbert Schindler has shown with reference to early modern Germany that nicknames were often used within marginal groups, reflecting "the complexity of social and cultural circumstances."[17] Chausson's nickname, "Des Estangs" or "De l'Estaing," clearly refers to his status: as is specified in the seventeenth-century "plumitif" (AN X2A 1027), he is "fils d'un marchand linger" (son of a cloth merchant, [82]), and the 1611 Cotgrave dictionary defines "Estain" as "fine woollen (or linnen) yarne, thread." The association of his nickname with his family background, which was a common feature of nicknames given to criminals and outsiders at the time,[18] indicates that others from different classes (possibly of higher standing) might have used this name when referring to him. With his family in the textile trade, it is likely that he would have been brought up around the Saints-Innocents Cemetery, now the Place Joachim-du-Bellay beside Les Halles and the Rue Saint-Denis, where all textile artisans were located during the early modern period.[19] At the time of the interrogation in 1661, he is said to have resided in the Rue de la Boucherie, which was one of the streets destroyed in the nineteenth century by Haussmann to create the Boulevard Saint-Germain,[20] and at his brother-in-law's house, also in the Faubourg Saint-Germain, which in the seventeenth century was an up-and-coming area popular with the aristocracy,[21] indicating that members of his family might have married above their station. While living in that area, Chausson was close to the Pont Neuf and its song-producing culture; indeed, the second volume of songs by the famous singer-songwriter Philippot le Savoyard was published in a printing house situated on the Rue de la Boucherie in 1656.[22] The origin of Jacques Paulmier's nickname, Fabry or Fabri, is harder to ascertain, but it could mean that he came from Italian stock. It could also, as with Chausson, refer to his father's occupation, deriving from the Latin "faber," meaning "craftsman."

Chausson is mentioned in the short interrogation (AN X2A 1027) as having previously "servi dans le regiment de La Vieuville" (served in La Vieuville's regiment [not "Veiville," as wrongly transcribed elsewhere]), which almost certainly would have been the regiment commanded by Charles II de La Vieuville (ca. 1616–1689), based in Champagne between 1651 and 1663. De La Vieuville was the son of Charles I de la Vieuville, who had held the prestigious post of *surintendant des finances* until his death in 1653, and who was replaced as *surintendant* by the ill-fated Nicolas Fouquet. Charles II remained in good favor with Louis XIV, eventually being appointed Chevalier du Saint-Esprit in 1688.

The circumstances of the 1661 case against Chausson as brought out in the short interrogation show that Chausson "est accusé d'impieté et prostitution de jeunes garçons et commettre le peché de sodomie et le faict commettre a douleur et a cet effect a cherché d'aultres jeunes garçons qui sont venus plusieurs fois ché luy avec autres personnes" (is accused of impiety and prostitution of young boys and of committing the sin of sodomy and having inflicted pain, and to do this he searched for more young boys who came several times to his house with other people),[23] an accusation that he refutes, replying that "il n'y est venu que ses amis" (only his friends came to visit him there). Moreover, he calls those who have reportedly testified against him "faulx temoings" (false witnesses [83]), and, apart from Paulmier, whom he acknowledges having met three or four times, claims not to know any of the other people named in the interrogation.

Another of the accusations that Chausson refutes is that he sent a servant to the Collège de Montaigu, a constituent college of the Faculty of Arts at the University of Paris, to fetch a young pupil. Immediately after this, he is asked "quelle cognoissance il a" (what acquaintance he has) with a man called Godefroy, which elicits another denial from Chausson. Of the various names mentioned in the transcript, Godefroy is one of the few people about whom there is some documentary evidence. Five and a half years after Chausson's trial, on 2 August 1667, in the same parliamentary court, a fifty-year-old priest and "bachelier en la Faculté de Paris" (Bachelor of Arts at the Paris Faculty), René Godefroy, was also tried for sodomy. The interrogation transcript makes mention of two previous occasions (1652 and 1665) on which he had been accused of sodomy. Moreover, it is suggested that Godefroy "estoit dans le proces de Chausson, qui a esté brulé vif" (was involved in the trial of Chausson, who was burned alive).[24] Given the previous accusations against Godefroy and the notoriety of Chausson's trial, it is possible that each man was interrogated about the other simply because the authorities were trying to establish if there were any networks or connections between men who were associated with the crime of sodomy. However, given Godefroy's position at the University of Paris and the preceding mention of the Collège de Montaigu in the Chausson transcript, it indicates at the very least that Chausson had university contacts.

Another interesting point in common between the Chausson and Godefroy trials is that each man was accused of singing songs—"des chansons impies" (impious songs) in Chausson's case and "des chansons dissolues et impies" (dissolute and impious songs) in the Godefroy transcript (which both men deny). This allegation brings to the fore some interesting details about sodomy cases in the period and offers intriguing possibilities about Chausson's own situation. Notwithstanding the severity of the legal language used to condemn sodomy, men were very rarely executed for sodomy alone; often the crime of sodomy was accompanied by accusations of blasphemy or impiety or of other crimes, such as having venereal disease (which Chausson is forced to deny having had [84]), so it was inevitable that Chausson (and, later, Godefroy) would have been questioned in this way, just as Paulmier was asked if "il a dit des impietés à chaque parolle" (he spoke impieties with every word [85]). However, Chausson in particular is interrogated about singing blasphemous songs rather than simply speaking profanities, which may explain, as we shall see, why a number of writers seemed particularly touched by his fate: Chausson possibly composed poems or songs for which he was known in literary circles, and he may even have performed them in the vicinity of where the singer would so poignantly sing about Chausson's own fate at the end of 1661. In the eighteenth-century transcript, Chausson states that in the two and a half years since he had left his post as a customs officer, he "etoit obligé de vivre d'ecritures et de copies qu'il faisoit pour les uns et les autres qui vouloient l'employer" (was obliged to live off writings and copies that he made for various people who wished to employ him [63]), which, however much credence one might give to the document, shows that the eighteenth-century imagination represented Chausson as a writer of some kind.

Paulmier, who tells the law court that he only recently returned from working for an English gentleman, is asked questions about his relationship with Chausson, whom he claims to have met in the Luxembourg Gardens and with whom he had eaten a meal once, spending one night at his home but not meeting anybody else. Most of the other questions center on his connection with page boys (84–85), a subject we will revisit in chapter 6.

Two names, difficult to decipher in the scribe's handwriting, are given in relation to Paulmier's previous employment, both seemingly related to time spent in England: "A servy le sieur de Montague. A servy le sieur de Pessage" (Served Lord Montagu. Served Lord Pessage). After this information is recorded, the first question posed to him is, "Interrogé si c'est en ce pays qu'il a commis le peché de sodomie" (Interrogated if it was in that country that he committed the sin of sodomy [84]), to which he gives the reply, "Dit qu'il ne sçait que c'est de cela" (Said that he does not know what that is). Later in the interrogation, he mentions that he had only just returned from England during the last week of Lent (85), which would have been in the first half of April 1661. It is therefore likely that Paulmier was in England during 1660 and the early part of 1661. The diverse members of the Montagu family were prominent in seventeenth-century England, and it is difficult to know with certainty which of them would have employed Paulmier. However, the example of the most distinguished member, Sir Edward Montagu, Earl of Sandwich, is particularly intriguing, as details of his daily life are available through his cousin and protegé Samuel Pepys, who had begun writing his diary on 1 January 1660. Paulmier's name does not appear in the diary, but this in itself is not unusual, as many servants in aristocratic households would have remained unnamed in writings such as journals and diaries, even in such a remarkably personal document as Pepys's celebrated work. Nonetheless, it is striking that the diarist mentions on 20 October 1660 that when dining with Lord Montagu, the latter "did talk very high how he would have a French Cooke and a Master of his Horse,"[25] and again on 15 November of the same year, Pepys writes that his wife had to help interpret for Lady Sandwich, who had just acquired a new French maid.[26] The Montagues were clearly proud at the time of acquiring French servants, and Paulmier may have been one of those in their employment. Only a few weeks later, at the beginning of 1661, while Pepys was on a journey with Lady Montagu, he mentions sharing his bed with one of Lady Montagu's pages on two successive nights.[27] Men sharing beds at the time was common practice, and even though Pepys writes only a few months earlier of sharing a bed with the clerk Will How, leading to the point that "he and I fell to play with one another,"[28] sleeping in bed with another man did not ordinarily mean that sexual activity was involved. Paulmier (in his twenties) was probably too old to be a page boy, but Pepys may be using the term generally to mean a male servant, so it is not beyond the bounds of possibility that Pepys shared a bed with Jacques Paulmier.[29]

The eighteenth-century longer interrogation (MS fr. 10969) purports to transcribe not only the questioning of the accused men but also various witness statements over a number of days between August and November 1661. Certain factual details vary widely enough from the shorter seventeenth-century interrogation to throw doubt on the veracity of the later document; for example, whereas the two men are said to be aged twenty-six (Chausson) and twenty-eight (Paulmier) in the earlier text, here they are listed as aged forty-three and thirty-six. In the Paris archives, a contract of marriage made on 30 April 1634 between Alexandre Chausson, named as "bourgeois de Paris," and Marie Mariot, daughter of the late Jean Mariot, "marchand verrier" (glazier merchant), residing in Rue Cassette, now part of Paris's sixth arrondissement, may corroborate Chausson's age as twenty-six, as he would have been born in 1635, within a year of Alexandre and Marie's marriage.[30] Moreover, contradicting Paulmier's claim that he hardly knew Chausson in the short text, in the eighteenth-century manuscript he is depicted as saying that they had worked together as customs officers and had spent much time together (66). Most of the allegations in the longer transcript revolve around the attempted rape by Chausson and Paulmier of young men and boys, most prominently a seventeen-year-old aristocrat named Octave

Julien des Valons.³¹ They were also accused of procuring boys for two noblemen, named as the baron de Belleforte and the marquis du Bellay.³²

Although there is no further direct evidence to substantiate this association with de Belleforte and du Bellay, one other connection between Chausson and a member of the aristocracy is evoked in a 1670 song from the *Chansonnier Maurepas*, which might at least give credence to the possibility that there were other more highly placed men involved. A man named in the eighteenth-century note as the marquis de Nantouillet, and described in derogatory terms as "un mary barbon" (something like "an old codger"), seems to have been linked with the Chausson trial:

> Du Chemin fait la fiere
> D'epouser un mary barbon,
> Qui fut mis dans l'affaire
> Du malheureux Chausson.³³

(Du Chemin is bragging / About marrying an old codger, / Who was involved in the affair / Of the unfortunate Chausson.)

Nowhere else does Nantouillet's name appear in connection with Chausson, but the mention of him demonstrates that noblemen, who inevitably escaped punishment and remained beyond the suspicion of the court because of their class status, were implicated in various ways in the Chausson/Paulmier case.

Whatever crimes Chausson and Paulmier did commit, their death sentence met with surprising sympathy and even solidarity, as the words "malheureux Chausson" in the above song indicate and as we shall see later in this chapter.

Executions in early modern Paris belonged to a very particular and vivid sound world,³⁴ and the two prisoners would have been assailed by various words and noises from the outset on the day of their deaths. Even before the prisoner emerged into the public space of the execution, the *greffier* (court clerk) would take the prisoner from his or her cell and, with other prison officials present, read the entire judgment aloud to the prisoner, who would have been made to listen while in a kneeling position.³⁵ In Chausson and Paulmier's case, the following judgment was likely to have been read aloud:

> Avons déclaré et déclarons lesdits Jacques Chausson, dit Des Estangs, et Jacques Paulmier, dit Fabry, prisonniers es prisons du Chastelet, bien et duement atteints et convaincus d'avoir dit et proféré les

blasphèmes et impietez mentionnez au procès; et en outre d'avoir commis et fait commettre le crime de sodomie et péché contre nature, pour réparation desquels cas et crimes énormes, les avons condamnez a faire amende honnorable nuds en chemise, la corde au col, devant l'Eglise de Notre Dame de Paris, où etans dans leurs tombereaux, et nuds teste à genoux, et tenant en leurs mains chacun une torche de cire jaune ardente du poids de deux livres, ils diront et déclareront à haute et intelligible voix que mechament, malicieusement et malheureusement ils auroient dit et proféré les blasphèmes et impietés mentionnées au procès, dont ils se repentoient, et demanderont pardon à Dieu, au Roy, et à la Justice. Ce fait, seront conduits à la place de grève pour être attachés chacun à un poteau et avoir la langue coupée, et ensuite leurs corps brûlez et réduits en cendres, lesquelles cendres seront jettées dans la Rivière de Seine. Déclarons en outre tous et un chacun des biens appartenans auxdits Jacques Chausson et Jacques Paulmier acquis et confisqués au profit de qui il appartiendra, sur lesquels néanmoins sera prélevée la somme de seize cent livres parisis d'amende, applicable moitié à l'Hôpital gênéral, et l'autre moitié au grand hôtel Dieu de Paris, et aussi la somme de huit cent livres parisis d'amende envers le Roy, au cas que confiscation n'ait pas lieu au profit dudit seigneur Roy.[36]

(We have found the said Jacques Chausson, called Des Estangs, and Jacques Paulmier, called Fabry, prisoners in the Châtelet prisons, duly guilty and convicted of having spoken and uttered the blasphemies and impieties mentioned in the trial, and moreover for having committed and enabled the crime of sodomy and sinned against nature, in reparation for which enormous offense and crimes, they are condemned to make honorable amends naked in a shirt, with a rope around their necks, in front of the Church of Notre-Dame of Paris, and placed in their open carts, naked and bowing low on their knees, each of them holding a burning yellow wax candle of two pounds in weight in their hands, they shall speak and declaim in a loud and intelligible voice that they spoke and uttered those blasphemies and impieties mentioned in the trial wickedly, maliciously, and wretchedly, for which they repented, asking forgiveness from God, the King, and Justice. Having done this, they will be taken to the Place de Grève and each will be tied to a stake and have his tongue cut out, and then their bodies will be burned and reduced to ashes, with those ashes being thrown into the River Seine. Further, we declare that all the goods belonging to each of the said Jacques Chausson and Jacques Paulmier will be acquired and confiscated from each appropriate person, upon which nonetheless will be levied a fine of the sum of sixteen hundred livres parisis, of which half will be given to the General Hospital and the other half to the great Hôtel Dieu of Paris, with the additional sum of eight hundred livres parisis as a fine for the King, in the case where the confiscation is not to the profit of the said Lord King.)

Once engaged on the procession to the scaffold (with the prisoner usually sitting in an open cart), the *greffier* would play a pivotal role in such proceedings, reading out the sentence at successive stages of the journey. As Pascal Bastien describes it, "Like a veritable orchestral conductor of the ritual, the court clerk would organize the unfolding process of the capital execution; as master of the written, he was also master of the spoken word."[37] No bell was rung or official announcement made in advance, and even *colporteurs* were expressly forbidden from selling news of executions until the official procession to the gallows was underway. Figure 7 shows a seventeenth-century depiction of a prisoner (accompanied by executioner, clerk, and confessor) being led to the stake.

For eagerly anticipated executions, it is likely that crowds would have gathered already, but often the first official announcement of such events would have been heard when the executioner cried out for silence and the sentence was read aloud by the clerk at the various stages of the procession, constituting the main method of drawing crowds to the place of execution. Evidence as to the likely identity of Chausson's executioner can easily be found, as throughout France, and in much of northern Europe, executioners came from family dynasties, widely regarded as social outcasts who enjoyed special privileges.[38] At the time of Chausson's and Paulmier's deaths, Jean Guillaume was the second in a long line of executioners from the same family and was coming to the end of his career, having been executioner in Paris since 1620, to be replaced in 1666 by his son François.[39] With the Place de Grève being one of the busiest thoroughfares in Paris at the time, people of all ages and from all levels of society would also have flocked naturally to the visual and auditory spectacle of the execution: from the seventeenth century onward, executions tended to be regarded primarily as a form of

Fig. 7 "Brunel dit Bétancourt conduit au supplice." Photo: BnF.

entertainment.[40] Although kings and queens stopped attending executions in the sixteenth century, members of the aristocracy were just as likely to be present as the wider populace.[41] Windows overlooking the Place de Grève were hired out, and for the most notorious executions, crowds (numbering as many as one hundred thousand people, according to contemporary reports)[42] would stretch for miles. The sound made by the crowd would therefore have been overwhelming, certainly competing with the voices of the executioner and scribe, and in some cases crowds were known to call for harsher sentences or to express sympathy for those on the scaffold.[43] Mercier's vivid observation of the different voices and crowds at the time of an execution in the second half of the eighteenth century would surely hold true for the seventeenth also:

> Quelle voix sinistre et retentissante emplissant les rues et les carrefours, se fait entendre jusqu'au sommet des maisons, et crie qu'un

homme plein de jeunesse va périr, égorgé de sang-froid par un autre homme, au nom de la societé? Le colporteur, en courant et hurlant, vend la sentence encore humide; on l'achete pour savoir le nom du coupable, et apprendre quel est son crime; on a bientôt oublié l'un et l'autre. C'est une condamnation subite qui vient épouvanter les esprits au moment où l'on ne s'y attendoit pas.

La populace quitte les atteliers et les boutiques, et s'attroupe autour de l'échafaud, pour examiner de quelle maniere le patient accomplira le grand acte de mourir en public au milieu des tourmens.[44]

(What sinister and echoing voice filling the streets and crossroads is making itself heard right to the rooftops of houses, crying out that a man in the first flush of youth is about to die, his throat cut in cold blood by another man, in the name of society? The peddler, running and shouting, sells the sentence, with the ink not yet dry; people buy it to find out the name of the guilty person and to learn the nature of his crime; both are soon forgotten. It is a sudden condemnation that comes to frighten people's spirits at the very moment that they did not expect it.

The people leave their workshops and shops, and crowd around the scaffold, in order to examine how the suffering man will accomplish the act of dying in agony in public.)

At the gallows, through the din of the growing crowd, Chausson would have heard the clerk reading out his death sentence one final time.

In addition to the voice of the executioner calling for silence, and that of the clerk, Chausson would have been obliged to listen to another person's voice, that of the confessor, who accompanied condemned criminals from prison to the scaffold. Indeed, the confessor in figure 7 to the right of the prisoner is depicted as speaking aloud to the prisoner. From the medieval period to the propagation of the revolutionary penal code in 1791, it was a requirement for local officials to provide condemned criminals with a priest (in Paris usually a doctor at the Sorbonne) for the purpose of confession.[45] For criminals who had willingly confessed to their crime, or for those terrified of their impending death, the priest might have offered some kind of solace, but for those refusing to acknowledge their crime or hardened to spiritual exhortation, the confessor's entreaties must have added to the hostility of the surrounding sounds. We know from treatises of the time, written for confessors of criminals condemned to death, that prisoners were spoken to at length by their confessors. It is easy for us now to view these priests as accomplices in the violent deaths of many people who were innocent or would be deemed innocent under the laws of most modern countries. However, if we consider a work such as that by Pierre de Besse, *La Practique chrestienne pour consoler les malades et assister les criminels qui sont condamnez au supplice*, published in 1638, the dominant word when instructing confessors is "consolation," and there seems a genuine attempt to make the condemned prisoner's death more bearable on both a spiritual and emotional level.[46] That said, the decisions reached by the law courts are deemed by de Besse to be unimpeachable and divinely ordained. Therefore, he is able to opine that "c'est encore une chose grandement desplorable en l'estat des criminels, que de ne vouloir jamais confesser leurs fautes" (it is still a hugely deplorable thing in the condition of criminals that they never wish to confess their errors [Book IX, 421]), adding that declarations of innocence are "sans doute une invention diabolique, et un artifice de Satan" (undoubtedly a diabolic invention, and a deceitful ploy by Satan [422]):

> A raison dequoy le Pere spirituel, ou celuy qui les entreprendra leur gouvernement, et leur conduite, s'efforcera par tous moyens, mais sur tout par la douceur, et avec une compassion toute chrestienne, de leur oster ces folles opinions, les en combatre par raisons, et les reduire en fin à la recognoissance de leur aveuglement, de s'estimer innocens estans si criminels, et coulpables de tant de forfaicts et de delicts, qu'en les condamnant à cette mort, on leur a fait plus de misericorde que de justice. (422)

> (For this reason the spiritual Father, or the person who undertakes their guidance and conduct, will endeavor by all means, but always with gentleness and a completely Christian compassion, to disabuse them of their mad opinions and to counter them with rational arguments, reducing them finally to a recognition of their blindness in considering themselves innocent when they are so criminal and capable of so many crimes and misdemeanors, and to argue that in condemning them to death, they will have been treated with greater mercy than justice.)

Other confessors clearly do not consider "douceur" to be the most effective way of persuading criminals to turn to God. Antoine Beaugendre's life of Benigne Joly, published in 1700, for example, depicts Joly, who was known as "Le Père des pauvres" (Father of the poor), at the scaffold first haranguing one condemned man, "toujours criant à ses oreilles pour lui toucher le cœur" (at all times shouting in his ear in order to touch his heart), then calling on God's mercy and exhorting the crowd to implore God also. With such vocal pressure applied from all sides, the criminal—"par une grace toute extraordinaire" (through an extraordinary act of grace)—decides to confess and dies in a state of what is described as "une contrition sincere" (sincere contrition).⁴⁷

Although some execution sites allowed the prisoner to speak to the crowd, this right was denied to those being executed on the Place de Grève.⁴⁸ Yet this did not prevent those condemned from giving voice to their feelings as they were led to their execution. Pierre de L'Estoile, whose journals span from 1574 to 1611,⁴⁹ often bringing to life not only the spectacle but also the sound world of Parisian executions, records, for instance, the execution on 24 April 1600 of the Prévost de Sens, commencing with the reading aloud of his sentence by the executioner, followed by the shouted curses of the condemned man as he was carried in an open cart to the Place de Grève:

> Son cri (que j'ouïs) portoit: "Pour vols, meurtres, ravissemens de femmes et filles, et autres forfaits exécrables et excès en grand nombre, perpétrés par lui." Il estoit aussi chargé d'avoir volé le frère du Premier Président: ce qu'il nioit si asseurément et avec telle impudence, qu'estant en la charette, maudissoit là-dessus le Premier Président, le donnant tout haut au Diable, avec ceste vilaine adjonction et indigne d'un Chrestien qui s'en va mourir. "Foutre pour lui." Ce qu'il répéta plusieurs fois.⁵⁰

(His cry [which I heard] went: "For thefts, murders, rape of women and girls, and other numerous terrible crimes and excesses, perpetrated by him." He was also charged with stealing from the First President's brother, something that he denied with such assurance and impudence, that when he was in the open cart, he cursed the First President, sending him with loud cries to the Devil, with this injunction, base and unworthy of a Christian who is about to die: "Fuck him." This was something he repeated several times.)

As the judgment of Chausson and Paulmier shows, the only words the prisoners were officially allowed to speak were to admit their guilt (known as an "amende honorable"), kneeling at the entrance of Notre-Dame cathedral on their way to the scaffold. In some cases convicted criminals chose not to make any such confession at this point, and, given his refusal to admit any guilt during his questioning, Chausson may have remained silent or may even have proclaimed his innocence.[51] When they reached the Place de Grève, this removal of the right to speak became all too real with the cutting out of their tongues, which signified their punishment for uttering blasphemies. Just before entering the flames, they would have heard the singing by all present of the Marian hymn "Salve Regina," in which the Virgin Mary is invoked, as a "most gracious advocate," to turn her "merciful eyes toward us."

Of the two men who died on the scaffold on 29 December 1661, Chausson is the person who caught the imagination of poets, writers, and song composers for the remainder of the seventeenth century and much of the eighteenth. A number of other songs and poems were clearly being composed and performed at the time of Chausson's death. One such piece is titled "La Coquille" (The shell) and appears in MS fr. 12666 in the Bibliothèque Nationale. It is wrongly dated as 1651, but this could easily have been a handwritten error, or a copyist may have misread the actual date of 1661 or even assumed that the reference to "l'orage" concerned the political turmoil associated with the Fronde during the early 1650s. Its content suggests that it was written before Chausson's death sentence had been pronounced. In the song, sodomy is imagined as being at odds with more normative sexual practices, but an interestingly oblique reference is made to the thought that a negative outcome for Chausson would have a devastating effect on others both more respectable and of higher social status than Chausson who evidently shared his predilections. Even more damningly, they are referred to as "tous les gens de bien" (all goodly people); sodomy is thus described as a practice enjoyed not by a marginalized minority but by all people of good standing:

> Sçavez vous l'orage qui s'eleve
> Contre tous les gens de bien?
> Si Chausson perd son proces en Greve,
> Le Cu ne servira plus de rien;
> Si Chausson perd son proces en Greve,
> Le Con gagnera le sien.[52]

(Do you know about the storm that is rising / Against all goodly people? / If Chausson loses his trial and ends up on the scaffold, / The Ass will no longer have any use; / If Chausson loses his trial and ends up on the scaffold, / The Cunt will win its own trial.)

Another piece certain to have been written in close proximity to the event (given that its author died only a few months after Chausson) and deserving of closer examination is the young poet Claude Le Petit's eloquently subversive sonnet about Chausson's death. The poem, which uses both auditory and visual imagery, vividly captures the discrepancy between the official depiction of Chausson as a sinner and the courage displayed by him at the time of his execution:

Amis, on a brûlé le malheureux Chausson,
Ce coquin si fameux, à la tête frisée;
Sa vertu par sa mort s'est immortalisée:
Jamais on n'expira de plus noble façon.

Il chanta d'un air gai la lugubre chanson,
Et vêtit sans pâlir la chemise empesée,
Et du bûcher ardent de la pile embrasée,
Il regarda la mort sans crainte et sans frisson.

En vain son confesseur lui prêchait dans la flamme,
Le crucifix en main, de songer à son âme;
Couché sous le poteau, quand le feu l'eut vaincu,

L'infâme vers le ciel tourna sa croupe immonde,
Et, pour mourir enfin comme il avait vécu,
Il montra, le vilain, son cul à tout le monde.[53]

(Friends, they have burned the unfortunate Chausson, / That famous scoundrel with his curly hair; / Through his death his virtue has become immortal: / Never did anyone die in a nobler way.

Joyfully he sang the lugubrious song, / And without blanching he wore the starched shirt, / And from the flaming stake of the fire-consumed pile of wood, / He faced death without fear or trembling.

In vain his confessor continued to preach to him in the flames, / Crucifix in hand, telling him to think of his soul, / Lying at the foot of the stake, when the fire had vanquished him, /

The infamous man turned his filthy posterior toward the sky, / And in order to die finally as he had lived, / The villain showed his ass to all the world.)

The "Amis" who are invoked at the beginning indicate a wider circle of people who share the poet's unease at such an execution; on one level, the poet is simply informing his friends of Chausson's death, but on another level he is inviting them all to join him in showing their outrage. The unspecified identity of these "amis" may imply a small circle of the poet's friends, or a wider readership, or even a group of people who share Chausson's sexual predilections.[54]

The first two quatrains are dominated by terms that recall stoic fortitude, underlining the strength shown by Chausson when facing his imminent death. Thus, just at the moment that he is supposedly being punished for a heinous vice, the poet refers to "sa vertu" (3). Moreover, in his manner of dying he shows himself to be "noble" (4), a word that is made all the more ironic when one considers his bourgeois status as opposed to the nobly born condition of Guitaut, who appears in the *Chansonnier Maurepas* song. Chausson's stoic courage is further demonstrated by his refusal to show weakness or fear: he goes to his death "sans pâlir" (6), "sans crainte" (7), "sans frisson" (7). Le Petit is attentive to sound and song. The "lugubre chanson" (5) that he sings is in all probability the "Salve Regina" that was sung at executions, but rather than perform it with the expected sense of dread or terror, we are told that he sings "d'un air gai" (5). Here is the portrayal of a man who refuses to conform to the legal and religious image of him as a tormented sinner.[55]

Le Petit's skillful manipulation of tense both dramatizes the immediacy of the events and further depicts Chausson in heroic terms. The passé composé of lines 1 and 3, for example, highlights the very recent event of Chausson's death, but significantly, the moment that we are told that his virtue "s'est immortalisée," his story becomes inscribed in the passé simple, as if it is now part of an honorable, historic past, so at odds with the rebarbative imperfect of the confessor's "prêchait" in line 9, which calls to mind the description of a confessor such as Père Joly "toujours criant à ses oreilles" (at all times shouting in his ear).

Yet coexisting with these traditional images of constancy and strength are nouns that seem to go against the sense of courage and honor that prevails elsewhere in the sonnet, as Chausson is described in what might be viewed as abusive terms: "coquin" in line 2, and then in the final tercet "infâme" and "vilain." Significantly, all three negative terms were widely used at the time to designate same-sex desire, and Le Petit would seem to have chosen the terms deliberately to evoke Chausson's sexual preferences. In the *Chansonnier Maurepas*, for example, the three terms are all used in connection with same-sex love, usually when two famous men of Italian origin known for their sexual preferences, Cardinal Mazarin and Louis XIV's court composer, Jean-Baptiste Lully, are evoked.[56] Le Petit, who had initially trained as a lawyer in Paris, is likely to have known that sodomy was listed in legal writings as a "crime vilain" (villainous crime—alongside incest and infanticide), with the jurist Le Brun de La Rochette naming it "une si detestable et orde vilennie" (such a detestable and foul villainy).[57] The word "infâme" appears in a longer satirical piece by Le Petit, *Paris Ridicule*, significantly in a section devoted to "La Grève," the site of executions, where those who have been executed are depicted as having been "massacrés" in far greater numbers than those slain in battle. Even taking into account the exaggeration of satire, the "infâmes" who after death are imagined taking the boat to paradise rather than to hell (the Place de Grève was conveniently located close to the river Seine) are evoked in what can only be described as sympathetic terms:

> Malheureux espace de terre
> Au gibet public consacré,
> Terrain où l'on a massacré
> Cent fois plus d'hommes qu'à la guerre;
> Certes, Grève, après mainct délict,
> Vous estes, pour mourir un lict
> Bien commode pour les infâmes,
> Car ils n'ont qu'à prendre un batteau,
> Et d'un coup d'aviron leurs âmes
> S'en vont en Paradis par eau.[58]

(Unhappy patch of earth / Dedicated to the public gallows, / Land where one hundred times more men / Have been massacred than in war; / Truly, Execution-place, after countless crimes, / You are a very convenient bed / For infamous people to die in, / For all they have to do is take a boat, / And with one oar stroke, / Their souls go to Paradise by water.)

I would argue that such traditional terms of abuse are redirected by Le Petit for both polemical and political ends. In the sonnet, Chausson's final act of defiance makes him "vilain" or "infâme" with respect to normative practices but also "vilain" as someone who goes heroically to his death without apologizing for his sexual preferences. The body part that signals the sodomite's sexual difference, "son cul" (line 14), becomes the principal locus and focus of resistance at the very moment that he is consumed by flames, a final act of defiance against those who have condemned him.[59]

Le Petit's sonnet brings to the fore parts of the sound world surrounding the burning of Chausson. In addition to the condemned man singing and the confessor preaching, we should not forget those other competing sounds on the Place de Grève, such as the noise of the crowd and the crackling flames.

Le Petit himself was burned to death at exactly the same spot less than eight months later, ostensibly for writing a number of seditious pieces, including the sonnet on Chausson. Many of his scandalous poems were burned along with the poet, such as the collection of sexually explicit pieces known as *Le Bordel des Muses*, the title of which is named in his death sentence.[60] Thanks to the baron de Schildebek, whom Le Petit met while traveling in Germany, an edition of *Le Bordel des Muses* was published in Holland, probably in 1663.[61] However, only a few fragments of this edition remain, including a prefatory letter in which de Schildebek laments the death of his friend, a list of contents, and eight of the sixty or so poems listed. Among the poems that have been lost, we find titles of certain pieces devoted to sodomy, with one labeled "Sonnet apologétique de la sodomie" (Sonnet in defense of sodomy). Of those that have survived, Chausson's name appears at the end of the second quatrain of a sonnet titled "Sur mon livre" (Upon my book):

Courtisans de Priape et du père Bacchus,
Vigoureux officiers des nocturnes patrouilles,
Venerables fouteurs d'inépuisables couilles,
Experts depuceleurs, artisans de cocus.

Et vous, garces à chiens, croupions invaincus,
Qui de nos braquemards vous faites des quenouilles,

Dames du Putanisme, agreables gargouilles,
Vous, lâches empaleurs et chaussonneurs de cus.

Venez tous au bordel de ces Muses lubriques:
L'esprit qui prend plaisir aux discours satyriques
Deschargera sans doute, entendant ces accords.

Ce livre fleurira sans redouter les flammes;
On souffre icy des lieux pour le plaisir des corps,
On en souffrira bien pour le plaisir des âmes.[62]

(Courtiers of Priapus and father Bacchus, / Vigorous officers of nocturnal patrols. / Venerable fuckers with indefatigable balls, / Expert deflowerers, craftsmen of cuckolds.

And you, bitches, unconquered rumps, / Who make distaffs out of our penises, / Ladies of Whoredom, pleasant gutters, / You, cowardly impalers and chaussoneurs of asses.

Come all of you to the brothel of these lubricious Muses: / The mind that takes pleasure in satirical discourse / Will no doubt unload, hearing these chords.

This book will flourish without fear of the flames; / Some places are suffered here for bodily pleasure, / Soon they will be suffered for the pleasure of souls.)

The final sestet of the sonnet underlines the radicality of Le Petit's vision. As Michel Jeanneret puts it, "In an age when culture, like art, works to sublimate instinct, neutralize the body and intellectualize human discourse, here rises an aberrant voice proclaiming that the mind is sexual and subject to biological laws."[63] The neologism "chaussonneurs" in line 8 is the first example of Chausson's name being used to designate sodomites more generally. The added image of flames in the final tercet both recalls Chausson's death and anticipates the destiny of both poet and book: Le Petit seems fully aware of the dangers he, too, faces. As Chausson was executed at the very end of 1661 and Le Petit met the same fate in 1662, it is possible to locate the poem's composition as sometime during the early months of 1662. Evidently Chausson's death made a profound impression on Le Petit's late poetry.

Writing in his *Mémoires*, the Huguenot scholar Jean Rou (1638–1711), who in later years adopted a moralizing tone that seems at odds with his younger self,[64] mentions that Le Petit was present at Chausson's execution and claims to have anticipated Le Petit's fate in a conversation Rou had with him:

> Eh bien, mon pauvre ami, lui dis-je, encore une fois, vous êtes un homme perdu et j'ai grand'peur que vous n'ayez anticipé votre propre peinture lorsque vous composâtes, il y a quelques mois, le sonnet de l'infâme Chausson.[65]

> (Well, my poor friend, I said to him once again, you are a lost man and I very much fear that you have anticipated your own portrait when a few months ago you composed the sonnet about the infamous Chausson.)

Unlike Chausson, whose tongue (the organ of the body that enabled him to be heard and understood by listeners) was cut out for blasphemy, Le Petit had his writing hand amputated, and he was afforded the dubious dignity of being secretly strangled before being placed on the pyre. As his friend François Colletet noted (with surprising detachment) in his *Mémoires des choses arrivées de notre temps,*

> Ce jourd'hui premier jour de septembre (1662) fut bruslé dans la place de Grève, à Paris, après avoir eu le poing couppé, fait amende honorable devant Nostre Dame de Paris et esté étranglé Claude Petit, advocat en Parlement, auteur de l'*Heure du Berger* et de *L'Escole de l'Interest*, pour avoir fait un livre intitulé: *Le Bordel des Muses*, escrit l'*Apologie de Chausson*, le *Moyne renié* et autres compositions de vers et de prose pleines d'impiétés et de blasphèmes contre l'honneur de Dieu, de la Vierge et de l'Estat. Il estoit âgé de 23 ans et fut fort regretté des honnestes gens à cause de son bel esprit qu'il eust peu employer à des choses plus dignes de lecture.[66]

> (This first day of September [1662] Claude Petit, lawyer at the parlement, author of l'*Heure du Berger* and *L'Escole de l'Interest*, was burned on the Place de Grève in Paris after having had his fist cut off and made honorable amends in front of Notre-Dame de Paris and then strangled for having created a book titled *Le Bordel des Muses*, written the *Apologie de Chausson*, and the *Moyne renié*, and other verse and prose compositions full of impieties and blasphemies

against the honor of God, the Virgin Mary, and the State. He was twenty-three years old and was greatly regretted by civilized people because of his fine mind that he may have been able to use for things that were more worthy of being read.)

Le Petit's own death was commemorated in writings by friends and sympathizers,[67] but it was Chausson's execution that had a particularly interesting afterlife in the sound world of France. Five years after Chausson's death, for example, his name was mentioned during the interrogation in the Châtelet of an elderly man called Grisy who had a history of molesting adolescent boys.[68] We have already seen the connection made between René Godefroy and Chausson in the interrogation for Godefroy's 1667 trial for sodomy. In 1671 a song about the musician and poet Charles Coypeau d'Assoucy (or Dassoucy), whom we met in part 1 of this book and who himself had strong ties with the song-producing culture of the Pont Neuf, compares him to Chausson and Tarneaut (possibly a misremembered or mistranscribed form of Paulmier, but perhaps also a variation of the name Fesnaut, which appears in a version of the same song in another manuscript, and whose name we will return to later).[69] In this imagined bawdy setting of Chausson's execution, it is significant that the condemned man is given a voice, perhaps before having that voice taken away from him with the removal of his tongue:

> Si le B . . . d'Assouci,
> Eût été pris, (bis)
> Il auroit êté roti,
> Tout au travers des flammes,
> De Chausson de Fabri.
>
> Chausson s'ecria tout haut,
> Où est Tarneaut? (bis)
> Ah! Monsieur le Lieutenant
> Avant que l'on me brûle;
> Souffrez que je l'encule,
> Et je mourai content.[70]

(If the Bugger d'Assouci / Had been caught, [to be sung twice] / He would have been roasted / Right through in the flames / Of Chausson and of Fabri.

Chausson cried out aloud, / Where is Tarneaut? [to be sung twice] / Ah! Mister Lieutenant, / Before I am burned, / Please let me fuck him, / And I will die happy.)

By this time the term "Chaussons" in the plural form had become synonymous with sodomites more generally.[71] Thus, in 1674 a reference to Chausson's name and trial in a song from the *Chansonnier Maurepas* is almost certainly not an anachronism but rather an allusion to the trial of other sodomites, here called "Chaussons." In June of that year, the composer Jean-Baptiste Lully (who himself had the reputation for being a sodomite) had charged members of the public half a louis each to watch a firework display that he had staged and that turned out literally to be a damp squib:

Excusés Messieurs si Batiste
Vous a fait un feu si lugubre, et si triste,
Et vous a mal servis pour vos demis Louis,
Le procés des Chaussons se poursuit, s'il s'acheve
Il vous en fera voir un autre en greve,
Dont vous serez plus rejouis.[72]

(Gentlemen, apologies if Baptiste / Has put on such a lugubrious and sad fire for you, / And has done you a disservice for your demis-louis, / The trial of the Chaussons is continuing, and if it finishes / He will allow you to see another fire on the scaffold / With which you will be much happier.)

Chausson and Lully are placed together in a later song from the *Chansonnier Maurepas* (1690), celebrating not only their sexual choices but also their hedonism. The plural form of Chausson again indicates that not only Chausson himself but sodomites more generally are being described here. Although the tone of the song may be ironic, coming as it does during the more austere later years of Louis XIV's reign, the indication that all listeners are encouraged to follow the two men's epicurean example suggests that moral condemnation is not the central message of the song:

Imitons Baptiste et Chaussons,
Point de Religion
Que celle des flacons.
N'aimons que les garçons

Sans Parens,
Crédit aux Marchans,
De l'Argent comptant,
Le v... bien bandant,
Sans Employ;
N'obeir qu'a soi,
C'est être ma foy,
Plus heureux que le Roy.[73]

(Let us imitate Baptiste and the Chaussons, / No Religion / Other than that of the bottle. / Let us love only boys / Without Parents, / Credit to the Tradesmen / Counting their money, / With a fully erect cock, / And no employment; / Obey only oneself, / That will be my belief, / To be happier than the King.)

In the same year as the song, Chausson's name again appears, this time in the journal of voyager Robert Challe, who reflects on the awfulness of death by fire and who provides another possible piece of sonic evidence to add to the sound world that we have been able to reimagine surrounding Chausson at the time of his execution, this time giving Chausson a voice in opposition to those judges who sent him to his death:

En effet plus j'envisage cette sorte de mort et plus je la trouve horrible. Chausson avant que d'être brûlé vif disait à ses juges qu'ils le damnaient par avance et qu'il n'y avait point de constance ni d'âme à l'épreuve du feu. (28 April 1690)[74]

(In effect, the more I envisage this kind of death, the more I find it horrible. Before being burned alive, Chausson said to his judges that they had condemned him in advance and that there was neither constancy nor soul in trial by fire.)

The term "Chausson" continues to be a byword for sodomy in songs about other people who lived long after the 1661 execution, firmly embedding itself in the eighteenth-century imagination and sound world of song. Just as the dubious eighteenth-century "transcript" of Chausson and Paulmier's trial might be seen to help fulfill that age's desire to be fed as much sordid detail as possible, sodomites from that century are immediately given added color either by being compared to Chausson or by being deemed to have surpassed Chausson's "crimes," such as in the piece from 1716 addressing Philippe de Courcillon, marquis de Dangeau, in which it is claimed that "On croit que tu l'emportes / Sur feu Monsieur Chausson Bougrillon" (It is believed that you outdo / the late Mr. Chausson the Bugger).[75] At times, the example of his execution is dangled before the listeners and/or readers as a warning of the fate that may befall them, such as in a 1716 song where we are informed that Thomas Goyon de Matignon "mene la vie de Chausson, / Et finira plus mal encore" (leads the life of Chausson, / And will finish up even worse),[76] or in the 1730 song about the pursuit of boys by the Bishop of Nîmes, Jean César de la Parisière ("on craint pour le derriere / De ce beau jeune garçon" [we fear for the behind / Of this beautiful young boy]), which ends with the words (referring to the bishop), "Comment le sauvera-t-on / Du feu qui brusla Chausson?" (How will he be saved / From the fire that burned Chausson?)[77]

Well into the eighteenth century, Voltaire alludes to Chausson on a number of occasions. In two poems, he couples Chausson with his (Voltaire's) enemy the Abbé Desfontaines, who had been imprisoned for sodomy, and associates Chausson with the sin of sodomy. In his satire "Le Père Nicodème et Jeannot" (1771), for example, he describes both men as being "dans le fond des enfers" (in the depth of hell), evoking also Chausson's "âme impure" (impure soul) in the ode "Sur l'ingratitude" (1736). However, when he ponders the manner of Chausson's death, Voltaire is more compassionate. Not only does he mention in a letter to the marquise du Deffant that he fears that the translator La Bastide du Chiniac "sera brûlé, vous dis-je, comme Chausson" (will be burned, I tell you, like Chausson [6 January 1769]), but also, in the heroic poem "La Guerre Civile de Genève" (1768), he portrays Chausson more sympathetically by associating him with the early fifteenth-century Czech priest and reformer Jan Hus, who was also executed:

> J'aimerais mieux mourir avec Jean Hus,
> Avec Chausson, et tant d'autres élus,
> Que m'avilir à rendre à mes semblables
> Un culte infâme et des honneurs coupables. (Chant I)[78]

(I would prefer to die with Jan Hus, / Chausson, and so many other select people, / Than to make myself so abject as to give to my fellow people / An infamous cult and guilty honors.)[79]

Perhaps the most telling, if transitory, remark that Voltaire makes about Chausson appears in his notebooks, for Chausson is listed among others (including Desfontaines and Rousseau de la Parisière) as someone whose name has become synonymous with derision and hatred, a convenient punching bag, one might add, for the prejudices of others:

> Roussau, Ravaillac, Chausson, [. . .] Desfontaines sont des hommes livrez à l'infamie. L'arest qui les condamne permet à tous les particuliers de les punir en les détestant, ce sont des morts livrez par la justice pour qu'ils soient disséquez.[80]

> (Rousseau, Ravaillac, Chausson, Desfontaines are men delivered to infamy. The ruling that condemns them allows all individuals to punish them while detesting them, and their corpses are delivered by justice so that they can be dissected.)

For a man such as Chausson to die at the hands of a moralistic and, if the songs are to be believed, hypocritical elite, it could be argued that the sound world of the Pont Neuf and the threat posed by scurrilous songs were less dangerous and rather easier to repress than I suggested in the first part of this book. Yet the example of the Chausson song and of the proliferation of pieces by other songwriters, poets, and commentators that Chausson's fate elicited shows us quite how quickly a sense of outrage or simply a heartfelt response to injustice can spread beyond the remit of those trying to suppress such dissent. Nor should we forget the countless other songs on similar topics, heard by many passersby on the streets and on the Pont Neuf, which were never captured on paper or have not survived.

Given the impression of prejudice enacted against a bourgeois sodomite that has been the subject of this chapter, it is only appropriate that in the next chapter, we trace the steps of the other, more fortunate person mentioned in the Chausson song: Guitaut.

CHAPTER 5

Guitaut, Condé, and the *Cordon bleu*

Just three days after Chausson and Paulmier were executed and their ashes deposited in the river Seine, if a spectator were to walk from the Place de Grève (now the Place de l'Hôtel de Ville, on the top right of fig. 8) over the Seine via the Pont Neuf (at the center left of fig. 8), perhaps even listening to a song or two being performed as she crossed the river, negotiating at the same time the competing sounds of street sellers, quacks, and trundling carriages, punctuated by the chimes of the Samaritaine pump, she could still reach the Église des Grands-Augustins (just to the bottom right of the Pont Neuf in fig. 8) within around fifteen minutes. It was here that the elaborate investiture of Louis XIV's newly appointed Chevaliers de l'Ordre du Saint-Esprit took place, on 1 and 2 January 1662.[1] The king had reinstated a tradition that had been abandoned since 1633 by selecting sixty Knights of the Order and presenting them with the *cordon bleu*. Eight ecclesiastic members of the order were nominated at the same time, along with four officers—chancellor, provost and master of ceremonies, treasurer, and clerk (*greffier*). As Louis writes in his *Mémoires* about those chosen to join the order, "Nulle récompense ne coûte moins à nos peuples, et nulle ne touche plus les cœurs bien faits que ces distinctions de rang" (No reward costs less to our people, and nothing touches upright hearts more than these distinctions of rank).[2]

In addition to nominating Louis de Bourbon, prince de Condé, known as le Grand Condé (at the time usually referred to as Monsieur le Prince), Condé's son the duc d'Enghien, and his brother the prince de Conti to become

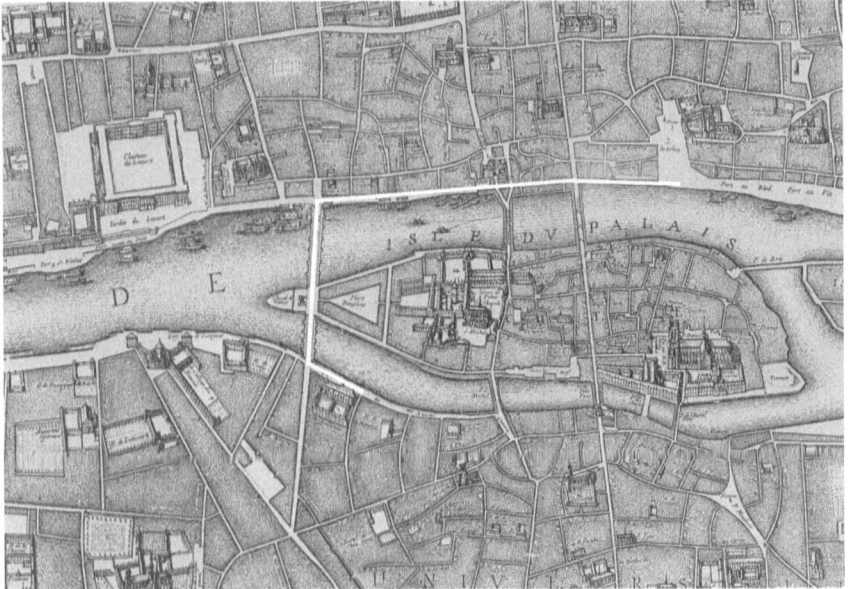

Fig. 8   Map of Paris (1675) by Jouvin de Rochefort. Photo: Cambridge University Library.

Knights of the Order, Louis XIV allowed Condé the privilege of naming one other person. His choice was Guillaume de Pechpeyrou-Comminges, comte de Guitaut, five years his junior and widely acknowledged as his favorite.

Given the magnificence of the occasion, and in order to underline the very different treatment meted out to Guitaut from that suffered by Chausson, a number of visual, as well as auditory, elements about the ceremony need to be mentioned. According to the very complicated rules of etiquette on such an occasion, Condé, as a "prince du sang" (prince of royal blood), would have been able to process down the aisle by himself, whereas Guitaut would have walked in a pairing with another member of the nobility.[3] In addition to the Chausson song where Guitaut's elevation is mentioned, other street songs from the time comment on the ceremony, including one quatrain in which the choice of the marquis de Bellefonds to hold the end of the king's cloak is questioned.[4] Loret reports in *La Muze historique* the ceremonial procession of the principal recipients of the order:

> Mais, placé comme un Patriarche,
> Je vis deux fois leur belle Marche,
> Où, du Roy, l'adorable aspect

Qui semé par tout le respect,
La grace de Monsieur son Frère,
Orné d'un plus doux caractère,
Et la mine fiére, en leur rang,
Des deux Premiers Princes du Sang,
Sembloient effacer tout le reste
Des Messieurs au Ruban céleste,
Qui les précedoient deux à deux,
Quoy que l'on pût voir entre-iceux
Des mines hautaines et graves,
Des Polis, des Galans, des Braves,
Et, pour le moins, aussi vaillans
Que des Renauds et des Rolans.⁵

(But, positioned like a patriarch, / I saw their beautiful procession twice, / Amongst whom the King whose adorable countenance, / Inspiring respect everywhere, / The grace of Monsieur his brother, / Adorned with a gentler character, / And the proud demeanor, each in their row, / Of the first princes of royal blood, / Seemed to erase all the rest / Of the gentlemen wearing the celestial ribbon, / Who all preceded them two by two, / Although one could see between them / The haughty and grave demeanors of the Polite, the Gallant, and the Fine, / And all at least as valiant / As Renauds and Rolands.)

Loret dwells on not only the visual magnificence of the spectacle but also the sumptuous sound world created to accompany the parade of the newly chosen Knights of the Order:

Puis le doux bruit des instrumens,
Trompettes, Hautsbois et Tymbales,
Qui rézonnoient par intervales,
Réglant par ordre et par compas,
Leurs contenances et leurs pas,
Pour rendre leurs démarches fières
Etoient d'assez rares matières.⁶

(Then the sweet noise of the instruments, / Trumpets, Oboes, and Timbrels, / Which resonated at intervals, / Regulating through order and through compass, / Their countenances and their footsteps, / To make their step appropriately lofty, / Was a rare event.)

In his history of the order, the eighteenth-century dramatist and royal historiographer Germain-François Poullain de Saint-Foix painstakingly maps out every vestimentary detail, of which the following quotation is only a fraction, as the soon-to-be chevaliers (known as novices) approach the king:

> Leur habillement de Novices consiste dans un pourpoint et trousses d'étoffe d'argent, caleçon, bas de soie et souliers blancs; le fourreau de l'épée est de la même couleur; la garde et la poignée sont d'argent; ils ont au cou un rabat de point d'Angleterre, et sur les épaules un capot de velours-ras noir; leur toque, au lieu de chapeau, est noire, garnie d'un bouquet de plumes blanches et d'une masse de héron. Ils se prosternent aux genoux du Roi qui est assis sur son trône, placé dans le sanctuaire du côté de l'Evangile, et après qu'ils ont fait et signé le serment, on leur ôte le capot, et Sa Majesté leur donne le grand manteau et le collier de l'Ordre.[7]

> (The newly appointed knights' dress consists of a doublet and hose of silver cloth, breeches, silk stockings, and white shoes; the sheath of the sword is the same color; the hilt and the handle of the sword are silver; they have around the neck a ruff of English thread, and around the shoulders a cloak of jet-black velvet; their cap, instead of a hat, is black, adorned with a cluster of white feathers and a bunch of heron feathers. They prostrate themselves at the feet of the king who is seated on his throne, which is placed in the sanctuary on the side of the Gospel, and when they have sworn and signed the oath, their cloak is removed, and His Majesty gives them the great cloak and collar of the Order.)

The engraving by François de Poilly (fig. 9) shows a similar eye for detail, with the large cross of the order matched by a cross embroidered into the cloak.

Saint-Foix then elaborates on the stage of the ceremony where the cross, supported by the "cordon bleu," is placed by the king around the new knight's neck:

Fig. 9
François de Poilly, "Chevalier de l'Ordre du Saint-Esprit." Photo: Abbeville, Musée Boucher de Perthes.

Après qu'ils ont fait la serment, Sa Majesté leur passe au cou, comme aux quatre grands Officiers, la croix de l'Ordre pendante à un ruban bleu céleste; cette croix, faite en croix de Malte, est d'or, émaillée de blanc sur les huit raies; il y a une fleur de lys d'or à chacun des quatre angles, et une colombe au milieu, les aîles déployées.[8]

(After they have sworn the oath, His Majesty puts the cross of the order hanging from a sky-blue ribbon around their necks as well as around the necks of the four grand officers; this cross, created in the shape of a Maltese cross, is made of gold, with white enamel on the eight lines of the cross; there is a golden fleur-de-lis in each of the four angles, and a dove in the middle, with its wings spread.)

As figure 10 shows, the iconography on the cross itself highlights the religious foundations of the honor bestowed on the knights, with the central dove denoting the Holy Spirit, the eight rounded corners representing the

Fig. 10
Diagram of the Cross of the Ordre du Saint-Esprit. Artwork: Tashiana Marday.

Beatitudes, the four fleurs-de-lis signifying the Gospels, and the twelve petals of the fleurs-de-lis symbolizing the apostles. Since the foundation of the Order of the Holy Spirit in 1578 by Henri III, these religious symbols had been widely satirized and had indeed been associated with sexual favors, especially in reference to Henri III and his *mignons*, leading Pierre de Brantôme to report a joke doing the rounds: "A aucuns on disoit: 'Qui eust jamais pensé que ceste croix eust passé si aysément par le cul pour venir se pendre au col?'" (To some it was said: "Who would ever have thought that this cross would have passed with such ease through the arse to come and hang around the neck?")[9]

Notwithstanding the satirical history of the order, Guitaut, dressed in his new robes and listening to the magnificent array of musical instruments, which may have been just loud enough to drown out the disordered sound world of the Pont Neuf a matter of yards away from the ceremony, would have been in no doubt as to the special favor shown to him by Condé in designating him for membership in the order. It was certainly a far cry from his relatively modest beginnings.

Of Gascon origin, Guitaut started work as a page boy to Cardinal Richelieu shortly before the latter's death, was then transferred to Louis XIII's household, and, after the king's death a few months later, continued in the service of the Maréchal de Gramont. Bussy-Rabutin writes in his *Mémoires* that Condé, a close friend of Gramont,[10] came across Guitaut at this point and, "le trouvant à son gré, prit de l'affection pour luy et fit sa fortune" (finding him to his liking, took him into his affection and made his fortune).[11] Bussy, who was the lieutenant captain of Condé's light cavalry and who had cause to resent Guitaut, implies strongly here and elsewhere that Guitaut's elevation owed more to his physical charms than to his professional capability. A few years later, in 1647 (when Guitaut would have been twenty-one), Bussy recounts that Condé "avoit jetté les yeux sur le petit Guitaut" (cast his eyes on the little Guitaut) in order to make him his standard-bearer ("cornette").[12] In 1651 Bussy was finally forced by Condé to sell his lieutenancy to Guitaut, to be paid for by Condé himself, prompting Bussy to declare: "J'avois toûjours fort aimé ce Prince jusqu'à ce qu'il se fût refroidi pour moi, et qu'il m'eût preferé Guitaut" (I had always loved this prince deeply until he became cold toward me and preferred Guitaut to me).[13] Whatever the nature of the relationship between the two men, Guitaut was injured while serving under Condé during the Fronde and subsequently followed him into exile to the Spanish Netherlands, acting as his "premier gentilhomme" (first gentleman) while his master was fighting on Spanish soil, often against the French army. He was assisted by Jean de Coligny-Saligny, a brave but irascible soldier nine years older than Guitaut, who had also started as a page to Richelieu, and whose own resentment of Condé's preference for the younger man would erupt a few years later.[14]

After the Treaty of the Pyrenees was signed between France and Spain in November 1659, Condé was allowed to return to France on terms favorable to him but also on the condition that he swear allegiance to the king. Keen to restore the networks of influence he had established before his exile, Condé sought on a number of fronts to reward his allies, to beautify his estate at Chantilly, and to surround himself with leading literary and scientific figures, including Boileau, the young Racine, Bossuet, and Malebranche. The particular regard in which he held Guitaut can be seen in the advantageous marriage that he procured for his protégé in 1660 with Madeleine de La Grange, daughter of the marquis d'Époisses, restoring also the governorship of the Lérins Islands to him. In later years, when Guitaut's wife died unexpectedly young in 1667, Condé arranged the transfer of the marquisate of Époisses (worth around 200,000 livres) from Guitaut's wife's family to Guitaut himself and organized his second marriage to the daughter of a counselor of state, Antoinette-Élisabeth de Verthamon.[15]

Soon after Guitaut's first marriage, Condé made him his choice as the newly created Chevalier de l'Ordre du Saint-Esprit. His selection of Guitaut scandalized many, including Coligny-Saligny, who had expected the nomination. As Coligny-Saligny wrote in his *Mémoires*, "Nous eusmes une grande escarmouche sur ce sujet" (We had a great falling-out about this matter),[16] which led to him leaving Condé's service and remaining virulently opposed to his former master for the rest of his life: "Tout cela s'est terminé en une guerre mortelle et une haine irréconciliable entre nous; car s'il me hait en diable, je le hais en diable et demi" (All that ended in mortal war and irreconcilable hatred between us; for if he hates me as a devil, I hate him as a devil and a half).[17] Coligny-Saligny was in no doubt about Condé's reasons for choosing Guitaut, excoriating him in another section of his *Mémoires*:

> Le bougre qu'il est, et je le maintiens bougre sur les Saints-Evangiles que je tiens en ma main, le bougre donc, avéré, fieffé, n'a que deux bonnes qualités, à savoir de l'esprit et du cœur.[18]

> (The bugger that he is—and I maintain, upon the Holy Gospels that I am holding in my hand, that he is a bugger—this verified, dyed-in-the-wool bugger has only two good qualities, namely, his spirit and heart.)

With such an accusation by Coligny-Saligny, it is necessary to put the alliances and friendships of Condé into brief context during the 1640s, when Guitaut first came to Condé's attention. While his father, Henri, was still alive, the duc d'Enghien (his title before succeeding his father as prince de Condé) was celebrated for a number of stunning military successes, not least the battle of Rocroi on 19 May 1643, when the twenty-one-year-old led the French army in a resounding defeat of the Spanish only weeks after the accession of the young Louis XIV to the throne under the regency of his mother, Anne of Austria. In the early years of the regency, after Richelieu's death, many writers hoped to be associated with the Condé family, not necessarily for financial patronage alone but also because the powerful family represented political stability and military valor.[19] The duc d'Enghien's marriage in 1641 to a niece of Cardinal Richelieu, Claire-Clémence de Maillé-Brézé, was, to quote Mark Bannister, "entirely a union of dynasties, with no feeling on Enghien's part,"[20] and helped consolidate his political prominence, even if it was regarded by the Condé family as a wedding to someone of lower birth than the usual alliances with ancient noble families. Although she bore him three children, his disregard for her resulted in her eventually being banished to Châteauroux, on what were generally considered to be trumped-up charges of infidelity with servants.[21]

Based at the Hôtel de Condé in Paris during the winter months of the 1640s, Condé both hosted and frequented literary salons (a world where verbal skills displayed in speaking aloud and in witty conversation predominated),[22] surrounding himself with young men known as "petits-maîtres" (little masters—in many cases his military companions during the summer campaigns), who became associated with *libertinage*—freethinking in both thought and action. As Katia Béguin describes them, "The society of little masters, above all made up of freethinking, hedonistic, and brave grand lords, with little inclination to endure the prohibitions of the authoritarian state and religious zealots regarding dueling, found in Louis II Bourbon a natural and powerful spokesman."[23]

This indifference to rules was reflected in the sexual excesses for which Condé and his friends became known. Although it is surely anachronistic to view Condé and the "petits-maîtres" as knowingly part of a homosexual subculture, it is clear that, as Jonathan Dewald sees it, "their experiences reflected the ease with which members of courtly society moved from fully acceptable to dangerous modes of behavior."[24] Just like his father before him,[25] Condé's same-sex exploits were widely known and celebrated or satirized in anecdotes, letters, poetry, and song, and he made little attempt to conceal his sexual preferences.[26] One of Condé's nonmilitary companions who frequented the salons at the Hôtels de Rambouillet and de Condé in the 1640s, Denis Sanguin de Saint-Pavin, who himself readily embraced his nickname of "Roi de Sodome" (King of Sodom),[27] devotes two poems to Condé's military and sexual conquests. In the first tercet of one sonnet, he writes,

> Tu vois qu'il vit en galant homme,
> Dans tous les sentiments de Rome,
> Pour lui Vénus est sans attraits.[28]

> (You see that he lives as a Gallant, / In all the sentiments of Rome, / For him Venus holds no attraction.)

In one version of another poem, addressed to le Grand Condé himself, Saint-Pavin compares him, in both predictable and less expected ways, to an ancient warrior:

> Quand on parle de vos emplois,
> Et dans l'amour, et dans la guerre,
> On vous compare quelquefois
> À celui qui donna des lois
> Au maître de toute la Terre;
> De votre honneur, je suis jaloux,
> Ce parallèle me fait peine;
> César, à le dire entre nous,
> Fut bien aussi bougre que vous,
> Mais jamais si grand capitaine.[29]

(When people speak of your endeavors / In both love and war, / They compare you sometimes / To the person who gave laws / To the master of the entire Earth; / I am jealous of your honor, / This parallel troubles me; / Just between you and me, Caesar / Was as much of a bugger as you, / But never so great a captain.)

Although much was made of Condé's heterosexual exploits, supposedly in keeping with his image as an all-conquering hero, they seldom seem to have been as deeply felt as the bonds he formed with his "petits-maîtres." In the 1640s, for example, the salons celebrated his love for Marthe du Vigean, but, as Mark Bannister describes it, the relationship seemed more idealized than real: "He, the invincible, and she, the virginal beauty wielding power over him by her modesty and her unaffected manner, formed the ideal romantic couple in novel-reading circles."[30] The liaison ended in 1645, apparently after Condé lost interest, and no other woman replaced her in his affections. Even a rumored dalliance with the great beauty of the day, Ninon de Lenclos, led to her circulating the Latin maxim *vir pilosus vel fortis vel libidinosus* (a hairy man is either valiant or libidinous), and she was overheard saying, "Pour avoir la valeur d'Hercule, il n'en avoit pas la vigueur" (He had the courage of Hercules, but he did not have his vigor).[31]

In the correspondence between Condé and his earlier favorites, by contrast, little attempt is made to conceal the homoeroticism that formed an important component of their friendships. The imagined exchange of verses in macaronic Latin between the prince and Amaury-Goyon de la Moussaye in 1643, for example, relating to a storm that surprised the pair when they were traveling on the river Rhône, brings out a playful awareness of their sexual preferences, something that appealed sufficiently to Proust to make him quote the poems in *La Prisonnière*.³² As the refrain "Landerirette" indicates, this dialogue is very likely to have been sung, possibly to a tune that both correspondents would have sung together on their shared travels and military campaigns, or even in Parisian salons. The fragmentary quality of "landeridi" hints at a sonic acknowledgment of camaraderie; in Michel de Certeau's elegant phrase, such fragments are "sonorous caskets of forgotten meanings and present memories":³³

Condé:
Carus amicus Mussaeus!
Ah! Deus bone! Quod tempus!
Landerirette,
Imbre sumus perituri,
Landeridi.

La Moussaye:
Securae sunt nostrae vitae,
Sumus enim s[odomitae].
Landerirette,
Igne tantum perituri,
Landeridi.³⁴

(Condé: Dear friend La Moussaye, / Good God! What weather! / Landerirette, / We are going to perish by drowning, Landeridi.

La Moussaye: Our lives are safe, / because we are sodomites. / Landerirette, / Only fire can make us perish, / Landeridi.)

Another of Condé's favorites, Gaspard de Coligny, duc de Châtillon, satirizes the linguistic conventions of preciosity by writing in a 1646 letter to his friend that he would communicate (by word of mouth) to Condé "plus de douceurs que n'en a jamais dit le plus passionné amant à sa maîtresse" (more sweet nothings than the most passionate lover has ever said to his mistress) and that "il n'est pas de feu si ardent dans lequel je ne me brûle pour l'amour de vous ni de mer si profonde et si salée dans laquelle il ne se noie avec plus de joie que n'en aura le chevalier [de Gramont] s'il fout Marion [Delorme] à son voyage" (there is no fire so ablaze as that in which I burn with love for you nor no sea so deep and salty as that in which the Chevalier de Gramont drowns with joy when he fucks Marion Delorme on his travels).³⁵ When Châtillon was killed on Charenton bridge during the Fronde, fighting in Condé's army, a song commemorating both his death and the close kinship between the two men was sung very soon afterward on the Pont Neuf:

> Il etoit le grand mignon,
> De Condé chose asseurée,
> Mais pour lui a Charenton,
> Fut tué dans la meslée.³⁶

(He was assuredly the great darling / Of Condé, / But at Charenton, / He was killed in combat.)

The language used by the comte de Toulougeon in a letter to Condé from 1649 is even more overtly erotic. Calling himself "le prince de l'amour" (the prince of love) and referring to himself in the third person, he writes: "Il espère de vous embrasser la cuisse bien tost et il est tout à vous" (He hopes to embrace your thigh soon and belongs entirely to you).³⁷

Another member of Condé's close circle at this time was François de Chevery, the Chevalier de Rivière, who had caught Condé's eye at the battle of Rocroi, leading to his becoming his "premier gentilhomme" (first gentleman—a post that was later filled by Guitaut when Condé went into exile). De Rivière, who never married, was well known as a libertine and atheist. There are a number of exchanges in song between him and his fellow libertine Claude de Chauvigny, baron de Blot, at the time that he was in Condé's household, and, as the following song set to the tune "Il a battu son petit frère" strongly implies, his sexual interests were not directed toward women:

> Mon cher Chevalier que je t'aime;
> Tu n'as jamais fait le carême.
> Tu vuides fort bien le flacon;
> Bible pour toy n'est que chimere.
> Tu n'as jamais f. . . . tu de C. . . .
> Et si tu ne vaus pas ton pere.³⁸

(My dear Knight how I love you; / You have never observed Lent. / You empty your bottle with great ease; / The Bible for you is but a dream. / You have never fucked in the Cunt / And also you are not worthy of your father.)

Given the content of these documents, we must surely go further than Béguin, who writes that "this casual, libertine, or gallant tone is that of men taking time away from wartime exploits."[39] They certainly represent expressions of camaraderie, but it is a kind of companionship that is consciously eroticized by favorites who must have known that such a tone would appeal to Condé.

The nature of friendship at the time between noblemen and other men of noble rank but lower social status is one that has interested scholars. Some, such as Béguin, who concentrates on the preservation of systems of power through aristocratic patronage,[40] or Alan Bray, who argues that sodomy is not necessarily a constituent part of intense same-sex friendships in early modern Britain,[41] tend to downplay the erotic side to such friendships. Others, such as Dewald and Christian Kühner, bring out the often uneasy slippage between friendship and sexuality in the period. Kühner is less interested in the veracity of accusations of sodomy aimed at a person like Condé than in what he calls "the discursive link between friendship and homosexuality."[42] For Dewald, "both the intensity of seventeenth-century friendships and their origins in physical attraction posed a further ethical problem: friendship easily shaded into sexual feeling and activity."[43] The overt eroticism of Condé's companions' messages to him indicates that his relationship with these men relied at the very least on such an overlap between friendship and sexual expression (certainly in word and very possibly in deed).

Even if the strongly homoerotic flavor of those earlier letters is not present in the handwritten copies of 114 unpublished letters (ranging between 1650 and the late 1660s) from Condé to Guitaut,[44] their warmth and intimacy reveal a commitment that goes far beyond that of a patron and his client or even of close friends.[45] On initial examination, these letters would seem to have little to do with orality and sound worlds, but, as was discussed in chapter 2 in relation to the marquise de Sévigné, letters were often considered as extensions of or even forms of conversation. The practice of reading private correspondence aloud still existed in the seventeenth century, lending a sense of vocality and performance to both the writing and reading of letters. As we will see, the guardedness of some of Condé's comments in his letters, and his allusion to the need for the two men to speak together in private, in some ways makes the letters seem like intimate conversations, but they are conversations held while the door is open: the possibility that someone might be listening in the wings or intercepting their letters remains very real. Therefore, Condé always makes a distinction between what is written down and what is spoken, and the latter is invariably more valuable and urgent.

The earliest letter, written in 1650 during the Fronde when Condé was imprisoned in the Château de Vincennes, communicates Condé's "peine" (pain) at the wounds sustained by Guitaut while fighting for him and ends with his assurance of "la continuation de mon affection" (my continuing affection [fol. 218]).[46] As generic a *formule de politesse* as this may seem, Condé's expressions of tenderness and kinship become ever more passionate in the later correspondence with Guitaut, and he very rarely simply begins or ends letters with the same terminology, quite unlike the cooler and more formulaic utterances in his letters to most other correspondents.[47] Within a year, he is writing, "Assurez-vous que je vous aime audelà de ce que vous pensez" (Be assured that I love you more than you think [1651, fol. 217]), moving to such protestations as "J'ai des impatiences furieuses de vous voir pour vous pouvoir témoigner que je vous aime avec tout l'estime et toute la tendresse imaginables" (I am furiously impatient to see you so that I can let you know that I love you with all imginable esteem and tenderness [17 December 1656, fol. 177]) and, barely a week later, "Je vous prie de vous en revenir le plutôt que vous pourrez; car en vérité, j'ai peine à m'accoutumer à être si longtemps sans vous" (I beg you to return as soon as you possibly can, for, to be truthful, I have trouble accustoming myself to being without you for so long [23 December 1656, fol. 179]). Even when Guitaut was married and his first wife gravely ill, Condé was able to insist on his friend coming immediately to join him, explaining, "J'ai une affaire pressée, où je ne puis me passer de vous" (I have urgent business where I cannot do without you [undated, fol. 166]).[48]

In an undated letter, but proposed as 1663 by the Chantilly archivist—in other words, during the years immediately after Guitaut's elevation to the Ordre du Saint-Esprit—Condé's response to a letter he has received from his favorite reveals worry on Guitaut's part about the continuation of Condé's friendship:

> Votre Lettre me paraît si allarmée sur mon amitié, que vous me faites pitié. Pouvez-vous croire que j'en puisse jamais manquer pour vous et est-il possible que vous puissiez jamais en avoir le moindre

doute ? Soyez donc en repos là-dessus et soyez persuadé que je vous la conserverai toute ma vie. (undated, fol. 164)

(Your letter appears to express such alarm about my friendship for you that you make me feel pity for you. Do you really believe that I can ever fail you and how can you possibly have the least doubt about that? Therefore, put your mind at ease on this matter and be persuaded that I shall keep that friendship for you all my life.)

The volatility of Condé's previous friendships with his favorites and the precariousness of the prince's finances from the mid-1660s onward might explain the anxiety of Guitaut, who still relied on the older man's patronage.[49]

However, Condé's insistent affirmation of the two men's closeness in his letters brings to the fore a further dimension of intimacy, one that lies beyond the confines of the handwritten or printed text. Another undated letter reveals the importance attached to secret confidences and information that can only successfully be understood and decoded by the two friends:

J'ai reçu vos lettres et je ne vous ai pas fait réponse, puisque je croyais que vous viendriez. Mandez-moi si vous viendrez ou non. Je me suis mis dans la tête d'en deviner quelque chose. Mandez-moi seulement si l'homme qui vous a parlé, n'aime pas le chocolat. Par là je verrai si j'ai bien deviné ou non. [. . .] J'ai mille choses à vous dire d'ailleurs. (undated, fol. 163–64)

(I have received your letters and have not replied to you, because I thought you would be coming. Tell me if you will come or not. I put it in my head to guess something about it. Tell me only if the man who spoke to you does not like chocolate. Through that I will see if I have guessed correctly or not. I have a thousand things to tell you besides.)

The identity of the man who does not like chocolate cannot be guessed by any other reader but constitutes a cipher that only Guitaut and Condé will comprehend.[50] Moreover, not only does such coded language reinforce the intimacy of the relationship between the two men, it also demonstrates the dangers of revealing precisely and overtly what one thinks: letters can be intercepted and read by others. Those words that truly communicate desire or secret information must always therefore be kept away from the page and await the time that the two men are alone together and able to speak their thoughts. We find this in Condé's "je croyais que vous viendriez" (I thought you would be coming) and in the enticing final words, "J'ai mille choses à vous dire d'ailleurs" (I have a thousand things to tell you besides).

This theme of the advantage of spoken over written communication is one that informs many of the letters between the prince and his favorite: in one missive, written in 1656, for example, he refers to having had to change his "stile," before adding that these are things that "il vaut mieux remettre à vous les dire qu'à vous les écrire" (it is better to tell you about them rather than write to you about them [25 January 1656, fols. 171–72]). A few months later, when based in Brussels, he insists that "je meurs d'envie de vous voir et de vous entretenir de mille choses" (I am longing to see you and talk to you about a thousand things), adding, "Assurez-vous toujours de mon extrême amitié et croyez-moi plus à vous que personne du monde" (Please be assured always of my absolute friendship and believe that I belong to you more than anybody in the world [11 October 1656, fol. 175]), later even teasing him (calling it "raillerie" [jesting]) that Guitaut prefers being in the company of another unnamed man than spending time with Condé (23 December 1656, fol. 179). In another letter from 1662, relating to Guitaut's financial affairs, he mentions that such matters are best communicated "de bouche, car par écrit cela n'irait pas si bien" (by mouth, for in writing that would not go down so well), before concluding with the words, "Cependant, assurez-vous que je ne vous ai jamais aimé plus tendrement que je vous aime" (But rest assured that I have never loved you more tenderly than I love you now [23 October 1662, fol. 206]). Akin to the dangers of scurrilous songs being written down rather than being heard, Condé was aware that the most intimate of sentiments needed to be communicated orally and not on paper.

The lack of written correspondence between the two men from the late 1660s onward may indicate that later letters have not been preserved, but it also coheres with the fact that Guitaut left the close remit of Condé's household around 1670. The precarious state of Condé's finances and the evidence of some tension between the two friends in this regard—one letter from as early as 1662 relating to Guitaut's "affaires" starts with the words "De peur que vous ne me continuiez vos reproches, je vais répondre à votre Lettre" (As I fear that you might continue to reproach me, I am going to reply to your letter [23 October 1662, fol. 206])—may be a contributing factor, but a brief reference in a song from 1670 (with the eighteenth-century note attached to it in the *Chansonnier Maurepas*) offers a further clue. The song (set to the popular tune "Laissez paître vos bêtes") covers a range of the latest court gossip and refers in passing to "la cheute de Guitaut" (Guitaut's fall).[51] The note explains that the hatred of Condé's only son, the duc d'Enghien, for Guitaut forced his father to banish his favorite.

A valuable witness to Guitaut's predicament around this time is the marquise de Sévigné. As the cousin of Bussy-Rabutin, who, as we saw, had cause to resent Guitaut, Sévigné might seem an improbable friend. But after Guitaut's Paris house in Rue de Thorigny burned down during the night in February 1671 (described vividly by Sévigné in a letter to her daughter),[52] her help in safeguarding some of Guitaut's valuables and assisting his pregnant second wife led to the two developing a close friendship. Among the paintings, furniture, and belongings destroyed (estimated by Sévigné at "plus de dix mille écus de perte" [losses of more than ten thousand écus]),[53] she makes special mention of and speculates on a particular item: "Ils ont grand regret à des lettres; je me suis imaginée que c'étaient des lettres de Monsieur le Prince" (They are particularly sorry about the loss of some letters; I gained the impression that they were letters from Monsieur le Prince).[54] Evidently she notes the importance that Guitaut attached to these letters, whether relating to business or personal affairs, and the fire may indeed explain why there are no surviving letters between the two men in the two years preceding the fire. The warmth of the rapport between Guitaut and Sévigné is strongly evident in Sévigné's correspondence, from accounts of her making him giggle during the funeral service for the chancellor Pierre Séguier ("sans aucun respect de la pompe funèbre" [without any respect for the solemnity of the funeral],[55] as she mischievously puts it) to the delight she takes in her frequent visits to his château in Époisses. Much of their affinity relies on shared auditory delights, such as Sévigné's depiction of Easter sermons she has heard given by the *chanoine* of Époisses, Simon-Michel Treuvé, who was preaching in Paris in 1683 and whose simple oratorical style she praises.[56] When she recounts to Guitaut her visit to the newly built Versailles, it is not so much the visual magnificence of the palace that she praises but rather the music that she hears there.[57] And above all, she relishes the many conversations that she and Guitaut have. Describing their closeness to her daughter in 1677, for instance, Sévigné writes,

> Nos conversations sont infinies. Il aime à causer, et quand on me met à causer, je ne fais pas trop mal aussi, de sorte qu'on ne peut pas être mieux ensemble que nous y sommes.[58]

(Our conversations are infinite. He loves to chatter, and when I am made to chatter, I do not do too badly either, so that we are perfectly matched when together.)

In a letter from the same year to Guitaut himself, she states, "Je ne pense pas qu'on puisse jamais avoir un meilleur correspondant que vous" (I could not imagine a better correspondent than you), mentioning Condé also: "Cela fait aussi dire de plaisantes choses à Monsieur le Prince" (That makes one think of saying enjoyable things to Monsieur le Prince also).[59]

It is clear that Guitaut confided in Sévigné over his estrangement from Condé. One letter in particular shows that Guitaut saw himself as a favorite who was resented by others in Condé's circle, described by Sévigné as "une petite cour":

> J'ai extrêmement causé avec Guitaut; il m'a divertie par les détails dont je ne savais que l'autre côté. Il est bon d'entendre les deux parties. Il m'a flattée d'avoir pris plaisir à me donner pour lui toute l'estime qu'on aurait pu m'ôter, si je ne m'étais miraculeusement fiée à sa bonne mine. Il m'a paru sincère et fort honnête homme, et je trouve que l'on l'a voulu chasser de l'hôtel de Condé, seulement parce qu'il faisait ombrage aux autres; un tel favori n'est pas agréable dans une petite cour. Il y a des endroits bien extraordinaires dans son roman.[60]

(I have chatted at length with Guitaut; he diverted me with details about which I only knew the other side of the story. It is good to hear both sides. He flattered me in taking pleasure in showing me all the esteem that could have been denied me, if I had not miraculously trusted his open demeanor. He seemed to me sincere and every inch the civilized man, and I find that they wanted to chase him from the Hôtel de Condé only because he was making other people jealous; such a favorite does not appeal within a little court. There are some truly extraordinary excerpts in the tale of his life.)

As late as 1685, the year of Guitaut's death, Sévigné refers to further financial wrangles in the Guitaut family, which may still have been related to Condé.[61]

On 10 March 1687, barely fifteen years after Chausson and Paulmier had been forced to kneel in front of Notre-Dame cathedral to make their "amende honorable" (honorable amends) before being taken to their deaths, the renowned bishop and orator Jacques-Bénigne Bossuet (whose sermons preached before the young king were discussed in chapter 3) delivered in the same precincts a funeral oration (the last one he would give) to mark the death three months earlier of le Grand Condé. For all its many literary merits, we should not forget that the prime purpose of such an oration was first and foremost to be heard rather than read. Calling on the many people who filled the cavernous spaces of the cathedral, Bossuet declaimed in the sermon's peroration:

> Tous ensemble, en quelque degré de sa confiance qu'il vous ait reçus, environnez ce tombeau; versez des larmes avec des prières; et, admirant dans un si grand prince une amitié si commode et un commerce si doux, conservez le souvenir d'un héros dont la bonté avait égalé le courage.[62]

> (All of you together, in whatever degree of his confidence that he received you, gather round this tomb; shed tears with prayers; and, admiring in so great a prince so commodious a friendship and so sweet an acquaintance, preserve the memory of a hero whose goodness was the equal of his courage.)

For a significant period of his life, Guitaut, who had died of a fever a year before Condé's death, had been both a major recipient of Condé's "bonté" and a witness of his "courage" in battle, enabling him to live a life of privilege apparently completely removed from the life and death of Jacques Chausson and his friend Jacques Paulmier. Although we find fragments of sung words about Guitaut in the songs of the time, much of the orality of the lives of Condé and his favorite did not need to exist on the streets but rather flourished in the verbal dexterity of salons, in the shared enjoyment (and prioritization) of conversation between friends, in the ceremonial auditory splendor of both men becoming Chevaliers de l'Ordre du Saint-Esprit at the very beginning of 1662, and in the privacy of shared spoken intimacies between the two men. For Chausson and his supporters, the stakes and dangers associated with the Pont Neuf sound world were far greater.

CHAPTER 6

Different Worlds

The very different fates of Chausson and Guitaut as traced through part 2 again highlight the sense of injustice that the four-line song from the *Chansonnier Maurepas* communicates so effectively. It would seem that here are two men from very diverse Parisian milieux who reportedly have indulged in the same "vice": one of them has lost his life because of it, while the other has received great wealth and favor through it. In other words, the poet/singer's outrage appears to come from the perception that the two men are treated differently precisely because they belong to such different worlds. The irony that one of the men who pronounced the sentence of death by fire on Chausson and Paulmier, Jean-Jacques de Mesmes (*président à mortier* at the Parlement de Paris), himself became provost and master of ceremonies of the Ordre du Saint-Esprit in 1671 only underlines the apparent disparity.

However, I would like to suggest a very different reading: that the outrage emanates directly from the closeness of the worlds of both Chausson and Guitaut. Indications of this closeness can be found in the oral culture of the Pont Neuf.

Another song about Chausson's execution, contained in two manuscripts at the Chantilly archives, and probably performed around the same time as the "Grands Dieux" piece, offers an intriguing clue about the proximity of Chausson and Guitaut's environs. This song evokes with less concision and greater earthiness the unequal treatment meted out to aristocratic and lower-class sodomites, and gives a voice to Chausson:

Je suis ce pauvre garçon
Nommé Chausson (bis)
Et que si l'on m'a roti
A la fleur de mon age,
C'est pour l'amour d'un Page
Du prince de Conti.

Et si l'on bruloit tous ceux
Qui font comme eux (bis)
Dans bien peu de temps, hélas!
Plusieurs seigneurs de France,
Grand Prelats d'importance,
Souffriroient le trépas.

Prions donc tous dedans ce saint lieu
La mere de dieu (bis)
Et son bon fils Jesus,
Que tous les V . . . se grossissent,
Que les c . . . se retrecissent,
Pour ne plus f. . . . en c. . . .[1]

(I am that poor boy / Called Chausson [to be sung twice] / And if I was roasted / In the flower of my youth, / It was for the love of a page / Of the prince de Conti.

And if all those / Who act in the same way were burned [sung twice] / Alas! In a very short time, / Several lords of France, / And great and important prelates, / would suffer death.

Let us all pray therefore in this holy place / To the mother of God [sung twice] / And her good son Jesus, / That all cocks become bigger, / That cunts become smaller, / So that there is no more need to fuck in the ass.)

The reference to Chausson as "ce pauvre garçon" (that poor boy) and the statement that there would not be many high-ranking officials left alive if every sodomite were put to death suggest that this piece, like the "Grands Dieux" song, was composed by somebody sympathetic to Chausson's plight and aware of the different standards applied to those from different social strata. The final stanza rehearses a common misogynistic trope that supposedly justifies sodomites' sexual choices.

However, of particular interest here is the comment that Chausson is to be burned on the scaffold for loving a page who worked for the prince de Conti, the younger brother of le Grand Condé. The note in one manuscript of the song (MS fr. 15127), which is wrongly identified as being from 1651, names a certain M. de Fesnau, "actuellement lieutenant-general" (presently lieutenant general), as the page in question. Fesnau appears also in a manuscript variant of another song, mentioned earlier,[2] in which Dassoucy is compared to Chausson. Although Fesnau's name does not feature in any of the interrogation records of the Chausson/Paulmier trial, all the transcripts refer to Chausson and Paulmier's corruption of younger men and adolescent boys. The shorter seventeenth-century transcript from the Parlement (AN X2A 1027) includes questions posed to Paulmier about page boys in particular:

> Interrogé s'il a esté au bois de Vincennes avec un page et à St-Maur. Dit qu'il ne sçait ce que c'est de cela, ne cognoist point de page de Madame.
> Interrogé qu'il a donné des oranges à un page.
> Dit qu'il luy a donné une orange. Luy a ramené a la foire a la boutique de sa sœur.[3]

> (Interrogated whether he has been to the Bois de Vincennes with a page boy and to St-Maur. Said that he does not know about that, does not know any page boy of Madame. Interrogated if he gave oranges to a page boy. Said that he gave him an orange. Took him to the fair to his sister's shop stall.)

The first page whom Paulmier denies knowing or seeing is one said here to have served Henriette d'Angleterre (known as Madame), wife of the king's brother Philippe d'Orléans. However, he does admit giving an orange to an unnamed page while at a fair from a stall run by his sister: oranges were at that time largely imported from Portugal or Italy and were sold on the Pont Neuf as exotic delicacies, and they would therefore have been seen as a valued gift.[4] In early modern Europe, the offering of a gift by an older man to a young man or boy was often seen as a sign of part of a sexual exchange,[5] which may explain the interrogators' attempts to make Paulmier admit to giving gifts to the page boy. Taking into account Paulmier's statement in the interrogation that "il n'est revenu que la derniere semaine de Caresme d'Angleterre" (he only returned in the last week of Lent from England), it is probable that he would have taken the boy to enjoy the sights and sounds of the Saint-Germain fair, which took place immediately after the end of Lent, during Eastertide. Although the lack of detail in the interrogation and the desperate situation of Chausson and Paulmier (and their desire not to be found guilty) make it difficult to ascertain the factual truths of the case, the gossip contained in the "Je suis ce pauvre garçon" song makes it possible to speculate that the unnamed recipient of the orange might have been the prince de Conti's page. Given Paulmier's denial of knowledge of Madame's page, it is not beyond the bounds of plausibility that the boy with whom he (and perhaps Chausson also) spent time in the Bois de Vincennes (incidentally, located right by where Condé and his brother had been imprisoned during the Fronde) was in actuality Conti's page, Fesnau.[6] If this were the case, Paulmier would not have been lying if he said that he did not spend time with Madame's page boy. The possibility of an association between Paulmier and a boy working for Conti gains further credence if one takes into account the mention of Saint-Maur during the interrogation, for the château at Saint-Maur was owned by the Condé family, and it is likely that if Paulmier were with the boy at Saint-Maur, as suggested, the page would have been working for the Condé family there.[7]

Conti's own son Louis Armand de Bourbon, born in the year of Guitaut's elevation to Chevalier de l'Ordre du Saint-Esprit and Chausson's execution, shared the sexual preferences of his uncle and grandfather. He was to become embroiled in a scandal himself in 1682, involving the comte de Vermandois, Louis XIV's fifteen-year-old son (his mother was Louis's former mistress Louise de la Vallière), and a group of men who vigorously espoused same-sex sexual pursuits and called themselves the Italian Brotherhood.[8] Louis XIV banished a number of the participants, including his son, even though none of them, being aristocrats, faced death by fire.

But, returning to 1661, such proximity between the world of Condé/Guitaut and Paulmier/Chausson as shown in the song and seventeenth-century interrogation transcript[9] (both communicated orally) might conceivably be seen as coincidental and of little relevance to the juxtaposition of Chausson and Guitaut in the "Grands Dieux" song were it not for the crucial circumstance of Guitaut's own beginnings as a page. As mentioned earlier, Guitaut began working as a page boy in the entourages of Richelieu, Louis XIII, and the Maréchal de Gramont before he came to Condé's attention. Significantly, in all three households sexual relationships between pages or other members of staff and aristocratic men were strongly rumored to have taken place. Tallemant des Réaux, for example, tells a tale of one of Richelieu's pages, called Vandy, procuring another boy for the sexual gratification of Richelieu's friend Boisrobert.[10] Louis XIII reportedly fell in love with several men in his entourage, starting with his coachman and moving to his dog keeper, and "on l'accusoit de faire cent ordures" (they accused him of performing a hundred filthy acts) with an officer in the royal household, François de Baradas, according to Tallemant.[11] The same-sex proclivities of Gramont, who, like Guitaut, was from Gascony, were widely known and are satirized in a number of songs,[12] including one quoted by Tallemant in which Gramont is told, "Prenez courage, / Il vous reste encore un page" (Take courage, / You still have a page boy left to you).[13] Even Guitaut's uncle, François de Comminges, who arrested Condé during the Fronde on 18 January 1650 and who was captain of the guards in the household of Louis XIV's mother, Anne of Austria, was rumored in song to be sexually active with his ensign (named in a note from the *Chansonnier Maurepas* as La Raliere-Fenestraux), while the pages from the same household are depicted as engaging in shameless sexual activity:

Cette Maison est impudique,
Les Pages y branlent la pique,
Les Gardes f..... les Exempts;
Pour achever la bougriniere;
On dit que tres seurement
Guitaut f. ... en C. ... la Raliere.[14]

(This House is shameless, / The Pages jerk their cocks there, / The Guards fuck the Officers; / To complete this array of buggery, / It is said on good authority / That Guitaut is fucking La Raliere in the ass.)

Thus, when Condé employed Guitaut, it is unsurprising that observers, especially those like Bussy-Rabutin or Coligny-Saligny who felt slighted by Condé's preference for the younger man, might have speculated on a sexual relationship between the pair. Moreover, although sexual activity between masters and page boys seemed to be almost the norm in princely or aristocratic households, certainly never leading to prosecution,[15] those cases where more lowly ranked men were said to be having sexual relationships with page boys inevitably led to much more severe punishments. Earlier in the century, for example, the parliamentary court records detail the interrogation in 1626 of a *valet de chambre* called Charles Bourgoin who worked for Seigneur de Mayenne, the son of the duc de Nevers. Accused of sodomizing a page called Vendempierre, Bourgoin, like Chausson and Paulmier, was sentenced to death by fire.[16]

Condé and the Pont Neuf Song Culture

In December 1661 Condé was clearly preoccupied with his, members of his family's, and his favorite Guitaut's elevation to the Ordre du Saint-Esprit, so it may appear unlikely that he would have had knowledge of a four-line song about Chausson and Guitaut being sung on the Pont Neuf. Yet, as we saw in the first part of this book, members of the aristocracy such as the marquise de Sévigné took a keen interest in the street-song culture of the time, and indeed many aristocrats wrote songs themselves that would have been sung on the Pont Neuf.

Nonetheless, given his many military engagements, it may at first be surprising to learn that Condé remained captivated by what was being sung on the streets of Paris. Before a battle, clearly aware how military defeats were ruthlessly satirized in songs, Condé was reputed to have shouted, "Gare les *ponts-neufs*, enfants!" (Beware the *ponts-neufs*, children!)[17] A song that exists in many forms about Condé's unsuccessful siege of Lerida in 1647 was supposed to have resulted in the poet Saint-Amant (who by a quirk of fate died on the very day that Chausson was executed in 1661) being targeted for a thrashing on the Pont Neuf, ordered by Condé (whose title at the time, before his father's death, was the duc d'Enghien) himself.[18] Its opening stanza alludes both to Condé's failure at Lerida and his sexual practices:

> L'Espagnol n'eusse pas crû
> Que D'Anguien eut eu un cu
> S'il n'eut tourné le derriere.
> Laire la, laire lan laire,
> Laire la, laire lan la.[19]

(The Spaniard would not have believed / That D'Enghien had an ass / If he hadn't turned his behind. / Laire la, laire lan laire etc.)

Another version of the song ends with an allusion to the realization that the author of the song will be punished if his or her identity is discovered:

Celuy qui a fait la chanson
N'oseroit pas dire son nom,
Car il auroit les etrivieres.
> Laire la
> Laire lan laire,
> Laire la
> Laire lan la.[20]

(The person who wrote the song / Would never dare say his name, / For he would then be whipped. / Laire la etc.)

Many songs praising Condé's military successes were circulated throughout his career, and there is evidence to suggest that Condé employed writers to compose counter propaganda songs for a failure like that at Lerida.[21] Even the singer Philippot le Savoyard, whom we met in the first part of this book and whose published songs comprise mostly drinking songs, includes a piece in praise of Condé's early military successes, "Chanson amoureuse à la louange de Monseigneur le duc d'Anguien," commencing with the lines:

Nouveau Germanicus,
Vray sang de Charlemagne,
Tu les as tous vaincus
Ces peuples d'Allemagne.[22]

(New Germanicus, / True blood of Charlemagne, / You have conquered them all, / These peoples from Germany.)

Condé himself is purported to be the author of songs to be found in the *Chansonnier Maurepas*, usually in which he presents himself as a gallant heterosexual lover, at odds with the way he is portrayed by others.[23]

Condé's active involvement in the production of songs, and indeed in the sound world of the Pont Neuf in particular, demonstrates again the extraordinary closeness of the different classes on the Pont Neuf. That the king's cousin whose estates and palaces rivaled those of the king and a blind self-confessed drunkard like Philippot, who felt most at home among the paupers at the foot of Henri IV's statue, should both be focused on the crowds gathered to listen to the latest songs shows the far-reaching appeal and power of such an oral culture.

Given Condé's proximity to and awareness of the song-producing domain of the Pont Neuf, it is therefore quite possible that the Chausson song reached his or those in his circle's attention. The existence of a handwritten copy of the song among the manuscripts at Chantilly (of which there are several volumes of songs from the period)[24] cannot prove that Condé himself saw it or had it copied on his behalf, but it does show that the family was interested in the songs emanating from Paris and elsewhere.

Authorship

If, as I have argued, the four-line "Grands Dieux" piece does indeed constitute a wry commentary on the very different destinies of men whose lives and tastes came into such close contact with each other, one question remains: who was the author of the song? It may conceivably have been written by someone who knew about the particular circumstances and links between the men involved. Given the dangers associated with being identified as the person to have written a potentially incendiary song, identifying the author of such a piece will always be necessarily speculative, and unless clear documentary proof relating to the song presents itself, it is unlikely that we will ever be certain. However, I would suggest that two very plausible names present themselves as the possible author, with a third candidate who may have been closer to the song culture of the Pont Neuf than initially thought.

Candidate 1

We already know that Chausson's death had a deep effect on the poet Claude Le Petit: as we saw earlier, he wrote one sonnet devoted to the subject and mentioned Chausson's name in another poem. It is therefore quite possible that he wrote a third piece about the same subject. Although Le Petit is not known primarily as a writer of songs, one of the lost items that is named in the list of contents of *Le Bordel des Muses*, "Sur le carême," is designated as "Chanson." Moreover, two seventeenth/eighteenth-century commentators, Claude Brossette and Charles-Hugues Lefebvre de Saint-Marc, both mention that Le Petit was arrested for writing and publishing "des chansons impies et libertines" (impious and libertine songs).[25] Also, as discussed earlier in the book, the vast majority of song authors from the time remained anonymous, so it is perfectly plausible that Le Petit wrote as many songs as he wrote sonnets. The fact that Le Petit met the same fate as Chausson only a few months later adds poignancy to the story but cannot amount to proof that he wrote the "Grands Dieux" piece; however, it is probable that he knew that he could face execution if he were uncovered as the author of the Chausson sonnet and of the *Bordel des Muses*, where sexual excess and provocation are celebrated. His own humble origins (as the son of a tailor) would surely have made him sensitive to the irony that Guitaut was being made a Chevalier de l'Ordre du Saint-Esprit as a result of his perceived relationship with Condé at the very moment that the bourgeois Chausson was being condemned to die for sodomy. Indeed, Le Petit's friend Jean Rou goes so far as to say that Le Petit himself might well have been spared the death penalty were it not for his "naissance trop obscure" (too lowly birth),[26] and a similar thought is implicit in the Chausson four-line song.

Yet, while none of these aspects demonstrates that Le Petit was aware of Guitaut's elevation, another piece written by the poet, his satirical *Paris Ridicule*, includes a section dedicated precisely to the subject of the "Chevaliers du Saint-Esprit." Since there had been no promotions to the order for several years (well before Le Petit was born) until the end of 1661, it is almost certain that the whole book, or at the very least this section, was written by Le Petit in the weeks or months following the event and certainly before mid-1662, when Le Petit was executed; he would therefore have been reflecting on the new cohort of Knights of the Order that included both Guitaut and Condé. Although no names are mentioned, the poet gently mocks the pretensions of these "Sires nouveaux" and their clothing:

> Disons donc un mot de ces autres
> Qui font, ensemble en peloton,
> Bande à part dedans ce canton:
> Disent-ils leurs patenôtres?
> Ces vénérables Cordons bleus
> Font bien, avec leurs habits neufs,
> Les fiers parmi ces hallebardes;
> Ont-ils peur, ces Sires nouveaux,
> Que le Diable emporte leurs hardes,
> Qu'ils font des croix à leurs manteaux?[27]

(Let us say a word of these other people / Who together as a group are placed / As a separate band in this district: / Do they recite their Pater-Nosters? / These venerable Blue Ribands, / With their new clothes / Make themselves haughty in the midst of these halberds; /

Are these new Lords afraid / That the Devil will take away their accessories / If they do not put crosses on their cloaks?)

The religious iconography that covered the cross and vestments worn by the knights (which was discussed earlier) provokes the amused response of the poet here.

In complete contrast to Chausson, who wore nothing but a "chemise empesée" (as we saw in Le Petit's sonnet devoted to the event), a starched shirt signifying the garb of the penitent, here the knights parade the new and elaborate clothes that signal their elevation to the highest order of the land. Not only is the visual splendor of these privileged men evoked, but so too is an imagined sound world of the prayers that such people might utter. The question "Disent-ils leurs patenôtres?" forms an intriguing counterpoint to the portrayal of Chausson in Le Petit's sonnet, where the condemned man goes to his death singing the hymn "Salve Regina" in a joyous manner. Given our knowledge, therefore, that Le Petit is depicting two events that took place within three days of each other, the satire of elaborate religiosity here might be seen to take on a harder edge than at first appeared to be the case, and it is made even more cutting through the evocation of the religious prayers and hymns that each person was incanting aloud. Furthermore, if Le Petit were indeed the author of the "Grands Dieux" song, the direct conjunction in that piece of Chausson with the "cordon bleu" awarded to Guitaut brings together the two elements that he was exploring separately in the sonnet and in *Paris Ridicule*.

But there remains one other bitter irony that might have been all too evident to Le Petit. If we examine more closely one particular detail of the cloak worn by Guitaut as the newest Chevalier de l'Ordre du Saint-Esprit, we will find that the black velvet, as royal historiographer Saint-Foix describes it, "est semé de flammes, ou *langues* de feu, brodées en or" (is covered with flames, or *tongues* of fire, embroidered in gold), denoting the tongues of fire descending on the apostles at Pentecost.[28] While Chausson's own tongue had very recently been cut off and his body incinerated by flames, with his ashes thrown into the river Seine, Guitaut's body was enveloped by a sumptuous cloak adorned with elaborate tongues of fire, signifying his emergence into the highest echelons of society.

Candidate 2

Another plausible candidate for the authorship of the Chausson song is, like Le Petit, a name we have come across already in this book and who was wrongly credited as the author of a 1671 clandestine edition of *Paris Ridicule*:[29] Roger de Rabutin, comte de Bussy, better known as Bussy-Rabutin. Emanating from a much more illustrious background than that of the young poet, Bussy was, as we have seen, closely connected to the circle of le Grand Condé and resented Condé's preference for Guitaut.

Bussy was also well versed in the latest songs, peppering his memoirs with quotations from songs and poems: he often shows his knowledge of what is currently being sung in Paris, such as the time soon after the ill-fated siege of Lerida when he boasts of teaching "mille chansons" (a thousand songs) to the Chevalier de la Vallière, who had been out of France for three or four years.[30] We know also that he frequently discussed the most recent songs in his correspondence with the marquise de Sévigné.[31] But above all, he was a prolific songwriter, happy to compose satirical verses while in high society in Paris or on military campaigns, especially when he was serving under the prince de Conti, le Grand Condé's brother, in Catalonia.[32] A manuscript containing fifty-one songs written in his hand is kept at the Chantilly library,[33] and one can only assume that these form a small part of all the pieces he wrote. Those songs that can be dated go as far back as 1643, when he was twenty-five, while others detailing friends' names or battles show that they were written in the 1640s and 1650s, when he was closely attached to the Condé household. Indeed, Bussy may well have been one of the songwriters employed by le Grand Condé to compose pieces in praise of his military exploits.

One of Bussy's *bêtes noires*, Turenne, who was often compared unfavorably to Condé as a military commander, appears in a number of the songs written in Bussy's hand, including one from 1657 (set to the tune of a Christmas carol) when Turenne, commander of the French royal troops, was forced by Condé, who was commanding the Spanish troops, to raise the siege of Cambrai. Not only does Bussy display a detailed knowledge of the military maneuvers involved, but he also pokes fun at the two men's differing sexual tastes:

> Or nous dittes Turenne
> Ou etiés vous alors
> Que Condé ce grand Prince
> Entra dans les dehors,
> On etoit je vous jure,
> En un lieu haut et bas,

Ou par bonne avanture
Condé ne passa pas.³⁴

(Now tell us Turenne / Where were you / When this great prince Condé / Entered from behind, / I swear to you that we were / In a high and low place, / Where by good fortune / Condé did not pass through.)

Another song in Bussy's hand about a great military commander, the duc de Vendôme, makes reference to the general's sexual preference for men; his name proved a godsend for songwriters, who frequently rhymed it with "Sodome":

Dans notre quartier La Baume
On voit autel contre autel,
Chés le bonhomme Vendosme
Dans notre quartier La Baume
On y vit comme a Sodome,
Et chés nous comme au Bordel.
Dans notre etc.³⁵

(In our district of La Baume / We see altar against altar / At the house of the good Vendôme / In our district of La Baume / They live there like in Sodom, / And in our place like in a Brothel. / In our etc.)

One song that is not to be found in Bussy's handwritten manuscript played a crucial part in the disgrace suffered by Bussy and his friends Vivonne, Manicamp, and Guiche after a few days spent in Roissy during Holy Week of 1659, a stay that would be recounted in Bussy's satirical depiction of court life, *Histoire amoureuse des Gaules*. Not only did the men feast and carouse during traditional days of fasting, but they also amused themselves composing an obscene version of the Easter hymn "Ô Filii et filiae" (a hymn that was often parodied by both Bussy and other writers in songs from the time),³⁶ with the highest figures at the court (including the king; his mother, Anne of Austria; his brother, Philippe d'Orléans; Cardinal Mazarin; and la Grande Mademoiselle) being imagined in varying degrees of sexual congress.³⁷ News of these debauches reached the devout wing of the court, and all four men were exiled for a short period (Bussy was to be imprisoned in 1665 and then exiled for a much longer time after the circulation of the *Histoire amoureuse*). Bussy attempts to minimize their sacrilegious behavior in his memoirs, and he does not even mention the satirical song,[38] but a letter to his cousin near the end of his life corroborates the truth that he and his friends did indeed compose a setting of the hymn:

> Je vous dirai que je viens de faire une version du cantique de Pâques, O filii et filiae, car je ne suis pas toujours profane. Vivonne, le comte de Guiche, Manicamp et moi fîmes autrefois des *alleluia* à Roissy qui ne furent pas aussi approuvés que le seraient ceux-ci; aussi nous firent-ils chasser tous quatre.[39]

> (I will tell you that I have just composed a version of the Easter hymn "O filii et filiae," for I am not always profane. Vivonne, the comte de Guiche, Manicamp, and I previously composed some alleluias at Roissy, which were not as warmly approved as these ones would be; also they led to all four of us being banished.)

The scandal emanating from the Roissy incident and his short-term exile made Bussy determined to regain the king's approval. When Condé was allowed by the king to return to France at the end of 1659, Bussy clearly hoped to take advantage of his former master's newly favorable status by reuniting with him and being included in what Bussy calls in his memoirs Condé's "amnistie" from the king. However, if Bussy is to be believed, when the two men met again at Saint-Maur in 1660, Condé only made vague assurances that came to nothing, no doubt increasing Bussy's resentment.[40]

In November 1661, on hearing that the king was selecting the names of the sixty men whom he would choose as his Chevaliers de l'Ordre du Saint-Esprit, the ambitious Bussy spared no effort in trying to catch the king's attention in order to let him know of what he considered to be his own merits. As he recounts in his memoirs,[41] after consulting a number of dignitaries who were close to Louis XIV, including Turenne, La Mesnardière (dramatist and member of the Académie Française and "Lecteur du Roi"), and Le Tellier (secretary of state for war), all of whom were supportive but unable or unwilling to sway the king's decision making, Bussy finally secured through his friend Saint-Aignan (first gentleman of the king's bedchamber) the brief chance to contact the king, and significantly it was the opportunity to speak to the king in person at Fontainebleau. Clearly, he considered the oral communication of his needs to have a greater chance of being listened to seriously than any written request. During his "petite harangue" (little speech), which, according to Bussy, was received "fort paisiblement" (very reasonably) by Louis,[42] he declared that he had four qualities for which he deserved the promotion: a family of the most ancient lineage, twenty-seven years of military service, eight years as colonel general of the light cavalry, and never yet having been recompensed by the court. However, when the list of names was revealed on 3 December, Bussy's name was not among them. His claim that he was "un peu fasché" (a little angry) by this rejection is evidently an understatement,[43] for he was still writing about the rebuttal twenty-six years later in a letter to the marquise de Sévigné, on the occasion of the promotion to the order of her daughter's brother-in-law the comte de Grignan.[44]

Although Bussy does not mention Guitaut by name at this point in his memoirs, the fact that Condé's favorite, whom Bussy regarded as undistinguished and undeserving of preferment, was named as one of the new chevaliers must surely have irked him. As he proclaims, "toute la Cour sçavoit que je meritois cet honneur autant que personne" (the entire court knew that I deserved this honor as much as anyone).[45]

It is therefore possible that Bussy felt irritated enough at this point to write a satirical song about the approaching event: we know from his memoirs that he was in Paris on frequent occasions during this time, so he could plausibly have heard about Chausson's impending execution just as the investiture ceremony for the chevaliers was drawing near, enabling him also to compose and circulate the song at short notice. The rejection by the king of Bussy's attempt to communicate orally with him might plausibly have been countered by another oral riposte in the form of a song sung in public.

A further contributing factor to the theory that Bussy wrote the Chausson piece is that he had already mentioned Guitaut's possible same-sex preferences in another song, written in Bussy's own hand (from the collection now housed in the Chantilly archives). Rather than discussing Condé and Guitaut's putative relationship, Bussy writes here of Guitaut's "ardeur fidelle [...] pour son amy flamand" (faithful ardor ... for his Flemish friend).[46] We know that Guitaut accompanied Condé to Brussels in the 1650s, where he might have met his Flemish friend. What is more, Condé wrote from Brussels to Guitaut at the end of 1656, teasing him that he preferred to remain in the company of "Sr ...." than spend time with him (23 December 1656, fol. 179), which may mean that this unnamed person was the male friend evoked in Bussy's song. Given such evidence that Bussy had already been content to refer to Guitaut's friendships in such a way, it remains plausible that he may have felt moved to refer to such inclinations in another song at the time that Guitaut was about to be made a chevalier thanks to the patronage of Condé.

However, with no direct links to be found between Bussy and Chausson, it might seem improbable that a nobleman such as Bussy, with such a strong sense of aristocratic entitlement, would have felt sympathy for the plight of a bourgeois former customs officer. To counter this possible objection, one may argue that the "Grands Dieux" song can be interpreted not as an indictment of the unequal treatment of people from different classes but as an ironic reflection on how the "vice" of one man is severely punished while the same "sin" in another man is rewarded with the highest honor in the land. Bussy's depiction of the Roissy party in the *Histoire amoureuse des Gaules* demonstrates both that he himself was unjudgmental about same-sex liaisons and that he was able to mock religious teachings about such matters. For example, when discovering his friends Manicamp and Trimalet (Guiche) in bed together, the character Bussy is able to say, "Pour moi, je ne condamne point vos manières" (As for me, I do not condemn your ways), before adding playfully, "mais je suis bien assuré de n'aller point à la béatitude par le chemin que vous tenez" (but I am assured that you will not reach eternal beatitude through the path that you are taking).[47]

A Third Candidate?

I would like to conclude this chapter by offering a final possible author of the "Grands Dieux" song: Jacques Chausson himself. As I have mentioned already, Chausson's fate in particular touched various writers in the seventeenth and eighteenth centuries. Moreover, his assertion in one interrogation that he had been earning money from "écritures" of various sorts could indicate that he wrote creatively also. Frédéric Lachèvre raises the question of why Claude Le Petit chose through the medium of his infamous sonnet to champion Chausson's posthumous cause rather than Paulmier's and concludes that Chausson must have been "de ses compagnons de débauche" (one of his companions in debauchery).[48] While this may have been the case, it is equally possible that Chausson was writing similarly subversive material as that found in *Le Bordel des Muses* and that Le Petit recognized in him a fellow free spirit and a companion who came from a similarly lowly background. The reality that no published texts by Chausson survive might point to him being an active songwriter and/or performer on or around the Pont Neuf, largely managing to preserve the anonymity that was essential to avoid prosecution, and might also explain the accusation made against him that he sang "des chansons impies" (impious songs). Could he have earned money by selling handwritten flysheets of his songs ("écritures"), performing them to crowds on the Pont Neuf, creating his own sound world? And, if that is indeed what happened, it is not impossible that he passed a four-line song bemoaning the injustice of his fate from his prison cell to a friend who could have performed it on his behalf. In this sense, the omnidimensional and penetrative quality of sound that was discussed at the beginning of this book gains added significance, as sound is transmitted through prison walls and out onto the nearby Pont Neuf. This theory would undoubtedly put another song previously quoted, "Je suis ce pauvre garçon / Nommé Chausson" (I am that poor boy / Called Chausson), into a different context. Could the "je" have been not so much a literary persona as Chausson himself anticipating and imagining his own impending death?

As speculative as this idea of Jacques Chausson as author of the "Grands Dieux" song may be, the prominence that his name attained as a result of his execution and the reaction it elicited mean that his case has given him an authority that would have been denied others who were executed and immediately forgotten. In an age where such a crime was deemed so dangerous that even the written charges against people like him were supposed to be destroyed along with the criminal's body, and where his blasphemous utterances necessitated the removal of his tongue before he was burned on the scaffold, Chausson's voice remains astonishingly alive.

Conclusion

Almost a decade after Chausson and Paulmier were burned at the scaffold, the marquise de Sévigné was awakened in her residence (the present 8, Rue de Thorigny) during the night by loud noises. As she reported two days later to her daughter, after visiting her cousin Coulanges (the songwriter whom we met in chapter 2),

> Je revins me coucher; cela n'est pas extraordinaire. Mais ce qui l'est beaucoup, c'est qu'à trois heures après minuit, j'entendis crier au voleur, au feu, et ces cris si près de moi et si redoublés que je ne doutai point que ce ne fût ici. Je crus même entendre qu'on parlait de ma petite-fille; je ne doutai pas qu'elle ne fût brûlée. Je me levai dans cette crainte, sans lumière, avec un tremblement qui m'empêchait quasi de me soutenir. Je courus à son appartement, qui est le vôtre; je trouvai tout dans une grande tranquillité. Mais je vis la maison de Guitaut toute en feu; les flammes passaient par-dessus la maison de Mme de Vauvineux. On voyait dans nos cours, et surtout chez M. de Guitaut, une clarté qui faisait horreur. C'étaient des bruits épouvantables, des poutres et des solives qui tombaient.[1]

> (I returned home to go to bed; that is not extraordinary. But what is much more extraordinary, is that at 3 a.m., I heard cries of "Thief," "Fire," and these cries were so close to me and becoming louder

that I had no doubt that it was here. I even thought I heard people speaking of my granddaughter; I was sure that she had been burned. I got up in this state of fear, without any light, trembling so much that I was unable to remain upright. I ran to her apartment, which is yours; I found everything in a state of complete calm. But I saw Guitaut's house consumed by fire; the flames were passing above Mme de Vauvineux's house. We could see in our courtyards, and above all in M. Guitaut's house, a brightness that was horrifying. There were terrifying noises of beams and girders falling.)

The sounds coming from outside that awoke Sévigné, unlike the mundane act of going to bed, are described by her as extraordinary. Significantly, it is their penetrating, intrusive, out-of-the-ordinary qualities that disturb her sleep, but, more than that, the ambiguity attached to the sounds makes them particularly troubling. Hearing the word "fire," she is overwhelmed with fear that her granddaughter (who was living in the same house) is in danger. As she walks through her house, she is literally in the dark assailed only by the noise. The uncertainty of sound in the darkness is soon replaced by the certainty and brightness ("clarté") of sight: her neighbor Guitaut's house (4, Rue de Thorigny) is consumed by flames, and the view of it is horrifying to her, exacerbated by the "bruits épouvantables" (terrifying noises).[2]

Given the charmed life that Guitaut had led in the ten years since being made a Chevalier de l'Ordre du Saint-Esprit, one might be tempted to perceive a certain poetic justice in the idea of his house being consumed by flames only a few hundred meters from the spot where two men, accused of "le même vice" (the same vice) as that which supposedly enabled Guitaut's social elevation, perished by fire. While Chausson and Paulmier were forced, as the official judgment puts it, to be "nuds en chemise, la corde au col" (naked in shirts, a rope around their necks),[3] Guitaut and his wife are described by Sévigné as being "quasi nus" (almost naked) in the street.[4]

Yet this incident, which led to Guitaut forming a close friendship with Sévigné for the rest of his life, brings together also a number of the themes and personalities we have considered in the preceding chapters. The dangerous unknowability of sound and the difficulty in repressing it became a major concern for Louis XIV and his government in the years following his assumption of absolute power in 1661. By 1667 a police force was set up, under the leadership of its new lieutenant general, Nicolas de la Reynie, whose role included monitoring the lives of Parisians by placing spies (known as "mouches") in public places to listen to conversations and to take more formal note of songs sung about the king. It is ironic that we owe the very survival of the gently subversive song about Chausson and Guitaut that has dominated this book to the probability that it was noted down for records by the very people who were attempting to police and eliminate such unruly sounds.

The consolidation of Louis's power in the 1660s manifested itself in other ways. His appropriation of artistic control has already been discussed in chapter 3, where the cultural threat posed by Nicolas Fouquet as patron of writers, musicians, and artists was deemed to be possibly as dangerous as his political ambitions. On a moral level, the execution of Chausson and Paulmier for sodomy, and the notoriety of the case, might suggest a state resolve to clamp down on sexual deviance. However, the tiny number of sodomy cases tried by French criminal courts in the sixteenth and seventeenth centuries points to a level of sexual tolerance in practice that is matched by the remarkably relaxed attitudes toward same-sex love that can be found in songs, letters, memoirs, and prose narratives from the time, and which I have examined elsewhere.[5] Inevitably, aristocrats tended not to be executed for sodomitical inclinations but were often banished instead, as in the 1682 exile of a number of noblemen attached to what was known as the "Confrérie Italienne" (Italian Brotherhood), which involved Louis's own son by Louise de Vallière, the comte de Vermandois, and le Grand Condé's nephew, the prince de Conti.[6]

One aim of this book has been to reconsider a monarch and an epoch that have almost invariably been presented previously from an overwhelmingly visual standpoint. By examining the age through some of its sound worlds, we might be better placed to acknowledge complexities and difficulties that emerge through the sounds heard, the songs sung, the sermons preached, the legal points argued. And yet this book has emphatically not been just about political, cultural, or moral elites.

In one of his more moving pieces of writing, in which he discusses various early modern documents relating to crime and punishment, Michel Foucault (perhaps inadvertently) uses a number of sound-related terms when considering those examples of prisoners whose lives are only known to subsequent generations through the short and brutal descriptions of their trials and crimes: "It is no doubt because of the vibrations that I still feel today when I happen to meet these lowly lives that have become ashes through the few sentences that condemned them. [. . .] Neither quasi- nor sub-literature, it isn't even the sketch of a genre; rather, it is in the disorder, noise and sorrow, the workings of power over lives, and the discourse that emanates from it."[7]

The noisiness, vibrancy, and mixture of genders and classes in a public thoroughfare such as the Pont Neuf enable us to listen to the sounds made by those who all too often have been erased from historical and cultural records. We have been able to witness songs sung by a disabled man such as Philippot le Savoyard, to hear the street cries of ordinary workers, to listen to pieces performed that question traditional orthodoxies, and finally to give voice to people who would otherwise have remained silent.

Appendix

The following interrogation document from the trial of Chausson and Paulmier, from the Archives Nationales (AN X2A 1027), has previously been imperfectly transcribed by Frédéric Lachèvre in *Le Libertinage au XVII*ᵉ *siècle: les Œuvres libertines de Claude Le Petit, Parisien brûlé le 1er septembre 1662* (Paris: Honoré Champion, 1918), and by Dr. Ludovico Hernandez (Perceau and Fleuret) in *Les Procès de Sodomie au XVI*ᵉ, *XVII*ᵉ *et XVIII*ᵉ *siècles: Publiés d'après les documents judiciaires conservés à la Bibliothèque Nationale* (Paris: Bibliothèque des Curieux, 1920). Improved techniques for transcribing manuscripts and the help of Dr. Tom Hamilton have enabled me to produce a more accurate rendering. This interrogation forms a crucial part of the sound world of Paris, because, however biased the transcription may have been in favor of the interrogators, the text gives us the most vivid opportunity to "hear" the voices of prisoners, voices that otherwise would have been completely and permanently erased.

Parlement criminel, plumitif du 29 dec. 1661
Messieurs: Mr le president de Mesmes, Mr le president Le Coigneux, Mrs Ferrand R, Doujat, Menardeau, Le Conte, Catinat, Petau, Le Clerc, Troncon, Fayet, Bizet, De St Martin, Barillon, Brodeau, Broussel, De La Garde

Jacques Chausson dit de L'Estaing 26 ans, vivant de son bien, est fils d'un marchand linger, bourgeois de Paris a.h. la langue coupé bruslé vif.

Qu'il a porté les armes dans le regiment de La Vieuville. A demeuré ché son beau-frere, en la rue de Seine, au faulx bourg St. Germain, et en la rue de Boucherie.

Interrogé qu'il est accusé d'impietés et prostitution de jeunes garcons, et commettre le peché de sodomie et le faict commettre a douleur, et a cet effect a cherché d'aultres jeunes garcons qui sont venus plusieurs fois ché luy avec autres personnes.
Dict qu'il n'y est venu que ses amis.

Interrogé que les tesmoins quy luy ont esté confronté luy ont soubstenu. Dict que se sont faulx tesmoins. Que sa servante l'a vollé. N'a jamais envoyé son garcon au college de Montaigu querir un jeune escolier. Ne luy a point donné une double pistole. Que son laquais s'appeloit La Scelle, qu'il a trouvé vollant. Ne cognoist point Duval.

Interrogé quelle cognoissance il a avec Godefroy.
Dict qu'il ne le cognoist point.

Interrogé qu'il chante des chansons impiës.
Dict que non.

Interrogé quelle cognoissance il a de Fabry.
Dict qu'yl ne l'a jamais vu que 3 ou 4 fois.

Interrogé si c'est pas vrai qu'il luy a mené Vignon de mad.^lle.
A dict que non, qu'il a esté a la lingerie au college de Clermont.

Interrogé s'il a pas envoyé des bouteilles de vin d'Espagne a Vignon.
Dict que non, qu'il ne cognoist point le petit Marinault. N'a jamais eu le mal venerien.

Jacques Paumier dit Fabry 28 ans. A servy le sieur de Montague. A servy le sieur de Pessage. A esté a un gentilhomme anglois.

Interrogé si c'est en ce pays qu'il a commis le peché de sodomie.
Dict qu'yl ne sait que c'est de cela.

Interrogé quelle cognoissance il avoit avec de L'Estaing.
Dict qu'il le rencontra a Luxembourg, et le trouva malade et luy demanda qu'est qu'il avoit. Ne le cognoissoit pas auparavant.

Interrogé s'il a pas esté au bois de Vincennes avec un page, et a St Maur.
Dict qu'il ne scait ce que c'est de cela. Ne cognoist point de pages de Madame.

Interrogé qu'il a donné des oranges a un page.
Dict qu'il luy donna une orange. Luy a ramené a la foire a la boutique de sa sœur. N'a jamais esté qu'une fois au college de Clermont avec le sieur Capeau et [le sieur] autres.

Interrogé qu'il a dict des impietés a chaque parolle.
A dict que non, et n'a point esté jamais de ceste mauvaise vie. A mangé une fois avec de L'Estaing, et y coucha une nuict, et n'a jamais veu personne y coucher.

Interrogé s'il a pas corrompu un petit garcon qui sortoit du bain.
Dict que non, qu'il n'est revenu que la derniere semaine de Caresme d'Angleterre. Qu'il n'a jamais entendu parler de Gaboury. Ne l'a point pressé d'aller coucher ches luy. A frequenté Vauqueray et s'appelloit de Bievre, et que les tesmoins ont esté gagnés.

Arresté bien jugé, mal et sans grief appellé, et renvoyé.
Mr Ferrand, rapporteur

(Criminal parlement, court record of 29 December 1661.
Messieurs: Mr le president de Mesmes, Mr le president Le Coigneux, Mrs Ferrand R, Doujat, Menardeau, Le Conte, Catinat, Petau, Le Clerc, Troncon, Fayet, Bizet, De St Martin, Barillon, Brodeau, Broussel, De La Garde.

Jacques Chausson called de L'Estaing, twenty-six years old, living off his own means is the son of a cloth merchant, bourgeois of Paris condemned to have his tongue cut out and burned alive.

That he bore arms in La Vieuville's regiment. Lived at his brother-in-law's house, in the rue de Seine, in the St Germain district, and in the rue de Boucherie.

Interrogated upon the charge that he is accused of impiety and prostitution of young boys and of committing the sin of sodomy and having it committed with pain, and to do this he searched for more young boys who came several times to his house with other people.
Said that only his friends came to visit him there.

Interrogated over the fact that the witnesses who had testified against him maintained their story. Said that they are false witnesses. That his female servant stole from him. Never sent his boy to the Collège de Montaigu to fetch a young pupil. Did not give him two gold coins (pistoles). That his valet was called La Scelle, and he found that he stole from him. Does not know Duval.

Interrogated about what acquaintance he has with Godefroy.
Said that he does not know him.

Interrogated over whether he sings impious songs.
Said no.

Interrogated over how he knows Fabry.
Said that he had only ever seen him three or four times.

Interrogated whether it is not true that he brought Mademoiselle's Vignon to him.
Said no, that he was at the laundry of the Collège de Clermont.

Interrogated whether he did not send bottles of Spanish wine to Vignon. Said no, that he does not know the little Marinault. Has never had venereal disease.

Jacques Paumier called Fabry twenty-eight years old. Served Lord Montague. Served Lord Pessage. Was with an English gentleman.

Interrogated whether it was in that country that he committed the sin of sodomy.

Said that he does not know what that is.

Interrogated over how he knew de L'Estaing.

Said that he met him in the Luxembourg Gardens, and found him ill and asked him what was wrong. Did not know him before then.

Interrogated whether he has been to the Bois de Vincennes with a page boy, and to St Maur.

Said that he does not know about that, does not know any page boy of Madame.

Interrogated if he gave oranges to a page boy.

Said that he gave him an orange. Took him to the fair to his sister's shop stall. Has only ever been to the Collège de Clermont with Lord Capeau and [Lord] others.

Interrogated whether he spoke impieties with each word.

Said no, has never partaken in such bad living. Ate once with de L'Estaing and slept one night at his house, and has never seen anybody sleep there.

Interrogated whether he corrupted a little boy who was coming out of the bath.

Said no, that he only returned in the last week of Lent from England. That he has never heard talk of Gaboury. Did not urge him to come and sleep at his house. Has frequented Vauqueray and someone called de Bievre, and the witnesses were purchased.

Arrested, judged, unsuccessfully appealed without coercion, and dismissed. Mr Ferrand, Reporter

Notes

Introduction

1. See http://www.parisiansoundscapes.org for performances of these songs.
2. Many of these recent studies will be discussed in chapter 1.

Chapter 1

1. See Brandon Labelle, who describes sound as "the combination of intensity and ephemerality" in *Acoustic Territories*, xvi.
2. Ibid.
3. The term "soundscape" emerged largely from the pioneering work in sound studies by R. Murray Schafer in *Soundscape*. For examples of those who have questioned the visual terminology used to describe sound, see Revill, "Tren fantasma," 333–44, and Ingold, "Against Soundscape," 10–13. See also Mark M. Smith, who writes of the scholarly propensity to consider issues "through a largely unconscious ocularcentrist or retinalphilic 'lens,'" in *Sensing the Past*, 19.
4. This is the point made by Ian James in "Affection and Infinity," 26. See also James, *New French Philosophy*, 48–49.
5. Nancy, *Listening*, 13. "C'est un 'en présence de' qui ne se laisse pas objectiver ni projeter au-devant. C'est pourquoi elle est d'abord présence au sens d'un *présent* qui n'est pas un être (du moins pas au sens intransitif, stable et consistant du mot), mais plutôt un *venir* et un *passer*, un s'*étendre* et un *pénétrer*. Le son essentiellement provient et se dilate, ou se diffère et se transfère" (Nancy, *À l'écoute*, 31–32).
6. Nancy, *Listening*, 13; "omnidimensionnel et transversal à tous les espaces" (Nancy, *À l'écoute*, 32).
7. Revill, "Tren fantasma," 334. See also Roberto Barbanti, who writes, "Unlike sight, which is oriented and 'sequential,' listening presents itself immediately in a contiguous and continuous spatial totality. It does not assign a place; it is ambient" ("Listening to the Landscape," 74).
8. Labelle, *Acoustic Territories*, xvii.
9. Other scholars who have written on early modern orality have made different claims about their importance. For example, Robert Darnton argues that "we will never have an adequate history of communication until we can reconstruct its most important missing element: orality" (*Poetry and the Police*, 2); Bruce R. Smith's wide-ranging study of sound in early modern England makes the important claim that "the fact that our only access to the oral cultures of early modern England comes via written texts points up the political differences that separate one speech community from another. In a word: a small number of writers and readers control the representations of tens of thousands of other people" (*Acoustic World of Early Modern England*, 25) For a range of recent articles exploring early modern French sound worlds, see Hamilton and Hammond, "Soundscapes." .
10. Labelle, *Acoustic Territories*, xvii.
11. See Revill, "Tren fantasma," 335.
12. Attali, *Noise*, 3; some phrases have been omitted in the translation, so I have provided translation of those. "Notre science a toujours voulu surveiller, compter, abstraire, castrer les sens, oubliant que la vie est bruyante et que seule la mort est silencieuse: bruits du travail, bruits de fête, bruits de vie et de nature; bruits achetés, vendus, imposés, interdits; bruits de révolte, de révolution, de rage, de désespoir . . ." (Attali, *Bruits*, 11).
13. Atkinson, "Republic of Sound," 59. See also Atkinson, *Noisy Renaissance*. Cf. Bruce Smith's discussion of "shifting acoustic communities" in early modern London in *Acoustic World of Early Modern England*, 56.
14. For a depiction of the difficulties associated with "recording" sound in Paris from a previous age, see Boutin, *City of Noise*, 4–5.

15. This is the point made by Angela Leighton in her stimulating study of sound in literature, in *Hearing Things*, 27.
16. Barthes, "Listening," 245. "*Entendre* est un phénomène physiologique; *écouter* est un acte psychologique" (Barthes, "Écoute," 727).
17. Batcho, "Sonic Lifeworld."
18. Farge, "Sounds of Enlightenment Paris," 52.
19. See Pocock, *Boileau and the Nature of Neo-classicism*, 23, who suggests that Satire VI was written around the same time as Satire I, that is, between 1657 and 1664.
20. Boileau, *Œuvres*, 42.
21. See Wissmann, *Geographies of Urban Sound*, 55. Cf. Khadijah White: "a sonic event becomes noise when it is unpredictable, or when people are not accustomed to it and/or feel they cannot control it, regardless of its physical loudness [. . .]. Noise returns to being 'sound' once people adapt to its presence" ("Considering Sound," 236). See also Hendy, *Noise*, and Steven Connor at http://www.stevenconnor.com/noise/.
22. Nancy, *Listening*, 13; "propriété de pénétration et d'ubiquité" (Nancy, *À l'écoute*, 32).
23. Boileau, *Œuvres*, 43.
24. Ibid.
25. Ibid., 43–44.
26. I use Pocock's terminology here. Pocock insists that this satire is "far from an attempt at documentary realism" (*Boileau and the Nature of Neo-classicism*, 27).
27. Farge, *Vivre dans la rue à Paris*, 35. See also Gutton, *Bruits et sons*, 69.
28. Carré, "pour les appaiser ou les détourner," in *Recueil curieux et édifiant*, 28. See also Garrioch, "Sounds of the City," 11–13, and Blavignac, *Cloche*. Alain Corbin's *Cloches de la terre* (Village bells), while devoted neither to Paris nor to the early modern period, is a seminal work on the cultural significance of church bells in the nineteenth century.
29. See Milliot, *Cris de Paris*, esp. 230–34, for a discussion of the way in which these auditory stereotypes were manipulated.
30. See Denney, "Sounds of Population Fail."
31. Berthod, *Ville de Paris*, ii.
32. Le Petit, *Paris Ridicule*, 123.

33. Lachèvre, *Libertinage au XVIIe siècle*, 146.
34. Janequin's piece *Voulez ouyr les cris de Paris* dates from 1530 and involves the cries of different sellers of vegetables, fruit, wine, pastries, matches, wood, brooms, etc. See Gutton, *Bruits et sons*, 75–76.
35. See Milliot, *Cris de Paris*. See also Boutin, *City of Noise*, chap. 4, for nineteenth-century depictions of peddlers' cries in Paris.
36. Madame de Sévigné, Letter to Madame de Grignan, 6 March 1680, in *Correspondance*, 2:860.
37. Mercier, *Tableau de Paris*, 5:169–70, chap. dxvi.
38. Scarron, *Foire Saint-Germain*, 76.
39. Colletet, *Tracas de Paris*, 6.
40. Lister, *Journey to Paris*, 10. Lister, who seems far more alert to the sights rather than the sounds of the city, even expresses surprise at the "very little noise" made of "Publick Cries of things to be sold" (22), which certainly goes against the opinion of Parisian writers.
41. See Garrioch, "Sounds of the City," 10.
42. Evelyn, 24 December 1643, in *Diary*, 1:69–70.
43. Corbin, *Village Bells*, 110; "l'architecture temporelle de la vie, l'habitus" (Corbin, *Cloches de la terre*, 184).
44. Letter from 29 April 1672, in Sévigné, *Correspondance*, 1:494.
45. DeJean, *How Paris Became Paris*, 28. See also Newman, *Cultural Capitals*, 34–53. Both DeJean's and Newman's books are enormously insightful, giving vivid portraits of Paris at the time, but neither concentrates at length on the noisiness of the city. In a chapter titled "Filth, Stench, Noise" (76–91), Newman writes about the smells and mud of early modern Paris but omits any mention of Parisian noise, other than in a brief reference to Proust.
46. Boileau, *Art poétique*, Chant III, in *Œuvres*, 182.
47. DeJean, *How Paris Became Paris*, 22.
48. Mercier, *Tableau de Paris*, 1:156.
49. Brice, *Description nouvelle*, 321.
50. Berthod, *Ville de Paris*, 8–9.
51. See DeJean, *How Paris Became Paris*, 38.
52. Howells, *Epistolae Howelianae*, 42, 44.
53. Lithgow, *Totall Discourse*, 10.

54. La Mare, *Traité de la police*, 1:122. Cf. 202, where La Mare mentions the police's role in "la discipline des mœurs" (moral discipline) after the 1685 Revocation of the Edict of Nantes, acting against "les chansons ou libelles dissolus" (dissolute songs or libels). See also Le Floc'h, "Chanteurs chansonniers sous l'Ancien Régime," 34.

55. Mercier makes the point that "les mouchards se plantent là" (spies take their place) on the Pont Neuf, and if over the course of a few days they fail to see a criminal whom they are seeking on the bridge, they know that he or she must be away from Paris. *Tableau de Paris*, 1:156.

56. Depping, *Correspondance administrative*, 2:801.

57. Of the many works devoted to the *mazarinades*, it is worth singling out Christian Jouhaud's *Mazarinades* for its acute analysis of the role played by public opinion and the staging of political events through the pamphlets.

58. Scribe, *Œuvres complètes*, 7.

59. See Mason, *Singing the French Revolution*, 105. Robert M. Isherwood's analysis of the Pont Neuf song culture is also centered on the eighteenth century but offers valuable insight into the earlier traditions. See Isherwood, *Farce and Fantasy*, esp. 3–21.

60. For an engaging account of the labyrinthine ways in which later eighteenth-century songs in Paris were policed, see Darnton, *Poetry and the Police*.

61. B. R. Smith, *Acoustic World of Early Modern England*, 188.

62. Kay and Noudelmann, "Introduction," 5.

63. Cotgrave, *A Dictionarie of the French and English Tongues*. All references will be to this edition.

64. Callières, *Des bons mots*, 13.

65. Ibid., 321–22.

66. For very perceptive analysis of these passages by Callières, see Tabeling, "Écriture familière en France," 291–96.

67. See Darnton, *Poetry and the Police*, for discussion of the role played by chansonniers in the eighteenth century.

68. "L'esprit facétieux et mordant de son époque" (Raunié, preface, xlvii).

69. For a discussion of these kinds of songs, see Hammond, *Gossip, Sexuality, and Scandal in France*, 39–45.

70. See d'Estrée, "Origines du chansonnier de Maurepas," 332–45; Keilhauer, *Das französische Chanson*, 161–62; Seifert, *Manning the Margins*, 159–60.

71. *Chansonnier Maurepas*, 23:66. For *Chansonnier Maurepas*, see http://www.parisiansoundscapes.org. For a performance of this song, see https://www.parisiansoundscapes.org/profiles/Additional%20contributors/Chausson/LouisDeath/Lully/AuthorsofSongs/CourtGossip

72. These are the categories used by Éva Guillorel in *La complainte et la plainte*, 203–9.

Chapter 2

1. Boileau, *Œuvres*, 170.

2. Ibid.

3. Mercier, *Tableau de Paris*, 6:41.

4. Cf. Coirault, *Formation de nos chansons folkloriques*, 1:66, who imagines the typical anonymous singer: "Quelques-unes des pièces que, surveillé par la police il chantait, tâchant à en apprendre l'air à ses acheteurs, sont de lui" (Some of the pieces that he would sing as he attempted to teach the tune to his purchasers, all the while watched over by the police, were written by him).

5. See François de Callières's remark, quoted in chapter 1, that "ce sont aussi quelquefois des Dames peu charitables, qui font contre d'autres Dames ou contre des hommes qui leur auront déplû, de ces chansons ingenieuses et plaisantes" (there are also sometimes uncharitable ladies, who write these kinds of ingenious and enjoyable songs against other ladies or men who have displeased them), in *Des bons mots*, 321–22.

6. Tallemant des Réaux, *Historiettes*, 2:864.

7. See Mason, *Singing the French Revolution*, 20–22.

8. See Darnton, *Poetry and the Police*, 87.

9. See Massin, *Célébrités de la rue*, 75–81; Gétreau, "Philippot le Savoyard."

10. See Massin, *Célébrités de la rue*, 79–80; Le Floc'h, "Chanteurs chansonniers sous l'Ancien Régime," 39; Le Floc'h, "Chanteurs

de rue et complaintes judiciaires," 97; Isherwood, *Farce and Fantasy*, 6–8.
11. See Gétreau, "Guillaume de Limoges et François Couperin," 163–82.
12. Coirault, *Notre chanson folklorique*, 378–79.
13. Since Coirault, the only scholar to have paid Philippot significant attention is Florence Gétreau in "Philippot le Savoyard."
14. See Maistre et al., *Colporteurs et marchands savoyards*, 7.
15. I am grateful to John Romey, who mentioned this idea to me and who is developing it in his own work.
16. Le Savoyard, *Recueil général des chansons*, and Le Savoyard, *Recueil nouveau des chansons du Savoyard*. In 1665 another version of the second edition was published, and this was used by M. A. Percheron for his 1862 edition, *Recueil des chansons du Savoyard*.
17. See Milliot, *Cris de Paris*, 55.
18. Boileau, *Œuvres*, 60.
19. Ibid. Cf. Pocock, who calls Satire IX a "positive defense of satire," in *Boileau and the Nature of Neo-classicism*, 50.
20. See Gétreau, "Philippot le Savoyard," 286.
21. See, for example, Robert Mandrou, who in surveying the production of songs from collections of the period concludes that "deux genres dominent cette production: la chanson à boire et la chanson d'amour" (two genres dominate such a production of songs: the drinking song and the love song), in *De la culture populaire*, 120. See also 118–21.
22. Le Savoyard, *Recueil des chansons du Savoyard*, 16.
23. Ibid., 45–46.
24. Romey, "Court Airs," 171–89.
25. Le Savoyard, *Recueil des chansons du Savoyard*, 90.
26. Romey, "Court Airs," 176.
27. See ibid., 178.
28. See Le Savoyard, *Recueil des chansons du Savoyard*, 3 (where "la famine" is evoked), 15, 32.
29. Ibid., 13, 77.
30. Ibid., 77.
31. Ibid., 6.
32. See the introduction to Saint-Pavin, *Poésies*, esp. 17–22.
33. Le Savoyard, *Recueil des chansons du Savoyard*, 99–100.
34. Ibid., 113.
35. Sorel, *Histoire comique de Francion*, 200. See also Gétreau, "Philippot le Savoyard," 274.
36. Le Savoyard, *Recueil des chansons du Savoyard*, 114.
37. Ibid., 113.
38. Ibid., 114.
39. Ibid., 113, repeated 114, 115, 116.
40. Ibid., 114–15.
41. Ibid., 115. There were many famous tooth pullers on the Pont Neuf during the seventeenth century, such as Tabarin and his sidekick Mondor, Ferranti, Contugi, and, in the early years of the eighteenth century, le Grand Thomas. See Jones, *Smile Revolution*, 25–28 and 77–80, for an account of these antecedents of the modern dentist.
42. Le Savoyard, *Recueil des chansons du Savoyard*, 115.
43. Ibid.
44. Ibid., 116.
45. For a detailed account of Dassoucy's life, see Scruggs, *Charles Dassoucy*, 13–56.
46. DeJean, *Libertine Strategies*, 42.
47. Dassoucy, *Avantures burlesques de Dassoucy*, 81–82.
48. Ibid., 82–83.
49. Ibid., 84.
50. Ibid., 84–85.
51. Ibid., 85.
52. Ibid., 86.
53. Ibid., 86. See Gétreau, "Philippot le Savoyard," 285–87, for analysis of other features of Dassoucy's account and for later theatrical representations of Philippot. She also argues that Philippot's nostalgia for the Christianity of Henri IV's time and criticism of present-day religion in the Dassoucy text indicates that Philippot was likely to have been Protestant.
54. See DeJean, *How Paris Became Paris*, 29.
55. The exact figures are difficult to ascertain, owing to the destruction of many important archives, but we know that literacy was much higher in Paris than in the provinces. However, as most studies rely on the percentage of people signing marriage certificates or wills, this would still have excluded the poorest citizens of Paris. Mercier writes in the later years of the eighteenth century that "on lit certainement dix fois plus à Paris qu'on

ne lisait il y a cent ans" (certainly people read ten times more in Paris than they used to one hundred years ago [*Tableaux de Paris*, 12:151]). See Roche, *Peuple de Paris*, 204–41; Chartier, "Pratiques de l'écrit," 3:109–15.

56. Bussy-Rabutin, *Histoire amoureuse des Gaules*, 197–98. Madeleine de Scudéry was even more forthcoming in her praise for Sévigné's singing voice, even in her final years, writing of her "voix douce, juste et charmante" (sweet, true, and charming voice) and adding that "elle chante d'une manière passionnée" (she sings passionately); see Duchêne's note in Sévigné, *Correspondance*, 1:996–97n7. In this section, all page references to Sévigné will appear within the main text and will be taken from the Duchêne three-volume edition.

57. *Chansonnier Maurepas*, 3:365.

58. For a brief consideration of Sévigné as aural witness to life in Paris, see Couvreur, "Oreille de Madame de Sévigné," 191–204.

59. See, for example, 14 June 1675, 1:733; 25 October 1679, 2:719; 28 February 1689, 3:518. For discussion of the orality of letters, see Bray and Strosetzki, *Art de la lettre*.

60. See Hammond, *Gossip, Sexuality, and Scandal in France*, 25–26. See also Chartier, *Lectures et lecteurs*, 129.

61. See Duchêne, *Bussy-Rabutin*, chap. 25, 151–55.

62. It was only from the late eighteenth century onward that urban elites developed their own class-conscious classical musical culture distinct from popular song. See Garrioch, "Sounds of the City," 24.

63. "Enfin Philisbourg est pris. J'en suis étonnée; je ne croyais pas qu'ils sussent prendre une ville. J'ai demandé d'abord qui l'avait prise, si ce n'était point nous, mais non, c'est eux. Le Pont-Neuf a fait ce couplet sur l'air: *Or écoutez, peuple français*:

> Le maréchal de Luxembourg
> Allait secourir Philisbourg,
> Car il est fort grand capitaine;
> Mais lorsqu'il fut près de donner,
> Il survint un bois dans la plaine
> Qui l'empêcha de dégainer."

(18 September 1676, 2:401)

(Finally Philippsburg has been taken. I am astonished by this as I did not think they had the wherewithal to take a town. I asked first who had taken the town, if it wasn't us, but no, it is them. The Pont Neuf composed this couplet to the tune "Or écoutez, peuple français": The marshal Luxembourg / Was going to save Philippsburg, / Because he is a very great captain; / But when he was near to delivering, / A wood in the plain arrived, / Preventing him from unsheathing his sword.)

For examples of other songs on the same topic that were sung at the time, see *Chansonnier Maurepas*, 4:347–48, 353.

64. A slightly different version of the same verses can be found in the *Chansonnier Maurepas*, 3:421: "De par Monseigneur de Paris, / On fait scavoir a tous maris, / Que leurs femmes l'on baisera / Alleluia" (Through Monseigneur de Paris, / All husbands are informed / That their wives will be fucked / Alleluia).

65. She quotes a song by Blot elsewhere, 25 December 1675, 2:199.

66. Herbert Schneider provides an incomplete list of parodies of Lully operas that appear in manuscript or printed sources in *Chronologisch-thematisches Verzeichnis*, but he does not analyze the link between these parodies and street culture. Much more complete (albeit in a later time frame of 1672 to 1745) is the magisterial study by le Blanc, *Avatars d'opéras*.

67. Le Cerf de La Viéville, *Comparaison de la musique*, 1:326–27.

68. Ibid., 1:327–28.

69. See Couvreur, "Oreille de Madame de Sévigné," 195.

70. See, for example, *Chansonnier Maurepas*, 4:291 (*Alceste*) and 389 (*Atys*).

71. Titon du Tillet, *Parnasse françois*, 395. See Romey, "Court Airs," 171–72.

72. Sévigné, 12 February 1683, in *Correspondance*, 3:101. A slightly different version of the same song and set to the same tune, dated also from 1683, can be found in the *Chansonnier Maurepas*, 5:293.

Chapter 3

1. See, for example, Apostolidès, *Roi-Machine*; Bély, *Louis XIV: Le plus grand*

roi; Bluche, *Louis XIV*; Burke, *Fabrication of Louis XIV*; Goubert, *Avènement du Roi-Soleil*; Marin, *Portrait du roi*; Petitfils, *Louis XIV*. Other works, such as Lucien Bély's *Secrets de Louis XIV* and Michel de Grèce's *Louis XIV*, are concerned with the hidden sides of Louis's reign but do not prioritize the auditory.

2. Mademoiselle, *Mémoires*, 277.
3. Loret, *Muze historique*, 3:338.
4. De Choisy, *Mémoires*, 99.
5. Performance of the melody can be found at https://www.parisiansoundscapes.org/jobs/Recordings.
6. *Chansonnier Maurepas*, 23:362.
7. See ibid.:

Du Cardinal mis au Cercueil,
On dit qu'on va prendre le deuil;
S'il te prend une telle envie
Tu aurois, ô France grand tort,
Tu porterois le deuil de sa vie;
Le porterois-tu de sa mort?

(Of the cardinal placed in the grave, / They say that people are going to mourn; / If such a desire takes your fancy, / You would be making a great mistake, oh France, / You will be mourning his life; / Why would you mourn his death?)

8. Ibid., 23:367.
9. De Choisy, *Mémoires*, 99.
10. See ibid., 123, and Bély, *Secrets de Louis XIV*, 194.
11. De Brienne, 11 March 1661, in *Mémoriaux du Conseil de 1661*, 1:18.
12. See Gutton, *Bruits et sons*, 40. Later in the century the chief of police, Gabriel de la Reynie, would employ public criers (accompanied by beating drums) to announce edicts; see Tucker, *City of Light*, 22–23. For the contribution of town criers in earlier ages, see Telliez, "À cor et à cri," 73–98.
13. Louis XIV, *Mémoires*, 72. For discussion of the multiple authorship of the text, see Cornette's introduction, 21–27.
14. Saint-Simon, *Mémoires*, 5:478.
15. Louis XIV, *Mémoires*, 73.
16. Lockwood, *Reader's Figure*, 219. Lockwood is making a distinction here between deliberative and epideictic rhetoric.
17. Bayley, *French Pulpit Oratory*, 6.

18. Bossuet, *Sermons*, 244.
19. Ibid., 245.
20. The Sermon on Death in the same series explores with particular acuity different ideas of spectatorship and the visual. See ibid., 146–61. Cf. Anne Régent-Susini, who writes of "le dialogisme et le spectaculaire" (the dialogic and the visual) in Bossuet's sermons, adding that "*Voir et entendre sont non seulement souvent associés, mais ils apparaissent chez Bossuet comme des équivalents*" (*Seeing* and *hearing* are not only often juxtaposed, but they appear in Bossuet's writing as equivalents), in *Bossuet et la Rhétorique*, 479, 480.
21. Bossuet, *Sermons*, 73.
22. Ibid.
23. For reference to the acoustics of the Oratory (now the Temple Protestant de l' Oratoire), see http://hugoparis.over-blog.com/2016/04/visite-de-l-oratoire-du-louvre-protestant-histoire-histoire-de-france.html. For analysis of acoustics and preaching in early modern Venetian churches, see Howard and Moretti, *Sound and Space in Renaissance Venice*, esp. 91–94.
24. Green's performance of Bossuet's Sermon on Death is available on CD under the Alpha label, part of the Voce Umana series (2002).
25. Green, sleeve note to his recording of the Sermon on Death.
26. See in particular the Virtual Saint Paul's Cathedral project, https://vpcp.chass.ncsu.edu.
27. "Voix du prédicateur et voix prêtée à Dieu lui-même se confondent." Régent-Susini, *Bossuet et la rhétorique*, 477.
28. Bossuet, *Sermons*, 81–82.
29. Ibid., 88.
30. Ibid., 87–88. Cf. "Il faut écouter attentivement Jésus-Christ, qui vient troubler notre fausse paix," 85.
31. Ibid., 82.
32. Ibid., 85.
33. Ibid., 90.
34. Ibid.
35. See Fraser, *Love and Louis XIV*, 81–82, and de Grèce, *Louis XIV*, 174–77.
36. Bossuet, *Oraisons funèbres* (Poujoulat), 286. The marquise de Sévigné, who was disappointed not to be able to attend the service, writes to her daughter, expressing

surprise that Bossuet's sermon "ne fut point aussi divin qu'on l'espérait" (was not as divine as was hoped), in *Correspondance,* 1:723. Earlier, she had written to her friend Guitaut (who will play a prominent role in the second part of this book) that, after a tearful parting from her children and her friends at court, Louise de la Vallière was content to be in a state of solitude, even if "elle caquète et dit merveilles" (she gossips and tells wonderful things), in *Correspondance,* 1:695.

37. Bossuet, *Oraisons funèbres* (Truchet), 409.

38. The abbé de Choisy writes many years later that, in a discussion between Mazarin and Louis, "on dit que le cardinal mourant lui avait conseillé de se défaire de Fouquet" (they say that when the cardinal was dying, he had advised him to get rid of Fouquet [*Mémoires,* 118]). At another point (120), de Choisy claims that a loud argument about money between Fouquet and his brother in the cardinal's antichamber two months before Mazarin's death turned the king against Fouquet.

39. La Fontaine, letter to Maucroix, in Molière, *Œuvres complètes,* 1:1133.

40. André Félibien, "Relation des magnificences de Vaux," in Molière, *Œuvres complètes,* 1:1141.

41. Ibid.

42. Ibid., 1:1139.

43. Ibid., 1:1140.

44. Ibid., 1:1141.

45. La Fontaine, letter to Maucroix, 1:1136–37.

46. "Le mécénat devient, avec la politique de prestige menée par Colbert et Louis XIV, un système étatique, et la censure se renforce à son tour" (Patronage became, with the policy of prestige led by Colbert and Louis XIV, a state system, and censorship was reinforced in tandem with this). See Viala, *Naissance de l'écrivain,* 9–10.

47. See the chapter titled "Fouquet mécène" in Petitfils, *Fouquet,* 258–79. Petitfils calls the various residences belonging to Fouquet between 1654 and 1661 "le principal foyer du rayonnement littéraire et artistique du royaume" (the principal center of literary and artistic influence in the kingdom [259]). See also Fumaroli, *Le poète et le roi,* who writes of the wide circle of architects, gardeners, painters, sculptors, musicians, dramatists, and poets that formed around Fouquet (135).

48. Pierre Corneille, "Au Lecteur," *Œdipe,* in *Œuvres complètes,* 3:17.

49. Molière, *Œuvres complètes,* 1:149.

50. See Forestier and Bourqui's analysis in ibid., 1:1271.

51. "L'occasion d'un entremêlement inédit entre théâtre parlé et théâtre dansé, qui fraya la voie à un genre mixte dont Molière et Lully allaient se faire une spécialité." Ibid., 1:1266.

52. Ibid., 1:161. All stage and page references to *Les Fâcheux* will appear in the main text and are from this edition.

53. Chansonnier Maurepas, 23:265 (wrongly dated to 1658):

> Peut on voir de Nimphe plus gentille,
> Qu'estoit Béjar l'autre jour?
> Dès que l'on vit ouvrir sa coquille,
> Tout le monde croit à l'entour.
> Dès que l'on vit ouvrir sa coquille
> Voicy la mere d'Amour.

(Is it possible to see a kinder Nymph / As Béjart was the other day? / As soon as she was seen opening her shell, / Everybody cried out around her. / As soon as she was seen opening the shell, / There's the mother of Love)..

54. For a nuanced analysis of the complexities of the term "mécène," see Jouhaud and Merlin-Kajman, "Mécènes, patrons et clients," 47–62.

55. For discussion of this, see Moyes, *Furetière's "Roman Bourgeois,"* 100–101.

56. Louis XIV, *Mémoires,* 64.

57. See Mousnier and Mesnard, *Age d'or du mécénat.*

58. Moyes, *Furetière's "Roman Bourgeois,"* 94.

59. Ibid., 96–99.

60. La Fontaine, letter to Maucroix, 1137.

61. For a more sustained analysis of the vocabulary relating to gossip and rumor, see Hammond, *Gossip, Sexuality, and Scandal in France,* 5–49. See also Butterworth, *Unbridled Tongue.*

62. Gourville, *Mémoires,* 133.

63. De Brienne, *Mémoires inédits,* 2:200.

64. See Goubert, *Avènement du Roi-Soleil*, 128–30.
65. Pellisson was to spend five years in the Bastille before his fortunes were transformed, eventually becoming *historiographe du roi* in 1670. He is also credited with cowriting the sections devoted to 1661 and 1662 in Louis's *Mémoires*. See Cornette's discussion of this in his edition of the *Mémoires*, 22–25.
66. See Swann, who makes the point that "the idea of a family council plotting the mobilization of kinship and clientele networks in order to shore up an endangered position was consistent with earlier aristocratic reactions to disgrace," in *Exile, Imprisonment, or Death*, 78.
67. D'Ormesson, *Journal*, 1:xxvii.
68. This is the argument of Georges Mongrédien, who in *Affaire Fouquet* suggests that if the trial had been focused on Fouquet from the outset, Colbert's wish for his rival to be executed may well have been fulfilled (95).
69. Many excellent studies have been devoted to Fouquet's trial. In English, the most recent and useful overview of all aspects related to the trial is Pitts, *Embezzlement and High Treason*. In French, Daniel Dessert's *Fouquet* is exceptional for its close examination of all the financial details relating to the accusations against Fouquet; Jean-Christian Petitfils's *Fouquet* gives a vivid picture of Fouquet's personality; Mongrédien's *L'Affaire Fouquet* remains an invaluable guide, especially for its reproduction of the many pieces about the trial that circulated at the time. Sévigné's correspondence about the trial has also elicited a number of perceptive scholarly pieces, many of which tend to prioritize Sévigné's interest in the visual aspects of the trial. For a subtle analysis of the intertexts between history and literature in the various accounts of the judicial process, see Hawcroft, "Historical Evidence and Literature," 57–75. For examination of ways in which Sévigné fictionalizes or theatricalizes the trial, see Barnwell, "Art épistolaire de Madame de Sévigné," 387–94; Thommeret, "Du greffe," 597–610; Dostie, "Fouquet sur la sellette," 584–95. Two useful explorations of public opinion in Sévigné, including the Fouquet letters, are Welsh, "State Truths," 170–83, and Freidel, *Conquête de l'intime*, 30–35.
70. See Hamscher, *Parlement of Paris*, 124–26.
71. "A méticuleusement monté toute l'horlogerie de la machination destinée à l'abattre," in Dessert, *Fouquet*, 231.
72. Bossuet, "Sermon sur la charité fraternelle," in *Sermons*, 129. See Constance Cagnat-Debœuf's analysis of this sermon, and the possible reference to Colbert and Fouquet, in the same edition, 23–28.
73. See Pitts, *Embezzlement and High Treason*, 63–67.
74. Ibid., 83–85.
75. Hamilton, *Pierre de L'Estoile*, 47. For analysis of what Hamilton calls "the social world of the Palais de Justice," see 47–60.
76. See McIlvenna, "Chanteurs de rues."
77. See Mongrédien, *Affaire Fouquet*, 99, and Petitfils, *Fouquet*, 381–82.
78. *Chansonnier Maurepas*, 23:371.
79. Ibid., 392. The word "adroit" (which is used in other versions of the quatrain) is mistakenly transcribed as "accord" in the manuscript.
80. D'Ormesson, *Journal*, 2:117.
81. Letter of 10 September 1661, in Ravaisson, *Archives de la Bastille*, 2:360.
82. Sévigné, *Correspondance*, 1:58.
83. Elizabeth C. Goldsmith argues persuasively that Sévigné's Fouquet letters, "as carefully constructed extensions of her daily exchanges with others, demonstrate the creative power of conversation, and its function in her world as a means of presenting reality in a way that is acceptable to all of her interlocutors," in *Exclusive Conversations*, 122.
84. Condé and Jules, *Lettres inédites*, 112. See also 70, 96, 97, 113, 116–19.
85. D'Ormesson, *Journal*, 2:120.
86. See Chéruel's edition of the d'Ormesson journal for detailed extracts of Foucault's account of the trial.
87. D'Ormesson, *Journal*, 2:233.
88. Sévigné, *Correspondance*, 1:58. See also her remarks over the course of the trial: "il y a très bien répondu" (he replied very well to it [59]), "il s'est très bien défendu" (he defended himself very well [60]), "il a fort bien répondu" (he replied very well [62]), "M. Foucquet s'est fort bien tiré d'affaire"

(M. Foucquet has acquitted himself very well [63]), "on l'a écouté; il a dit des merveilles" (they listened to him; he said some wondrous things [65]); "il a dit des merveilles" (he said wondrous things [67]), "[il] a parlé [...] si admirablement bien" (he spoke so admirably well [68]), "M. Foucquet a très bien dit" (M. Foucquet spoke very well [69]).
89. Ibid., 1:58.
90. Ibid., 1:59.
91. Ibid., 1:72. Ellen R. Welsh makes the helpful point that, when Sévigné refers to the opinion of the wider world, "public murmuring may not always be factually accurate, but it is a credible witness to popular sentiment," in "State Truths," 176.
92. Hawcroft, "Historical Evidence and Literature," 65.
93. Sévigné, Correspondance, 1:68. For discussion of the rich tradition of parliamentary rhetoric, see Fumaroli, Âge de l'éloquence, 427–74.
94. D'Ormesson: "M. le chancelier parut s'endormir" (The chancellor seemed to fall asleep), in Journal, 2:254; Sévigné: "Mais, au lieu d'être alerte, Monsieur le Chancelier sommeillait doucement" (But, instead of being alert, the chancellor was quitely dozing), in Correspondance, 1:62.
95. Sévigné, Correspondance, 1:65. Cf. d'Ormesson: "Par la conduite que j'observe de M. le chancelier, il ne presse pas cette affaire" (From the chancellor's conduct as I observe it, he is not hurrying this business), in Journal, 2:255.
96. Sévigné, Correspondance, 1:73.
97. D'Ormesson, Journal, 2:255–56.
98. Ibid., 2:257.
99. Ibid., 2:271.
100. Sévigné, Correspondance, 1:70.
101. D'Ormesson, Journal, 2:271. He continued to avoid speaking about the trial until after the final judgment. Writing on 17 December, for example, he mentions that "quelques-uns de mes amis de la cour m'estant venu voir, je leur ay imposé silence" (some of my friends from the court came to see me, and I imposed silence on them [276]).
102. Sévigné, Correspondance, 1:74.
103. Ibid.
104. D'Ormesson, Journal, 2:272.
105. Ibid., 2:279.
106. Ibid., 2:277.
107. Ibid., 2:281.
108. Ibid., 2:288.
109. Ibid., 2:283.
110. Chansonnier Maurepas, 23:429.
111. D'Ormesson, Journal, 2:289.
112. Chansonnier Maurepas, 23:427. A slightly different version of the same madrigal appears also on 23:387.
113. Ibid., 23:415–16.
114. Ibid., 23:416–17. Another longer song, set to the melody "A la venue de Noël," employs the same structure, ending in praise of the "grand d'Ormesson," 424.
115. D'Ormesson, Journal, 2:287.
116. See Pitts, Embezzlement and High Treason, 166–67.
117. D'Ormesson, Journal, 2:283–84.
118. Chansonnier Maurepas, 2:447.
119. Ibid., 2:463.
120. Petitfils, Fouquet, 526.
121. D'Ormesson, Journal, 2:290.
122. Ibid., 2:325.
123. Ibid., 2:572.
124. See Armogathe, "Bossuet, orateur sacré," 257–69, esp. 264. See also Armogathe, "Témoignage d'un prédicateur," 215–20.
125. See Burke, Fabrication of Louis XIV, 135–50.

Chapter 4

1. Chansonnier Maurepas, 3:369. A performance of the song by mezzo-soprano Katie Bray and the period instrument ensemble Badinage can be found at https://www.parisiansoundscapes.org/profiles/Additional%20contributors/Chausson.
2. A vast corpus of scholarship deals with the difficulty of defining and describing sexuality during the early modern period, most of which responds to Michel Foucault's notion that prior to the nineteenth century homosexuality was conceived in terms of "acts" and not "identities," in Histoire de la sexualité, 1:59. Modern critical opinion tends to be divided between those (known as "social constructionists") who see the homosexual as historically and culturally determined, and therefore not to be conflated with later conceptions of sexuality, and those (called "essentialists") who argue that homosexuality crosses over all historical and cultural boundaries. For an excellent summary of

these different critical positions, see Ferguson, *Queer (Re)readings in the French Renaissance*, 1–54, and Poirier, *Homosexualité dans l'imaginaire*. For a discussion of the vocabulary relating to same-sex desire, see Hammond, *Gossip, Sexuality, and Scandal in France*, 55–56, and Hennig, *Espadons, mignons et autres monstres*. Jeffrey Merrick makes the very useful comment, when discussing eighteenth-century Parisian sodomites, that "they had no access to our categories, but we have some access to their mentalities, and we should not make them sound more modern than they were" (*Sodomites, Pederasts, and Tribades in Eighteenth-Century France*, 2).

3. MS 576, fol. 90, Archives de Chantilly.

4. For a wide-ranging recent consideration of execution ballads, see McIlvenna, "Power of Music," 47–89.

5. Mercier, *Tableau de Paris*, 10:255.

6. Ibid., 6:42–43.

7. Cf. Pascal Bastien: "Ces chansons ne tendaient pas nécessairement vers l'héroïsation du criminel; au contraire, cette orientation fut plutôt rare" (These songs did not necessarily tend toward depicting the criminal as hero; on the contrary, this approach was much rarer). See *Histoire de la peine de mort*, 193. See also Bée, who writes of the "leçon morale" (moral lesson) contained in the execution *complainte* but who argues also that it sometimes makes a kind of "héros noir" (black hero) out of the executed prisoner ("Spectacle de l'exécution," 848). For slightly later examples in London of condemned prisoners who attracted praise for their seeming indifference to their fate or their outright defiance as they were led to the scaffold, see Gatrell, *Hanging Tree*, 33–37. For late seventeenth-century executions in England, see McKenzie, *Tyburn's Martyrs*: "The degree to which the language of martyrology, legitimation and resistance were intertwined in this period, and that traitors, martyrs, murderers and robbers alike drew from a common eschatology in which the 'good death' was not only an ultimate goal, but a powerful political and metaphysical statement" (xvi).

8. McIlvenna, "Power of Music," 89.

9. Such a song performed before the event could be likened to what Vic Gatrell calls "flash ballads" in *Hanging Tree*, 123–26.

10. Le Brun de La Rochette, *Procès civil et criminel*, 1:42–43.

11. Bruneau, *Observations et maximes*, 403.

12. Ibid., 404–5.

13. Ginzburg, preface to *The Cheese and the Worms*, xv.

14. Hernandez, *Procès de sodomie*.

15. Soman, "Pathologie historique," 152.

16. Ibid., 160.

17. Schindler, *Rebellion, Community and Custom*, 84. For an analysis of the culture and practice of nicknames from the period, see 48–92.

18. See ibid., 79–80.

19. See Roussel, *Violences et passions*, 31.

20. Piganiol de La Force describes the Rue des Boucheries as follows: "Cette rue aboutit d'un côté à la rue des Fossés S. Germain, et de l'autre au coin de la rue de Bussy, vis-à-vis la barriere des Sergens" (This street ends on one side of the Rue des Fossés St-Germain, and on the other side at the corner of the Rue de Bussy, facing the sergeants' gate). See *Description de Paris*, 6:440.

21. See Roussel, *Violences et passions*, 33.

22. Le Savoyard, *Recueil nouveau des chansons du Savoyart*.

23. Hernandez, *Procès de sodomie*, 83. All references to this text and the other trial transcripts will be from the Hernandez edition, with page numbers in brackets. However, for the imperfectly transcribed interrogation document (AN X2A 1027), the text that will be used is that found in the appendix of this book, transcribed by Tom Hamilton and the author.

24. Archives Nationales X2A 1032, 2 August 1667.

25. Samuel Pepys, 20 October 1660, in *Diary of Samuel Pepys*, 1:269.

26. Pepys, *Diary of Samuel Pepys*, 1:293.

27. Ibid., 2:15, 17.

28. Pepys, 15 August 1660, in *Diary of Samuel Pepys*, 1:222.

29. Cotgrave's translation of the French word *page* is instructive in this regard: "A page; a waiting, or serving boy (in France, where he hath often good breeding, he ought to be a Gentleman borne)." The implication here is that a page could also be a servant

and that in England, unlike in France, noble breeding was not an expectation.

30. Archives Nationales MC/ET/I/107. My thanks to Tom Hamilton for this information.

31. Listing people with double Christian names is another anachronism that Soman points out, as this practice only became common in the eighteenth century, "Pathologie historique," 151.

32. Charles Du Bellay, prince d'Yvetot, was known for his sexual exploits with men: Tallemant des Réaux devotes one of his *historiettes* to him, detailing Du Bellay's infatuation with various lower-class younger men and mentioning his generosity to them. He was separated from his wife, whom he had married in 1622, and left no heirs. See Tallemant des Réaux, *Historiettes*, 2:616–18. Cf. Lever, *Bûchers de Sodome*, 140–41 and 210–15, where Lever accepts unquestioningly the veracity of the various documents and gives a summary of the accusations against Chausson and Paulmier.

33. *Chansonnier Maurepas*, 3:310.

34. See Pascal Bastien's analysis of what he calls "l'univers sonore du supplice" (the sonic universe of the scaffold), in *Histoire de la peine de mort*, 183–243.

35. See Friedland, *Seeing Justice Done*, 92.

36. The jurist and writer Mathieu Marais (1664–1737), who was a lawyer at the Parlement of Paris and who perhaps had access to the records there, confirms many of the details of their sentence in his *Journal et mémoires*, with the added mention of another accused person, an eighteen-year-old named Mauger, student at the Collège de Montaigu, who was sentenced to six months in Saint-Lazare prison. See Marais, *Journal et mémoires*, 3:65.

37. "Véritable chef d'orchestre du rituel, ce fut le greffier qui organisa le déroulement de l'exécution capitale et qui, maître d'écriture, fut aussi un maître de paroles" (Bastien, *Histoire de la peine de mort*, 220).

38. See Friedland, *Seeing Justice Done*, 71–76.

39. See Demorest and Demorest, *Dictionnaire historique et anecdotique*.

40. See Friedland, *Seeing Justice Done*, 101, and Joris, *Mourir sur l'échafaud*, 112–14. Michel Bée writes eloquently of the different classes and ages of people in the crowds that attended executions in "Spectacle de l'exécution," 845.

41. See Friedland, *Seeing Justice Done*, 132.

42. Ibid., 144.

43. See Hamilton, "Contesting Public Executions," 179–202, esp. 195–98, for examples of crowd disturbances at public executions.

44. Mercier, *Tableau de Paris*, 2:192.

45. See Friedland, *Seeing Justice Done*, 90, 101.

46. Cf. Chaduc, who writes that "la consolation telle qu'elle est présente dans la direction spirituelle n'est pas uniquement l'expression de la sympathie liée à une peine circonstancielle: elle a un sens spirituel" (consolation insofar as it is present in spiritual direction is not uniquely the expression of sympathy linked to a circumstantial affliction: it has a spiritual meaning), in *Fénelon*, 287. See also Delumeau, *Aveu et le pardon*, 41–49.

47. Beaugendre, *Vie de Messire Benigne Joly*, 170–71. For an extraordinarily detailed account by a confessor of a criminal's execution, see Edme Piro's description of the notorious Brinvilliers execution in Roullier, *Marquise de Brinvilliers*.

48. See Ward, *Global History of Execution*, 132.

49. L'Estoile described more than three hundred executions during the Wars of Religion, selecting them either for their political import or for the unusual nature of the crimes. See Hamilton, "Contesting Public Executions," 181. See also Friedland, *Seeing Justice Done*, 132–36.

50. Hamilton, *Mémoires-Journaux de Pierre de L'Estoile*, 7:224. For a recent discussion of the rituals involved in the execution of men in same-sex relationships in early modern Italy, see Ferguson, *Same-Sex Marriage in Renaissance Rome*, esp. 73–83.

51. See Friedland, *Seeing Justice Done*, 98. For examples of prisoners who publicly questioned their sentences and refused to perform the "amende honorable," see Hamilton, "Contesting Public Executions," 184–86. See also Sévigné, *Correspondance*, who describes the execution of murderer Catherine Deshayes, known as la Voisin: "A Notre-Dame, elle ne voulut jamais prononcer l'amende honorable et, à la Grève, elle se défendit autant qu'elle put de sortir du

tombereau" (At Notre-Dame, she did not want to speak her honorable amends, and at the Place de Grève, she refused as much as she could to leave the open cart [23 February 1680, 2:846]). By contrast, as Sévigné sees it, the poisoner Marie-Madeleine-Marguerite d'Aubray, marquise de Brinvilliers, would seem to have performed the "amende honorable" before her execution: "A six heures on l'a menée nue en chemise et la corde au cou, à Notre-Dame faire l'amende honorable" (At six o'clock, she was led naked in a shirt with the rope around her neck to Notre-Dame to make her honorable amends [17 July 1676, 2:343]). Standing too far from the scaffold on the Notre-Dame bridge (no doubt owing to the crowds witnessing the event), Sévigné mentions that others reported Brinvilliers's courage at the moment of her execution.

52. Quoted in Hernandez, *Procès de sodomie*, 5–6.

53. Reproduced by Frédéric Lachèvre in *Libertinage au XVIIe siècle*, xli. Lachèvre speculates that Le Petit chose to commemorate Chausson rather than Paulmier because only Chausson was "de ses compagnons de débauche" (one of his debauched companions [xlii]).

54. For an excellent account of the complexity of seventeenth-century friendships in France, see Dewald, *Aristocratic Experience*, 104–45.

55. See Gatrell, *Hanging Tree*, 33–37 and 138–44, for analysis of similar courageous or nonchalant behavior (what he calls the "dying game") by condemned prisoners when faced with the scaffold in eighteenth-century London.

56. In the case of Lully, see 5:405, where he is called "ce vilain Baptiste" (that villain Baptiste) in conjunction with same-sex desire, and 5:176, where Lully himself is named as the supposed author of a song in which he speaks of "baiser un si vilain Bardache" (fucking so villainous a Bardash). He is also described as someone who "f . . . [. . .] en cu comme un infame" (fucks in the ass like an infamous man [5:419]). Another song evokes "l'infame plaisir chaque nuit / De jouïr d'un nouveau Bardache" (the infamous pleasure each night / Of taking pleasure in a new Bardash [1:386]). Cf. also 5:369. Mazarin is described as "le bougre de Sicile" (the bugger from Sicily) who "a fait de vilains coups" (has delivered villainous blows [3:135]), as well as "coquin" (scoundrel [3:153]). For discussion of the terms "vilain" and "infâme" in relation to same-sex love, see Hennig, *Espadons, mignons et autres monstres*, 333–41, 391–96. Hennig shows that from the twelfth century onward the words "vilain métier" referred not only to female prostitution but also to same-sex desire, to the extent that in the late sixteenth century, Calvin is able to speak of Catholic monks and "docteurs sorboniques" as being "menés de désirs si vilains et énormes, jusques à être bougres, comme cela est un métier commun entr'eux" (led by such villainous and enormous desires, to the extent of being buggers, as that is a common practice that they share ["Quatrième sermon sur la premiere Epître à Timothée," 1567]). Pierre de L'Estoile frequently uses the terms "vilain" and "vilenie" to denote sodomy in his *Mémoires-journaux* (e.g., 7:75, 8:14–15) and in his *Registre-journal du règne de Henri III*, 3:48, 55.

57. Le Brun de La Rochette, *Procès civil et criminel*, 1:43. I am grateful to Jonathan Patterson, who is currently writing a book on villainy, for this information.

58. Lachèvre, *Libertinage au XVIIe siècle*, 143.

59. For a similarly engaged poem from a few years earlier in which another sodomite on trial (named Vigeon) is defended by a poetic voice, see Saint-Pavin, *Poésies*, 30, 70. An obscene imitation of this poem by Saint-Pavin, but addressed to Chausson, can be found in the Bibliothèque nationale, MS fr. 10969, 720.

60. Archives Nationales X2B 657, reproduced by Frédéric Lachèvre in *Œuvres libertines de Claude Le Petit*, xlix–xlx.

61. For an account of the editorial history of *Le Bordel des Muses*, see Lachèvre, *Œuvres libertines de Claude Le Petit*, xlv–lvii.

62. Lachèvre, *Libertinage au XVIIe siècle*, 108.

63. "À une époque où la culture, comme l'art, travaille à sublimer l'instinct, à neutraliser le corps et à intellectualiser le discours sur l'homme, voilà que s'élève une voix aberrante pour proclamer que l'esprit est sexué et

soumis aux lois biologiques" (Jeanneret, *Éros rebelle*, 220).

64. In his edition of Le Petit's works, Thomas Pogu writes that Jean Rou "n'était moralement pas aussi droit qu'il veut nous faire croire dans ses mémoires" (was not as morally upright as he wants us to believe in his memoirs [Introduction to Le Petit, *Œuvres libertines*, 43]).

65. Rou, *Mémoires inédits et opuscules*, 2:316. See also the appendix, 2:17, at the end of the same volume, where Rou quotes Le Petit's sonnet, calling Chausson "un malheureux sodomite" (an unfortunate sodomite), whose bravery in the flames had impressed the poet as "une grandeur d'âme" (greatness of soul), which Rou dismisses as "un effet de stupidité brutale" (the effect of brutish stupidity).

66. Quoted in Lachèvre, *Œuvres libertines de Claude Le Petit*, lii. The manuscript of Colletet's memoir was destroyed in a fire at the Louvre library in 1871, but it had previously been cited elsewhere. See also Le Petit, *Œuvres libertines*, 9–47.

67. For examples, see Pogu's introduction to Le Petit, *Œuvres libertines*, 40–42. See also DeJean, *Reinvention of Obscenity*, 90–91, who argues that Molière's use of the word "obscénité" with respect to censorship came immediately in the wake of Le Petit's execution.

68. For a full account and transcription of this case, see Merrick, "Chaussons in the Street," 167–203. One witness in the trial of Grisy, Étienne Petre, claims that Grisy had been accused of sodomy at the same time as Chausson and Paulmier (180), and another witness, Louis Fleuret, asserts that he knows Grisy to have been "du Nombre de Ceux qu'on accusoit comme les Chaussons" (one of those who were accused of being Chaussons [195]).

69. This manuscript is MS fr. 12666 from the Bibliothèque Nationale, wrongly dated as from 1651, and reproduced by Hernandez, *Procès de sodomie*, 4–5.

70. *Chansonnier Maurepas*, 4:313.

71. See Merrick, "Chaussons in the Street," 177.

72. *Chansonnier Maurepas*, 4:101.

73. Ibid., 6:204. Another example of Chausson in the plural form can be found in the *Chansonnier Maurepas*: "Régiment de la Callotte," 2:144, where "les Mânes des Chaussons" (the spirits of the Chaussons) are evoked.

74. Challe, *Journal du voyage des Indes orientales*, 91.

75. *Chansonnier Maurepas*, 3:385.

76. Ibid., 3:375.

77. Ibid., 7: 156. Cf. ibid., 20: 32, where a 1738 song alludes to "les vices de deffunt Chausson" (the vices of the late Chausson).

78. Voltaire, *La Guerre Civile de Genève*, 8. See Deloffre, "Challe, Voltaire," 31–43.

79. Voltaire, *La Guerre Civile de Genève*, 8. The note that Voltaire himself added after these lines in the first edition places Chausson in a list of notorious historical sodomites: "Chausson, fameux partisan d'Alcibiade, d'Alexandre, de Jules César, de Giton, de Des Fontaines."

80. Voltaire, *Œuvres complètes*, 81–82:351. For Voltaire's attitudes toward homosexuality, see René Pomeau, "Voltaire, du côté de Sodome?" and David Wootton, "Unhappy Voltaire, or 'I shall never get over it as long as I live.'"

Chapter 5

1. See Saint-Foix, *Histoire de l'Ordre du Saint-Esprit*, 1:82–83.

2. Louis XIV, *Mémoires*, 137.

3. For the intricate rules of order of precedence, see Saint-Foix, *Histoire de l'Ordre du Saint-Esprit*, 1:84–88. See also Sternberg, *Status Interaction*, 17–19, for the prominent role played by "princes du sang" in the legitimate line of the Bourbons.

4. "Bellefonds porte queuë, à mine indifférente; / Du plus grand des Mortels, suivoit la marche lente, / Et montrant au public ce qu'il a de menton, / Faisoit dire au public, pourquoi le choisit-on?" (Bellefonds is carrying the train with an indifferent demeanor; / He was following the slow procession of the greatest of mortals, / And in showing the public the greater part of his chin, / Made the public say, why was he chosen? [*Chansonnier Maurepas*, 23:382]).

5. Loret, *Muze historique*, book 13, letter 1, 452.

6. Ibid.

7. Saint-Foix, *Histoire de l'Ordre du Saint-Esprit*, 1:72–73. Cf. Loret, who writes how "ces magnifiques Messieurs" (these magnificent gentlemen) were "ravis de leur riche encolure" (delighted with their rich neckpiece), with "leur pierrerie, / Leur Saint Esprit, en broderie, / Leurs beaux et somptüeux atours / Leur manteaux à fonds de velours" (their jewelry, / Their Cross of the Holy Spirit, as embroidery, / Their fine and sumptuous attire / Their cloaks with a velvet base), in *Muze historique*, book 13, letter 1, 452.

8. Saint-Foix, *Histoire de l'Ordre du Saint-Esprit*, 1:78.

9. Brantôme, *Œuvres complètes*, 5:107. For a discussion of the origins of the Order of the Holy Spirit and some of the satirical depictions of it during the reign of Henri III, see Ferguson, *Queer (Re)readings in the French Renaissance*, 308–12.

10. Even when they were fighting on opposing sides during the Fronde, Condé was able to write to Gramont on 28 September 1651, "Je souhaitte avec passion dans ces fâcheuses rencontres, qu'il ne fasse rien qui puisse diminuer notre amitié" (I passionately wish that these troublesome encounters will in no way diminish our friendship), in Archives de Chantilly, J IV, fol. 158.

11. Bussy-Rabutin, *Mémoires*, 1:190.

12. Ibid., 1:189. "Cornette [. . .] signifie l'estendart d'une Compagnie de Chevaux-legers [. . .] et se prend pour l'Officier qui porte la cornette" (Cornette means the flag of a company of light cavalry and is used for the officer who carries the cornette [*Dictionnaire de l'Académie Françoise*, 1694]).

13. Bussy-Rabutin, *Mémoires*, 1:254–55. In other versions of the *Mémoires*, Bussy refers to Guitaut as "ce petit garçon sans naissance" (that little boy without high birth). See Pujo, *Grand Condé*, 262. See also Duchêne, who describes Guitaut as "un parvenu sans noblesse, un intrigant qui flatte les vices du prince" (an upstart without nobility, a plotter who flatters the vices of the prince), in *Bussy-Rabutin*, 64. See also 91–95 for a discussion of Bussy's difficulties in obtaining the money from Guitaut and Condé for his lieutenancy. While Condé was in prison, with the sale of the lieutenancy still to be completed, Bussy found himself obliged to continue supporting Condé against the king, an obligation that, as he wrote to his cousin the marquise de Sévigné, "n'a pas été sans de grandes répugnances, car je sers contre mon Roi un prince qui ne m'aime pas" (has not been without great repugnance, for I am serving a prince who does not love me against my king [2 July 1650]), in Sévigné, *Correspondance*, 1:13.

14. See Pujo, *Grand Condé*, 228. For Guitaut's service under Condé during the Fronde, see Gourville, *Mémoires*, 1:61–76.

15. For details of Condé's generosity to Guitaut (and arranging both his marriages), see Béguin, *Princes de Condé*, 155–57, 208–9.

16. Coligny-Saligny, *Mémoires*, 64. See also 64–67.

17. Ibid., 18.

18. Ibid., xlix–xlx.

19. Béguin, *Princes de Condé*, 58. In the 1640s alone, nine works, including Pierre Corneille's *Rodogune* in 1647, were dedicated to the duc d'Enghien and thirty-nine works were written about him.

20. Bannister, *Condé in Context*, 66.

21. For the financial arrangements of the marriage, see Béguin, *Princes de Condé*, 41–42. See also Pujo, *Grand Condé*, 367, who speculates that all traces of Claire-Clémence de Maillé-Brézé were expunged from the Chantilly archives; it is his contention that she suffered from a mental illness, which may explain why she continued to be incarcerated in Châteauroux even after Condé's death (403–4). Various pieces were circulated in 1671 about Condé's wife's supposed affairs, which were said to have resulted in her being wounded while two of her servants fought over her. In one allegorical fable, we find the lines, "Ils caressoient souvent cette bonne maîtresse / Qui leur rendoit souvent caresse pour caresse" (Often they would caress this good mistress, / Who herself would often return caress for caress). See *Chansonnier Maurepas*, 3:397–401. See also the epigram on the subject, fol. 401. Saint-Simon writes about her incarceration in his *Mémoires*, 3:598.

22. This heyday of literary and artistic salon culture has been called "l'âge de la conversation" (the age of conversation) by Craveri, *Âge de la Conversation*.

23. "La société des petits-maîtres, avant tout composée de grands seigneurs libertins, hédonistes et valeureux, peu enclins à endurer les prohibitions de l'État autoritaire et des dévots en matière de duel, trouva en Louis II de Bourbon un porte-parole naturel et puissant" (Béguin, *Princes de Condé*, 84).

24. Dewald, *Aristocratic Experience*, 119. See also Bannister, *Condé in Context*, 55–78.

25. For discussion of Condé's father's same-sex pursuits, see Tallemant des Réaux, *Historiettes*, 1:417–22; Lever, *Bûchers de Sodome*, 137–39; Hammond, *Gossip, Sexuality, and Scandal in France*, 94–95.

26. See Mongrédien, *Grand Condé*, 60; Lever, *Bûchers de Sodome*, 154–55.

27. He is named "Roi de Sodome" in a song from the *Chansonnier Maurepas*, 2:221. Saint-Pavin wrote a sonnet that ends with the lines, "Et je conserve le nom / Que tout le monde me donne" (And I maintain the name / That everybody gives me), in Saint-Pavin, *Poésies*, XXXVI, 67.

28. Ibid., CX, 102.

29. Ibid., CLV, 134, 206.

30. Bannister, *Condé in Context*, 67. See *Chansonnier Maurepas*, 2:108 and 123 for songs about Marthe du Vigean.

31. See Goudal, *Ninon de Lenclos*, 41–42. Cf. also Dulong, *Amour au XVII*ᵉ *siècle*: "Ninon le trouva insuffisant et osa le lui dire, en des termes assez plaisants pour être rapportés" (Ninon found him lacking and dared tell him that, in agreeable enough terms for it to be reported [180]).

32. Proust, *A la recherche du temps perdu*, 3:303.

33. "Écrins sonores de sens perdus et de mémoires présentes" (Certeau, *Arts de faire*, 1:237).

34. These two poems are cited by Monmerqué in his edition to Coligny-Saligny's *Mémoires* (xlix), reportedly from a manuscript in Monmerqué's private collection, which I have been unable to locate.

35. Letter from Gaspard de Coligny to Condé, dated 3 August 1646, Archives de Chantilly M, vol. 3, fols. 199–202.

36. *Chansonnier Maurepas*, 2:149. Bussy-Rabutin writes that Condé "fut dans une grande affliction" (was in a desperate state) at Châtillon's death, "parce que Châtillon avait l'honneur d'être son parent et son premier ami" (because Châtillon had the honor of being his relative and his first friend [*Mémoires*, 127]).

37. Letter from Toulougeon to Condé, dated 2 May 1649, Archives de Chantilly, P III, ff. 438–39.

38. *Chansonnier Maurepas*, 2:246 (1650).

39. "Ce ton désinvolte, libertin ou galant, est celui d'hommes rompus aux travaux de Mars" (Béguin, *Princes de Condé*, 73).

40. For a list of Condé's clients, see ibid., 395–440. See also Mousnier, who views such friendships as partly emotional fidelity and partly self-interested clientelism in *Institutions de la France*, vol. 1, and Kettering, who concentrates on alliances between royal ministers and provincial elites as forms of power brokering in *Patrons, Brokers and Clients*, and who makes the point that "friendship and clientage varied in their emotional intensity and durability" in *Friendship and Clientage*, 150.

41. See Bray, *Friend*.

42. "Le lien discursif entre l'amitié et l'homosexualité" (Kühner, "Amitié nobiliaire," 221).

43. Dewald, *Aristocratic Experience*, 117.

44. The letters, which were copied and presented to the duc d'Aumale by the comte de Guitaut around 1820, are contained in a fifty-seven-sheet booklet and housed in the archives of the Château de Chantilly, O 1 161–219. All references in brackets in the main text will be to these unpublished letters.

45. Cf. Kühner, who, with respect to Condé and Guitaut in particular, writes,

> Cette relation illustre par excellence le fait qu'une relation peut très bien être décrite par les parties concernées comme une amitié alors que les catégories analytiques des sciences sociales la classent dans les relations de clientélisme et qu'elle est caractérisée par la différence de rang (ici entre un prince et un comte), par le soutien du client par son patron— ce qui s'illustre notamment en ce que Guitaut suit volontairement Condé en exil. S'il est un cas où l'on peut parler d'amitié entre inégaux, c'est bien celui-là. ("Amitié nobiliaire," 110)

> (This relationship illustrates par excellence the fact that a relationship can be

described by the concerned parties as a friendship while the analytical categories of the social sciences class it in relationships of clientelism, characterized by difference in rank [here between a prince and a count], and by support of the client by the patron, which is notably illustrated in the fact that Guitaut voluntarily followed Condé into exile. If there is a case of speaking of a friendship between nonequals, this was certainly of that kind.)

46. Pierre Lenet writes of Guitaut's courage in battle, describing him as "le jeune comte Guitaut, qu'on ne pouvoit empêcher de se trouver en toutes les actions d'honneur, quoiqu'il fût encore moribond de la grande blessure qu'il avoit reçue dans le marais de Blanquefort" (the young count Guitaut, who could not be prevented from being found in every kind of honorable military action, even though he was still on the point of dying from the deep wound that he had received in the Blanquefort swamp), in *Mémoires*, 54:52. Guitaut lost his brother in the same conflict.

47. See Kühner, "Amitié nobiliaire," 268–69.

48. This is a recurring theme in the correspondence. Cf. fol. 169: "J'ai une affaire fort pressée où vous m'êtes tout-à-fait nécessaire" (I have very urgent business where you are absolutely necessary to me).

49. At this time Condé had debts of 8 million livres, yet he continued to buy land and spend enormous sums on his estate at Chantilly. See Dewald, *Aristocratic Experience*, 153.

50. Kühner gives a compelling reading of this dimension of the letter in "Amitié nobiliaire," 270.

51. *Chansonnier Maurepas*, 3:330. A version of the same song, with the same line about Guitaut, can be found in Tallemant des Réaux's collection of poems and songs, *Manuscrit 673*, 444. It also can be found in the Chantilly archives, MS 574, fol. 32.

52. Sévigné, *Correspondance*, 1:164–66.

53. Ibid., 1:165.

54. Ibid. Duchêne suggests that these would have been business letters from Condé relating to the trust funds of Guitaut's first wife. *Bussy-Rabutin*, 1001n3.

55. Sévigné, *Correspondance*, 1:504.

56. See ibid., 3:110.

57. See ibid., 3:102.

58. Sévigné, 21 August 1677, in ibid., 2:531. See also her reference in a letter to Guitaut to their "douces et charmantes conversations" (27 April 1674, 1:695).

59. Sévigné, 23 December 1677, in ibid., 2:590.

60. Sévigné, 27 October 1673, in ibid., 1:605.

61. "Je plains fort M. et Mme de Guitaut; une transaction disputée me fait transir. Il n'y a donc rien de sûr" (I pity M. and Mme de Guitaut greatly; a disputed transaction is making me tremble. Nothing is certain [Sévigné, 28 February 1685, in ibid., 3:187–88]).

62. Bossuet, *Oraisons funèbres* (Truchet), 408–9.

Chapter 6

1. MS 574, Archives de Chantilly, fol. 478, and MS 576, fol. 91, which is wrongly dated as 1651. A slightly different version can also be found in MS fr. 15127, Bibliothèque Nationale, and this version is quoted by Hernandez, *Procès de sodomie*, 4.

2. MS fr. 12666, Bibliothèque Nationale, reproduced by Hernandez, *Procès de sodomie*, 4–5.

3. Hernandez, *Procès de sodomie*, 84–85.

4. Mercier, writing in the late eighteenth century, remarks that on the Pont Neuf the orange "abonde en pyramides, comme si l'on étoit en Portugal" (is abundantly laid out in pyramids, as if one were in Portugal), which contrasted markedly with forty years previously, where "ces belles pommes d'or étoient rares en France, et se vendoient vingt sous pièce" (these beautiful golden apples were rare in France and were sold for 20 sous ap iece [9:70, chap. 75]).

5. See, for example, Ferguson in *Same-Sex Marriage in Renaissance Rome*: "It was, in fact, an extremely common practice for a passive youth to receive or at least expect gifts—clothes, food and drink, money—or other favors in return for his willingness to satisfy an older partner's desires" (134).

6. If the page had indeed worked in Madame's household, he would probably have already been exposed to the same-sex

sexual intrigues involving the entourage of Madame's husband, Philippe d'Orléans. See Hammond, *Gossip, Sexuality, and Scandal in France*, 99–110.

7. Saint-Maur remained an important location for the Condé family. Defying the orders of both the king and his father, Condé had brought his friend Maurice de Coligny, mortally wounded in a duel, to Saint-Maur, where the latter died in 1644. He had also used Saint-Maur as a base in 1651 during the Fronde. After his return from exile, during which his representatives had zealously kept Chantilly and Saint-Maur from being confiscated by the king, Condé engaged in renovation work at Saint-Maur with the architect Daniel Gittard. Such work was being conducted at the time that Paulmier was accused of being with the page boy at Saint-Maur. For further details about Condé and Conti's dealings at Saint-Maur, see Béguin, *Princes de Condé*, 114–15, 130, 139–43, 331–32, 420.

8. For discussion of this, see Hammond, *Gossip, Sexuality, and Scandal in France*, 71–78.

9. The eighteenth-century transcript of Paulmier's interrogation brings out one further, rather more tangential, connection with Condé. Paulmier admits to having committed sodomy with an officer in the Piedmont Regiment, Doralier, who was killed in July 1659 in Flanders, fighting with the French army, led by Condé, against the Spanish. See Hernandez, *Procès de sodomie*, 79.

10. Tallemant des Réaux, *Historiettes*, 1:413–14. For discussion of Boisrobert, see Hammond, *Gossip, Sexuality, and Scandal in France*, 87–93.

11. Tallemant des Réaux, *Historiettes*, 1:339. Other favorites of Louis, with whom he was infatuated, include the duc de Luynes, Claude de Saint-Simon, and the marquis de Saint-Mars. See Hammond, *Gossip, Sexuality, and Scandal in France*, 95–97.

12. See, for example, *Chansonnier Maurepas*, 1:453–54 (quoted also by Tallemant des Réaux, *Historiettes*, 1:528) and 5:251.

13. Tallemant des Réaux, *Historiettes*, 1:528. Tallemant claims that Condé used to refer to him in the feminine as "Ma Guiche," 531. See also 528–33, esp. 532, in which an anecdote is told of how Gramont managed to make a certain vicomte du Bac, who had outstayed his welcome, leave his home promptly by offering to share his bed with him. Cf. Lever, *Bûchers de Sodome*, who describes him as "le plus grand sodomite du royaume" (the greatest sodomite of the kingdom [155]).

14. *Chansonnier Maurepas*, 2:215 (1649).

15. There are numerous cases of pages and their masters in the *Chansonnier Maurepas*: for example, the French ambassador to Rome, Charles de Créquy, who was involved in various diplomatic incidents in the year after Chausson's death, is depicted in one 1662 song as a person who "aime les plaisirs Romains" (enjoys Roman pleasures [3:398]), and later in the same volume is described as having "pris son beau Page, / [. . .] Prenant le masle pour la femelle" (taken his handsome page, / Taking the male as a female [3:402]). Also in England at a similar time, Samuel Pepys writes in his diary on 1 July 1663: "Sir J. Mennes and Mr Batten both say that buggery is now almost grown as common among our gallants as in Italy, and that the very pages of the town begin to complain of their masters for it. But blessed be God, I do not to this day know what is the meaning of this sin, nor which is the agent nor which the patient" (3:210). See also Tristan l'Hermite's *Le page disgracié*, believed to be autobiographical in inspiration, where the eponymous page writes of his master who "me trouva joli, et m'honora de caresses particulières" (found me pretty and honored me with particular caresses), in Prévot, *Libertins du XVIIe siècle*, 1:387. Cf. the page's account of another master, who calls him "mon petit mignon" (my little favorite) and "me pressa le visage de ses mains pour me caresser" (held my head in his hands to caress me [525]).

16. Archives Nationales X2A 989, 7 May 1626, and X2B 1331, 26 June 1626. I am grateful to Tom Hamilton for drawing my attention to these transcripts.

17. See Fournier, *Histoire du Pont-Neuf*, 2:312, and Dupuy-Demportes, *Histoire génerale*, 30.

18. The Saint-Amant scholar Jean Lagny argues in *Poète Saint-Amant* that it is unlikely that Saint-Amant was the author of the song. Bussy-Rabutin, who fought under

Condé at the siege of Lerida, wrote about the conflict in his *Mémoires*. Members of Condé's entourage believed that Condé had been given a hopeless task by Cardinal Mazarin in order to humiliate him. See Béguin, *Princes de Condé*, 97.

19. *Chansonnier Maurepas*, 2:27. The song is wrongly dated as being from 1644.

20. Saint-Amant, *Œuvres complètes*, 2:505.

21. See Béguin, *Princes de Condé*, 58.

22. Le Savoyard, *Recueil des chansons du Savoyard*, 45–46.

23. See, for example, *Chansonnier Maurepas*, 2:52, where he is purported to have written a song for a woman in Madame de Ricouart's entourage, or fol. 29, where he is supposedly addressing his sister the duchesse de Longueville, with whom he was rumored to be infatuated. Another song in the same volume is said to have been composed by Condé while in the army "en débauche, le verre à la main" (in a state of debauchery, glass in hand [fol. 63]). See also fol. 99 for a further song claimed to be by Condé.

24. The Chausson song is to be found in MS 576, fol. 90, Archives de Chantilly. MSS 574–93 are all volumes of songs from the seventeenth and eighteenth centuries. See *Chantilly le Cabinet des Livres*, 2:303–9.

25. See Lachèvre, *Œuvres libertines de Claude Le Petit*, xlvii, lviii.

26. Rou, *Mémoires inédits et opuscules*, 2:316.

27. Lachèvre, *Œuvres libertines de Claude Le Petit*, 116.

28. Saint-Foix, *Histoire de l'Ordre du S. Esprit*, 1:73. Cf. Loret in *Muze historique*, book 13, letter 1, from 7 January 1662, who refers to "Quantitè de flâmes luizantes" (a number of shining flames) on the cloaks of the Chevaliers, 452.

29. See Lachèvre, *Œuvres libertines de Claude Le Petit*, lvii–lviii, 196. Lachèvre speculates that Bussy was named as the author either to sell more copies in the aftermath of the *succès de scandale* of his *Histoire amoureuse des Gaules* or as some kind of "sotte vengeance" (stupid vengefulness) against him.

30. Bussy-Rabutin, *Mémoires*, 1:174.

31. For a particularly lively example of such discussions, see Sévigné, *Correspondance*, 2:635–37.

32. See Duchêne, *Bussy-Rabutin*, chaps. 19 and 25.

33. MS 565, Archives de Chantilly.

34. Song no. 13 in ibid. Isherwood, in *Farce and Fantasy*, writes of the eighteenth-century practice of courtiers supplying "the crowd with the malicious news that formed one of the cornerstones of marketplace culture" (11), a practice that was likely to be commonplace in the seventeenth century also.

35. Song no. 25, MS 565, Archives de Chantilly.

36. For examples of satirical versions of this Easter hymn, see song 44 in ibid., written in Bussy's hand; see also Sévigné, *Correspondance*, 1:193–94; *Chansonnier Maurepas*, 2:3–6, 11–14, 3:243, 335–36, 377–86, 413–42.

37. The song is reproduced in Bussy-Rabutin, *Histoire amoureuse des Gaules*, 191–93.

38. For Bussy's account of the Roissy incident, see Bussy-Rabutin, *Mémoires*, 2:179–85.

39. 17 April 1692, in Sévigné, *Correspondance*, 3:992.

40. See Bussy-Rabutin, *Mémoires*, 2:193–94.

41. For a detailed account of his attempt to become a Chevalier de l'Ordre du Saint-Esprit, see ibid., 208–20.

42. Ibid., 215.

43. Ibid., 217.

44. Letter from 18 December 1688, in Sévigné, *Correspondance*, 3:433. He claims that "j'en fus fâché alors, mais les regrets en sont passés" (I was angry about it at the time, but the sorrow has passed), but then he goes on to write that the news of Grignan's promotion "rouvrait un peu mes vieilles plaies" (managed to reopen my old wounds a little [433]).

45. Bussy-Rabutin, *Mémoires*, 2:220.

46. Song no. 20, MS 565, Archives de Chantilly. The full text of the song, purported to be written from the perspective of the comte de Gramont, is as follows:

Sarabande
Lors que Guitaut par une ardeur fidelle
Qu'il a toujours pour son amy flamand
Sceut obliger la personne que j'ayme
Au duc dicelle qui causa mon tourment,
Las je pensois comme il pensoit luy meme
Ne revoir Philis qu'au Jour du Jugement,

Mais ce n'est qu'un bannissement.

(When Guitaut, through a faithful ardor / That he still has for his Flemish friend, / Was able to oblige the person that I love / Through the duke of the person who caused my torment, / Weary, I thought as he himself thought / Of never seeing Philis again until the Day of Judgment, / But it is only an exile.)

47. Bussy-Rabutin, *Histoire amoureuse des Gaules*, 151.
48. Lachèvre, *Œuvres libertines de Claude Le Petit*, xlii.

Conclusion

1. Sévigné, 20 February 1671, in *Correspondance*, 1:164.
2. Boileau's Satire VI, which was discussed in chapter 1, includes a section on the sound world of a neighbor's fire that is strikingly similar to Sévigné's description: "Tremblant et demi-mort, je me lève à ce bruit" (Trembling and half-dead, I get up upon hearing this noise), in *Œuvres*, 45.
3. Hernandez, *Procès de sodomie*, 80.
4. Sévigné, *Correspondance*, 1:164.
5. Hammond, *Gossip, Sexuality, and Scandal in France*, esp. 51–113. Figures on the number of cases tried in the Parlement of Paris are part of forthcoming research by Tom Hamilton and Alfred Soman. While the number of prosecutions for sodomy was low in the seventeenth century, the early eighteenth century and especially the 1720s saw a significant increase in prosecutions in cities such as Paris, London, and Utrecht. Criminal archives beyond the Parlement of Paris include details of other sodomy trials, but these archives are far less systematic and it is impossible to give a definitive number of cases.
6. See ibid., 71–78, for discussion of the Confrérie.
7. "C'est sans doute à cause de cette vibration que j'éprouve aujourd'hui encore lorsqu'il m'arrive de rencontrer ces vies infimes devenues cendres dans les quelques phrases qui les ont abattues. [. . .] Ni 'quasi' ni 'sous-littérature,' ce n'est même pas l'ébauche d'un genre; c'est dans le désordre, le bruit et la peine, le travail du pouvoir sur les vies, et le discours qui en naît" (Foucault, *Philosophie anthologie*, 563–64).

Bibliography

Manuscript Sources

Bibliothèque Nationale, Fonds Français
"Recueil de Chansons, Vaudevilles, Sonnets, Epigrammes, Epitaphes, et autres vers satiriques." 30 vols. Known as the Chansonnier Maurepas.

Chantilly Archives
Série J (diverse pieces from the Condé household)
Série P (correspondence by le Grand Condé)
MSS 565 and 576 (collections of songs)

Secondary Sources

Apostolidès, Jean-Marie. *Le Roi-Machine: Spectacle et politique au temps de Louis XIV*. Paris: Éditions de Minuit, 1981.

Armogathe, Jean-Robert. "Bossuet, orateur sacré." In *Bossuet le verbe et l'histoire, 1704–2004*, edited by Gérard Ferreyrolles, 257–69. Paris: Honoré Champion, 2006.

———. "Témoignage d'un prédicateur: Action oratoire et visée pastorale." *Littératures classiques* 46 (2002): 215–20.

Atkinson, Niall. *The Noisy Renaissance: Sound, Architecture, and Florentine Urban Life*. University Park: The Pennsylvania State University Press, 2016.

———. "The Republic of Sound: Listening to Florence at the Threshold of the Renaissance." *I Tatti Studies in the Italian Renaissance* 16, no. 1 (2013): 57–84.

Attali, Jacques. *Bruits: Essai sur l'économie politique de la musique*. 1977. Paris: Fayard/PUF, 2001.

———. *Noise: The Political Economy of Music*. Translated by Brian Massumi. 1985. Minneapolis: University of Minnesota Press, 2009.

Bannister, Mark. *Condé in Context: Ideological Change in Seventeenth-Century France*. Oxford: Legenda, 2000.

Barbanti, Roberto. "Listening to the Landscape." In Kay and Noudelmann, "Soundings and Soundscapes," 62–78.

Barnwell, H. T. "L'art épistolaire de Madame de Sévigné dans les lettres sur le procès Foucquet." In *Correspondances: Mélanges offerts à Roger Duchêne*, edited by Wolfgang Leiner and Pierre Ronzeaud, 387–94. Tübingen: Gunter Narr, 1992.

Barthes, Roland. "Écoute." In *Œuvres complètes*, edited by Éric Marty, 3:727–56. Paris: Seuil, 1995.

———. "Listening." In *The Responsibility of Forms: Critical Essays on Music, Art, and Representation*, translated by Richard Howard, 245–60. Oxford: Blackwell, 1986.

Bastien, Pascal. *Une histoire de la peine de mort: Bourreaux et supplices 1500–1800*. Paris: Seuil, 2011.

Batcho, James. "The Sonic Lifeworld: A Phenomenological Exploration of the Imaginative Potential of Animation Sound." *Journal of Sonic Studies* 6, no. 1 (2014). http://journal.sonicstudies.org/vol06/nr01/a05.

Bayley, Peter. *French Pulpit Oratory, 1598–1650*. Cambridge: Cambridge University Press, 1980.

Beaugendre, Dom Antoine. *La Vie de Messire Benigne Joly, prestre, docteur de la faculté de Paris, de la Maison et Société de Navarre, Chanoine de l'Eglise Abbatiale et Collegiale de S. Estienne de Dijon, Instituteur des Religieuses Hospitalieres de la même Ville, où l'on le nommoit: Le pere des pauvres*. Paris: Loüis Guerin, 1700.

Bée, Michel. "Le spectacle de l'exécution dans la France d'Ancien Régime." *Annales: Économies, Sociétés, Civilisations* 38, no. 4 (1983): 843–62.

Béguin, Katia. *Les princes de Condé: Rebelles, courtisans et mécènes dans la France du grand siècle*. Paris: Champ Vallon, 1999.

Bély, Lucien. *Louis XIV: Le plus grand roi du monde*. Paris: Jean-Paul Gisserot, 2005.

———. *Les secrets de Louis XIV*. Paris: Tallandier, 2013.

Berthod, Claude Louis. *La ville de Paris en vers burlesques*. Paris: n.p., 1654.

Blavignac, J.-D. *La cloche: Etudes sur son histoire et sur ses rapports avec la société aux différents âges*. Geneva: Grosset & Trembley, 1877.

Bluche, François. *Louis XIV*. Paris: Fayard, 1986.

Boileau, Nicolas. *Œuvres*. Edited by Georges Mongrédien. Paris: Garnier Frères, 1961.

Bossuet, Jacques-Bénigne. *Oraisons funèbres*. Edited by Jacques Truchet. Paris: Gallimard-Folio, 1998.

———. *Les oraisons funèbres de Bossuet, suivies du sermon pour la profession de Mme de la Vallière*. Edited by M. Poujoulat. Tours: Alfred Mame et Fils, 1869.

———. *Sermons: Le carême du Louvre*. Edited by Constance Cagnat-Deboeuf. Paris: Gallimard-Folio, 2001.

Boutin, Aimée. *City of Noise: Sound and Nineteenth-Century Paris*. Urbana: University of Illinois Press, 2015.

Brantôme, Pierre de. *Œuvres complètes de Pierre de Bourdeille, seigneur de Brantôme*. Edited by Ludovic Lalanne. 11 vols. Paris: Librairie Renouard, 1864–82.

Bray, Alan. *The Friend*. Chicago: University of Chicago Press, 2003.

Bray, Bernard, and Christoph Strosetzki, eds. *Art de la lettre, art de la conversation*. Paris: Klincksieck, 1995.

Brice, Germain. *Description nouvelle de ce qu'il y a de plus intéressant et de plus remarquable dans la ville de Paris*. 1684. Paris: Nicolas Le Gras, 1698.

———. *Mémoriaux du Conseil de 1661*. Vol. 1. Edited by Jean de Boislisle. Paris: Renouard, 1905.

Brienne, Henri-Auguste de Loménie, comte de. *Mémoires inédits*. Edited by F. Barrière. 2 vols. Paris: Fonthieu, 1828.

Bruneau, Antoine. *Observations et maximes sur les matières criminelles*. Paris: Cavelier, 1715.

Burke, Peter. *The Fabrication of Louis XIV*. New Haven: Yale University Press, 1992.

Bussy-Rabutin, Roger de. *Histoire amoureuse des Gaules*. Edited by Jacqueline and Roger Duchêne. Paris: Gallimard Folio, 1993.

———. *Mémoires*. 2 vols. Paris: Jean Anisson, 1696.

Butterworth, Emily. *The Unbridled Tongue: Babble and Gossip in Renaissance France*. Oxford: Oxford University Press, 2016.

Callières, François de. *Des bons mots et des bons contes*. Paris: Claude Barbin, 1692.

Carré, Rémi. *Recueil curieux et édifiant sur les cloches de l'église*. Cologne, 1757.

Certeau, Michel de. *Arts de faire*. Vol. 1 of *L'Invention du quotidien*. Paris: Folio, 1990.

Chaduc, Pauline. *Fénelon, direction spirituelle et littérature*. Paris: Honoré Champion, 2015.

Challe, Robert. *Journal du voyage des Indes orientales*. Edited by Jacques Popin and Frédéric Deloffre. Geneva: Droz, 1998.

Chantilly le Cabinet des Livres. 2 vols. Paris: Plon, 1900.

Chartier, Roger. *Lectures et lecteurs dans la France d'Ancien Régime*. Paris: Seuil, 1987.

———. "Les pratiques de l'écrit." In *Histoire de la vie privée*, edited by Philippe Ariès and Georges Duby, 3:109–15. Paris: Seuil, 1999.

Choisy, François Timoléon, abbé de. *Mémoires*. Edited by Georges Mongrédien. Paris: Mercure de France, 1966.

Cobb, Richard. *The Police and the People: French Popular Protest, 1789–1820*. Oxford: Clarendon, 1970.

Coirault, Patrice. *Formation de nos chansons folkloriques*. 3 vols. Paris: Editions du Scarabée, 1953–59.

———. *Notre chanson folklorique: Etude d'information générale; L'objet et la méthode, l'inculte et son apport, l'élaboration, la notion*. Paris: Auguste Picard, 1942.

Coligny-Saligny, Jean de. *Mémoires*. Edited by Louis Jean Nicolas Monmerqué. Paris: Jules Renouard, 1841.

Colletet, François. *Le tracas de Paris*. Paris: Antoine de Rafflé, 1680.

Condé, Louis Prince de, and Henri Jules duc d'Enghien. *Lettres inédites à Marie-Louise de Gonzague, reine de Pologne, sur la cour de Louis XIV (1660–1667)*. Edited by Émile Magne. Paris: Émile-Paul Frères, 1920.

Corbin, Alain. *Les cloches de la terre: Paysage sonore et culture sensible dans les campagnes au XIXe siècle*. Paris: Albin Michel, 1994.

———. *Village Bells*. Translated by Martin Thom. New York: Columbia University Press, 1998.

Corneille, Pierre. *Œuvres complètes*. Edited by Georges Couton. 3 vols. Paris: Gallimard, 1987.

Cotgrave, Randle. *A Dictionarie of the French and English Tongues*. London: Adam Islip, 1611.

Couvreur, Manuel. "L'oreille de Madame de Sévigné." In *Madame de Sévigné (1626–1696): Provence, spectacles, "lanternes,"* edited by Roger Duchêne, 191–204. Grignan: Association d'Action Culturelle des Châteaux Départementaux de la Drôme, 1998.

Craveri, Benedetta. *L'âge de la conversation*. Paris: Gallimard, 2002.

Darnton, Robert. *Poetry and the Police: Communication Networks in Eighteenth-Century Paris*. Cambridge: Harvard University Press, 2010.

Dassoucy, Charles Coypeau. *Avantures burlesques de Dassoucy*. Edited by Emile Colombey. Paris: A. Delahaus, 1858.

DeJean, Jean. *How Paris Became Paris: The Invention of the Modern City*. New York: Bloomsbury, 2014.

———. *Libertine Strategies: Freedom and the Novel in Seventeenth-Century France*. Columbus: Ohio State University Press, 1981.

———. *The Reinvention of Obscenity*. Chicago: University of Chicago Press, 2002.

de La Force, Piganiol. *Description de Paris*. Paris: Theodore Legras, 1742.

Deloffre, Frédéric. "Challe, Voltaire et le brûlement de Chausson." In *Recherches et Travaux. XVIIIe siècle* 44 (1993): 31–43.

Delumeau, Jean. *L'aveu et le pardon: Les difficultés de la confession XIIIe–XVIIIe siècle*. Paris: Fayard, 1990.

Demorest, Danielle, and Michel Demorest. *Dictionnaire historique et anecdotique des bourreaux*. Paris: Editions généalogiques de la Voûte, 2011.

Denney, Peter. "The Sounds of Population Fail: Changing Perceptions of Rural Poverty and Plebeian Noise in Eighteenth-Century Britain." In *Experiences of Poverty in Late Medieval and Early Modern England and France*, edited by Anne M. Scott, 295–312. 2012. Abingdon: Routledge, 2016.

Depping, G. B., ed. *Correspondance administrative sous le règne de Louis XIV*. Paris: Imprimerie nationale, 1851.

Dessert, Daniel. *Fouquet*. Paris: Fayard, 1987.

Dewald, Jonathan. *Aristocratic Experience and the Origins of Modern Culture: France, 1570–1715*. Berkeley: University of California Press, 1993.

Dostie, Pierre. "Fouquet sur la sellette: Le procès d'un héros cornélien dans la Correspondance de Mme de Sévigné." *Papers on French Seventeenth-Century Literature* 22, no. 43 (1995): 584–95.

Duchêne, Jacqueline. *Bussy-Rabutin*. Paris: Fayard, 1992.

Dulong, Claude. *L'amour au XVIIe siècle*. Paris: Hachette, 1969.

Dupuy-Demportes, Jean-Baptiste. *Histoire génerale du Pont-Neuf en six volumes in-folio*. London, 1750.

Estrée, Paul d'. "Les origines du chansonnier de Maurepas." *Revue d'histoire littéraire de la France* 3 (1896): 332–45.

Evelyn, John. *Diary*. Edited by Austin Dobson. 3 vols. Cambridge: Cambridge University Press, 2015.
Farge, Arlette. "The Sounds of Enlightenment Paris." In Kay and Noudelmann, "Soundings and Soundscapes," 52–61.
———. *Vivre dans la rue à Paris au XVIIIe siècle*. 1979. Paris: Folio, 1992.
Ferguson, Gary. *Queer (Re)readings in the French Renaissance: Homosexuality, Gender, Culture*. Aldershot: Ashgate, 2008.
———. *Same-Sex Marriage in Renaissance Rome: Sexuality, Identity, and Community in Early Modern Europe*. Ithaca: Cornell University Press, 2016.
Foucault, Michel. *Histoire de la sexualité*. 4 vols. Paris: Gallimard, 1976–2018.
———. *Philosophie anthologie*. Paris: Gallimard-Folio, 2004.
Fournier, Edouard. *Histoire du Pont-Neuf*. 2 vols. Paris: E. Dentu, 1862.
Fraser, Antonia. *Love and Louis XIV: The Women in the Life of the Sun King*. London: Weidenfeld & Nicolson, 2006.
Freidel, Nathalie. *La conquête de l'intime: Public et privé dans la correspondance de Madame de Sévigné*. Paris: Honoré Champion, 2009.
Friedland, Paul. *Seeing Justice Done: The Age of Spectacular Punishment in France*. Oxford: Oxford University Press, 2012.
Fumaroli, Marc. *L'âge de l'éloquence*. Geneva: Droz, 1980.
———. *Le poète et le roi: Jean de la Fontaine dans son siècle*. Paris: Fallois, 1997.
Garrioch, David. "Sounds of the City: The Soundscape of Early Modern European Towns." *Urban History* 30, no. 1 (2003): 5–25.
Gatrell, V. A. C. *The Hanging Tree: Execution and the English People, 1770–1868*. Oxford: Oxford University Press, 1996.
Gétreau, Florence. "Guillaume de Limoges et François Couperin, ou comment enseigner la musique hors la Ménestrandise parisienne." In *Musik, Raum, Akkord, Bild / Music, Space, Chord, Image*, edited by Antonio Baldassarre, 163–82. Bern: Peter Lang, 2012.
———. "Philippot le Savoyard—Portraits d'un orphée du Pont-Neuf mêlés de vaudevilles, d'images et de vers burlesques." In *"L'esprit français" und die Musik Europas. Entstehung, Einfluss und Grenzen einer ästhetischen Doktrin. Festschrift für Herbert Schneider*, edited by Michelle Biget-Mainfroy and Rainer Schmuch, 269–88. Hildesheim: Olms, 2007.
Gétreau, Florence, and Michel Colardelle, eds. *Musiciens des rues de Paris*. Paris: Éditions de la Réunion des musées nationaux, 1997.
Ginzburg, Carlo. *The Cheese and the Worms: The Cosmos of a Sixteenth-Century Miller*. Translated by John and Anne C. Tedeschi. 1976. Baltimore: Johns Hopkins University Press, 2013.
Goldsmith, Elizabeth C. *Exclusive Conversations: The Art of Interaction in Seventeenth-Century France*. Philadelphia: University of Pennsylvania Press, 1988.
Goubert, Pierre. *L'avènement du Roi-Soleil 1661*. Revised edition by Jean-Pierre Goubert. Paris: Gallimard, 1967, 2014.
Goudal, Jean. *Ninon de Lenclos, amoureuse et courtisane*. Paris: Hachette, 1967.
Gourville, Jean Hérauld de. *Mémoires*. Edited by Arlette Lebigre. Paris: Mercure de France, 2004.
———. *Mémoires*. Edited by Léon Lecestre. 2 vols. Paris: Librairie Renouard, 1894.
Grèce, Michel de. *Louis XIV: L'envers du soleil*. Paris: Olivier Orban, 1979.
Guillorel, Éva. *La complainte et la plainte: Chanson, justice, cultures en Bretagne XVIe–XVIIIe siècles*. Rennes: Presses Universitaires de Rennes, 2010.
Gutton, Jean-Pierre. *Bruits et sons dans notre histoire*. Paris: PUF, 2000.
Hablot, Laurent, and Laurent Vissière, eds. *Les paysages sonores du Moyen Âge à la Renaissance*. Paris: Presses Universitaires de Rennes, 2015.
Hamilton, Tom. "Contesting Public Executions in Paris Towards the End of the Wars of Religion." In *Cultures of Conflict Resolution in Early Modern Europe*, edited by Stephen Cummins and Laura Kounine, 179–202. Farnham: Ashgate, 2015.

Hamilton, Tom, and Hammond, Nicholas, eds. "Soundscapes." Special issue, *Early Modern French Studies*, 41, no. 1 (2019).
———. *Pierre de l'Estoile and His World in the Wars of Religion*. Oxford: Oxford University Press, 2017.
Hammond, Nicholas. *Gossip, Sexuality, and Scandal in France (1610–1715)*. Oxford: Peter Lang, 2011.
Hamscher, Albert N. *The Parlement of Paris After the Fronde, 1653–1673*. Pittsburgh: University of Pittsburgh Press, 1976.
Hawcroft, Michael. "Historical Evidence and Literature: Madame de Sévigné's Letters on the Trial of Fouquet." *Seventeenth Century* 9, no. 1 (1994): 57–75.
Hendy, David. *Noise: A Human History of Sound and Listening*. London: Profile Books, 2013.
Hennig, Jean-Luc. *Espadons, mignons et autres monstres: Vocabulaire de l'homosexualité masculine sous l'ancien régime*. Paris: Le Cherche Midi, 2014.
Hernandez, Ludovico [Louis Perceau and Fernand Fleuret]. *Les Procès de sodomie au XVIe, XVIIe et XVIIIe siècles: Publiés d'après les documents judiciaires conservés à la Bibliothèque Nationale*. Paris: Bibliothèque des Curieux, 1920.
Howard, Deborah, and Laura Moretti. *Sound and Space in Renaissance Venice*. New Haven: Yale University Press, 2009.
Howells, James. *Epistolae Howelianae: The Familiar Letters of James Howell*. Boston: Houghton Mifflin, 1907.
Inglis-Jones, James John. "The Grand Condé in Exile: Power Politics in France, Spain and the Spanish Netherlands." DPhil thesis, Oxford University, 1994.
Ingold, Tim. "Against Soundscape." In *Autumn Leaves: Sound and the Environment in Artistic Practice*, edited by Angus Carlyle, 10–13. Paris: Double Entendre, 2007.
Isherwood, Robert M. *Farce and Fantasy: Popular Entertainment in Eighteenth-Century Paris*. Oxford: Oxford University Press, 1986.

James, Ian. "Affection and Infinity." In *Making Sense: For an Effective Aesthetics*, edited by Lorna Collins and Elizabeth Rush, 23–32. Bern: Peter Lang, 2011.
———. *The New French Philosophy*. Cambridge: Polity, 2012.
Jeanneret, Michel. *Éros rebelle: Littérature et dissidence à l'âge classique*. Paris: Seuil, 2003.
Jones, Colin. *The Smile Revolution in Eighteenth Century Paris*. Oxford: Oxford University Press, 2014.
Joris, Freddy. *Mourir sur l'échafaud: Sensibilité collective face à la mort et perception des exécutions du Bas Moyen-Âge à la fin de l'Ancien Régime*. Liège: Éditions du Céfal, 2005.
Jouhaud, Christian. *Mazarinades: La fronde des mots*. Paris: Aubier, 2009.
Jouhaud, Christian, and Hélène Merlin-Kajman. "Mécènes, patrons et clients: Les médiations textuelles comme pratiques clientélaires au XVIIe siècle." *Terrain* 21 (1993): 47–62.
Kastner, Georges. *Les voix de Paris: Essai d'une histoire littéraire et musicale des cris populaires de la capitale depuis le moyen âge jusqu'à nos jours*. Paris: G. Brandus, Dufour etc., 1857.
Kay, Sarah, and François Noudelmann. "Introduction: Soundings and Soundscapes." In Kay and Noudelmann, "Soundings and Soundscapes," 1–9.
———, eds. "Soundings and Soundscapes." Special issue, *Paragraph* 41, no. 1 (2018).
Keilhauer, Annette. *Das französische Chanson im späten Ancien Régime: Strukturen, Verbreitungswege und gesellschaftliche Praxis einer populären Literaturform*. Hildesheim: Olms, 1998.
Kettering, Sharon. "Friendship and Clientage in Early Modern France." *French History* 6 (1992): 139–58.
———. *Patrons, Brokers, and Clients in Seventeenth-Century France*. Oxford: Oxford University Press, 1986.
Kühner, Christian. "L'amitié nobiliaire en France au XVIIe siècle: Représentations et pratiques d'un lien social."

PhD diss., Albert-Ludwigs-Universität, 2010.

Labelle, Brandon. *Acoustic Territories: Sound Culture and Everyday Life*. London: Bloomsbury, 2010.

Lachèvre, Frédéric. *Le libertinage au XVIIe siècle: Les œuvres libertines de Claude Le Petit, Parisien brûlé le 1er septembre 1662*. Paris: Honoré Champion, 1918.

Lagny, Jean. *Le poète Saint-Amant (1594–1661): Essai sur sa vie et ses œuvres*. Paris: A. G. Nizet, 1964.

La Mare, Nicolas de. *Traité de la police*. Paris: Jean et Pierre Cot, 1705.

Le Floc'h, Joseph. "Chanteurs chansonniers sous l'Ancien Régime." In *Musiciens des rues de Paris*, edited by Florence Gétreau and Michel Colardelle, 34–40. Paris: Éditions de la Réunion des musées nationaux, 1997.

———. "Chanteurs de rue et complaintes judiciaires." *Le Temps de l'Histoire*, special issue (2001): 93–103.

———. "Les complaintes judiciaires." In "Histoire et justice, panorama de la recherche," special issue, edited by Frédéric Chauvaud. *Revue d'histoire de l'enfance "irrégulière"* (2001): 93–10.3

le Blanc, Judith. *Avatars d'opéras: Parodies et circulation des airs chantés sur les scènes parisiennes*. Paris: Classiques Garnier, 2014.

Le Brun de La Rochette, Claude. *Le procès civil et criminel*. 2 vols. Lyon: Jaques Roussin, 1610.

Le Cerf de La Viéville, Jean-Laurent. *Comparaison de la musique italienne et de la musique française, où, en examinant en détail les avantages des spectacles et le mérite des deux nations, on montre quelles sont les vraies beautés de la musique*. 2 vols. Brussels, 1704–5.

Leighton, Angela. *Hearing Things: The Work of Sound in Literature*. Cambridge: Harvard University Press, 2018.

Lenet, Pierre. *Mémoires*. Edited by A. Petitot and Monmerqué. Paris: Foucault, 1826.

Le Petit, Claude. *Œuvres libertines*. Edited by Thomas Pogu. Paris: Éditions Cartouche, 2012.

———. *Paris Ridicule*. In Lachèvre, *Le libertinage au XVIIe siècle*.

Le Savoyard, Philippot. *Recueil des chansons du Savoyard*. Edited by M. A. Percheron. Paris: Jules Gay, 1862.

———. *Recueil général des chansons du Capitaine Savoyard Faictes & composées par les meilleurs autheurs de ce temps par luy seul Chantées dans Paris*. Paris: chez Jean Promé, en sa boutique au bout du Pont neuf, 1645.

———. *Recueil nouveau des Chansons du Savoyart par luy seul chantées dans Paris*. Paris: chez la Veuve de Jean Promé, demeurant rue de la Boucherie, au bout du Pont Sainct-Michel, 1656.

L'Estoile, Pierre de. *Mémoires-journaux de Pierre de L'Estoile*. Vol. 7. Edited by Gustave Brunet, Aimé Louis Champollion-Figeac, Eugène Halpen, et al. Paris, 1888–96.

———. *Registre-journal du règne de Henri III*. Edited by Madeleine Lazard and Gilbert Schrenck. Geneva: Droz, 1992–2003.

Lever, Maurice. *Les bûchers de Sodome*. Paris: Fayard, 1985.

Lister, Martin. *A Journey to Paris in the Year 1698*. London: Jacob Tonson, 1699.

Lithgow, William. *The Totall Discourse of the rare adventures and painefull peregrinations of long nineteene years travayles from Scotland*. 1632. London: I. Okes, 1640.

Lockwood, Richard. *The Reader's Figure: Epideictic Rhetoric in Plato, Aristotle, Bossuet, Racine, and Pascal*. Geneva: Droz, 1996.

Loret, Jean. *La muze historique*. Vol. 3. Edited by Ch.-L. Livet. Paris: P. Daffis, 1878.

Lough, John. *France Observed in the Seventeenth Century by British Travellers*. Stocksfield: Oriel Press, 1985.

Louis XIV. *Mémoires de Louis XIV, ou le Métier de roi*. Edited by Joël Cornette. Paris: Tallandier, 2007.

Mademoiselle, La Grande [Anne-Marie, duchesse de Montpensier]. *Mémoires*.

Edited by Bernard Quilliet. Paris: Mercure de France, 2005.

Maistre, Chantal, Gilbert Maistre, and Georges Heitz. *Colporteurs et marchands savoyards dans l'Europe des XVIIe et XVIIIe siècles*. Annecy: Académie Salésienne, 1992.

Mandrou, Robert. *De la culture populaire aux 17e et 18e siècles*. Paris: Imago, 1999.

Marais, Mathieu. *Journal et mémoires sur la régence et le règne de Louis XV (1715–1737)*. 4 vols. Paris: Firmin Didot Frères, 1864.

Marin, Louis. *Le portrait du roi*. Paris: Éditions du Minuit, 1981.

Mason, Laura. *Singing the French Revolution: Popular Culture and Politics, 1787–1799*. Ithaca: Cornell University Press, 1996.

Massin, Robert. *Les célébrités de la rue*. Paris: Gallimard, 1981.

McIlvenna, Una. "*Chanteurs de rues*, or Street Singers in Early Modern France." *Renaissance Studies* 33, no. 1 (2019): 1–158.

———. "The Power of Music: The Significance of Contrafactum in Execution Ballads." *Past and Present* 229, no. 1 (2015): 47–89.

McKenzie, Andrea. *Tyburn's Martyrs: Execution in England, 1675–1775*. London: Hambledon Continuum, 2007.

Mercier, Louis-Sébastien. *Le tableau de Paris*. 12 vols. Amsterdam, 1782–88.

Merrick, Jeffrey. "Chaussons in the Street: Sodomy in Seventeenth-Century Paris." *Journal of the History of Sexuality* 15, no. 2 (2006): 167–203.

———, ed. *Sodomites, Pederasts, and Tribades in Eighteenth-Century France*. University Park: The Pennsylvania State University Press, 2019.

Milliot, Vincent. *Les cris de Paris ou le peuple travesti*. 1995. Paris: Publications de la Sorbonne, 2014.

Molière. *Œuvres complètes*. Edited by Georges Forestier and Claude Bourqui. 2 vols. Paris: Gallimard, 2010.

Mongrédien, Georges. *L'affaire Fouquet*. Paris: Hachette, 1956.

———. *Le Grand Condé: L'homme et son oeuvre*. Paris: Hachette, 1959.

Mousnier, Roland. *Les institutions de la France sous la monarchie absolue, 1598–1789*. Vol. 1. Paris: PUF, 1974.

Mousnier, Roland, and Jean Mesnard. *L'age d'or du mécénat (1598–1661): Actes du colloque international Le mécénat en Europe et particulièrement en France avant Colbert*. Paris: Éditions du CNRS, 1985.

Moyes, Craig. *Furetière's "Roman Bourgeois" and the Problem of Exchange: Titular Economies*. London: Legenda, 2013.

Nancy, Jean-Luc. *À l'écoute*. Paris: Galilée, 2002.

———. *Listening*. Translated by Charlotte Mandel. New York: Fordham University Press, 2007.

Newman, Karen. *Cultural Capitals. Early Modern London and Paris*. Princeton: Princeton University Press, 2007.

Ormesson, Olivier Lefèvre. *Journal d'Ormesson et extraits des mémoires d'André Lefèvre d'Ormesson*. Edited by Adolphe Chéruel. 2 vols. Paris: Imprimerie Impériale, 1856.

Pepys, Samuel. *The Diary of Samuel Pepys*. Edited by Robert Latham and William Matthews. 10 vols. 1971. London: HarperCollins, 2000.

Petitfils, Jean-Christian. *Fouquet*. 1998. Paris: Perrin, 2005.

———. *Louis XIV*. Paris: Perrin, 1995.

Pitts, Vincent J. *Embezzlement and High Treason in Louis XIV's France: The Trial of Nicolas Fouquet*. Baltimore: Johns Hopkins University Press, 2015.

Pocock, Gordon. *Boileau and the Nature of Neo-classicism*. Cambridge: Cambridge University Press, 1980.

Poirier, Guy. *L'homosexualité dans l'imaginaire de la Renaissance*. Paris: Champion, 1996.

Pomeau, René. "Voltaire, du côté de Sodome?" *Revue d'histoire littéraire de la France* 86, no. 2 (1986): 235–47.

Prévot, Jacques, ed. *Libertins du XVIIe siècle*. 2 vols. Paris: Gallimard, 1998–2004.

Proust, Marcel. *A la recherche du temps perdu*. Edited by Pierre Clarac and André Ferré. 3 vols. Paris: Pléiade, 1956.

Pujo, Bernard. *Le Grand Condé*. Paris: Albin Michel, 1995.

Raunié, Émile. Preface to *Recueil Clairambault-Maurepas: Chansonnier historique du XVIIIe siècle*, i–xcviii. Paris: A. Quantin, 1879.

Ravaisson, François, ed. *Archives de la Bastille*. 3 vols. Paris: Durand, 1866–68.

Régent-Susini, Anne. *Bossuet et la rhétorique de l'autorité*. Paris: Honoré Champion, 2011.

Revill, George. "El tren fantasma: Arcs of Sound and the Acoustic Spaces of Landscape." *Transactions of the Institute of British Geographers* 39, no. 3 (2014): 333–44.

Roche, Daniel. *Le peuple de Paris: Essai sur la culture populaire au XVIIIe siècl*. 1981. Paris: Fayard, 1998.

Romey, John. "Court Airs Performed in Seventeenth-Century French Streets." In *Tanz Musik Transfer*, edited by Hanna Walsdorf, Jelena Rothermel, and Christoph Koop, 171–89. Leipzig: Leipzig University Press, 2018.

Rou, Jean. *Mémoires inédits et opuscules*. Edited by Francis Waddington. 2 vols. Paris: Société de l'histoire du protestantisme français, 1857.

Roullier, G. *La marquise de Brinvilliers: Récit de ses derniers moments; manuscrit du P. Pirot, son confesseur*. 2 vols. Paris: Alphonse Lemerre, 1883.

Roussel, Diane. *Violences et passions dans le Paris de la Renaissance*. Seyssel: Champ Vallon, 2012.

Saint-Amant, Antoine Girard de. *Œuvres complètes*. Edited by Ch.-L. Livet. 2 vols. Paris: P. Jannet, 1855.

Saint-Foix, Germain-François Poullain de. *Histoire de l'Ordre du Saint-Esprit*. 2 vols. Paris: Pissot, 1775.

Saint-Pavin, Denis Sanguin de. *Poésies*. Edited by Nicholas Hammond. Paris: Classiques Garnier, 2012.

Saint-Simon, duc de. *Mémoires*. Edited by Yves Coirault. 8 vols. Paris: Gallimard, 1983–88.

Scarron, Paul. *La Foire Saint-Germain*. In Claude Berthod, *La ville de Paris en vers burlesques*, 75–84. Paris: Antoine Rafflé, 1654.

Schafer, R. Murray. *The Soundscape: Our Sonic Environment and the Tuning of the World*. 1977. Rochester: Destiny Books, 1994.

Schindler, Norbert. *Rebellion, Community, and Custom in Early Modern Germany*. Translated by Pamela E. Selwyn. Cambridge: Cambridge University Press, 2002.

Schneider, Herbert. *Chronologisch-thematisches Verzeichnis sämtlicher Werke von Jean-Baptiste Lully*. Tutzing: Hans Schneider, 1981.

Scribe, Eugène. *Œuvres complètes*. Paris: Delahays, 1858.

Scruggs, Charles Eugene. *Charles Dassoucy: Adventures in the Age of Louis XIV*. Lanham: University Press of America, 1984.

Seifert, Lewis C. *Manning the Margins: Masculinity and Writing in Seventeenth-Century France*. Ann Arbor: University of Michigan Press, 2009.

Sévigné, Madame de. *Correspondance*. Edited by Roger Duchêne. 3 vols. Paris: Pléiade, 1972–78.

Smith, Bruce R. *The Acoustic World of Early Modern England*. Chicago: University of Chicago Press, 1999.

Smith, Mark M., ed. *Sensing the Past: Seeing, Hearing, Smelling, Tasting, and Touching in History*. Berkeley: University of California Press, 2007.

Soman, Alfred. "Pathologie historique: Le témoignage des procès de bestialité aux XVIe–XVIIe siècles." In *Actes du 107e Congrès national des sociétés savantes: Section de philologie et d'histoire jusqu'à 1610*, 1:149–61. Paris: ENSB-CTHS, 1984. Reprinted in *Sorcellerie et justice criminelle: Le Parlement de Paris, 16e–18e siècle*. Hampshire, Vt.: Variorum, 1992.

Sorel, Charles. *Histoire comique de Francion*. In *Romanciers du XVIIe siècle*. Edited by Antoine Adam. Paris: Gallimard, 1958.

Sternberg, Giora. *Status Interaction During the Reign of Louis XIV*. Oxford: Oxford University Press, 2014.

Surmont, Jean Nicolas de. *Chanson: Son histoire et sa famille dans les dictionnaires de langue française*. Berlin: De Gruyter, 2010.

Swann, Julian. *Exile, Imprisonment, or Death: The Politics of Disgrace in Bourbon France, 1610–1789*. Oxford: Oxford University Press, 2017.

Tabeling, Brice. "L'écriture familière en France au XVIIᵉ siècle." PhD thesis, Université de Paris 3 Sorbonne Nouvelle, 2017.

Tallemant des Réaux, Gédéon. *Historiettes*. Edited by Antoine Adam. 2 vols. Paris: Pléiade, 1960–61.

———. *Le Manuscrit 673*. Edited by Vincenette Maigne. Paris: Klincksieck, 1994.

Telliez, Romain. "À cor et à cri: Le paysage sonore de la justice, en France à la fin du Moyen Âge." In *Les paysages sonores du Moyen Âge à la Renaissance*, edited by Laurent Hablot and Laurent Vissière, 73–98. Paris: Presses Universitaires de Rennes, 2015.

Thommeret, Loïc Y. "Du greffe à la mise en scène: Mme de Sévigné et le procès de Fouquet." *Papers on French Seventeenth-Century Literature* 22, no. 43 (1995): 597–610.

Titon du Tillet, Évrard. *Le Parnasse françois*. Paris: Coignard fils, 1732.

Tribout, Bruno. "La mémoire des mazarinades: Une critique politique sous Louis XIV." *Revue d'histoire littéraire de la France* 115, no. 4 (2015): 933–50.

Tucker, Holly. *City of Light, City of Poison: Murder, Magic, and the First Police Chief of Paris*. New York: Norton, 2017.

Viala, Alain. *La naissance de l'écrivain*. Paris: Minuit, 1985.

Voltaire. *Œuvres complètes*. Vols. 81–82. Edited by Theodor Besterman. Geneva: Voltaire Foundation, 1968.

———. *La Guerre Civile de Genève*. Besançon: Nicolas Grandvel, 1768.

Ward, Richard, ed. *A Global History of Execution and the Criminal Corpse*. London: Palgrave Macmillan, 2015.

Welsh, Ellen R. "State Truths, Private Letters, and Images of Public Opinion in the *Ancien Régime*: Sévigné on Trials." *French Studies* 67, no. 2 (2013): 170–83.

White, Khadijah. "Considering Sound. Reflecting on the Language, Meaning and Entailments of Noise." In *Reverberations: The Philosophy, Aesthetics, and Politics of Noise*, edited by Michael Goddard, Benjamin Halligan, and Paul Hegarty, 233–43. London: Continuum, 2012.

Wissmann, Torsten. *Geographies of Urban Sound*. Farnham: Ashgate, 2014.

Wootton, David. "Unhappy Voltaire, or 'I shall never get over it as long as I live.'" *History Workshop Journal* 50 (2000): 137–55.

Index

Page numbers in *italics* refer to illustrations.

Anne of Austria, 60, 132, 149
Argenson, Marc René d', 28
Armogathe, Jean-Robert, 92, 177n124
Artagan, comte d', 74
Atkinson, Niall, 11, 169n13
Attali, Jacques, 11, 169n12
Audran, Gérard, "Guillaume de Limoge", 34–35, *34*

Bannister, Mark, 133, 134
Baradas, François, 149
Barbanti, Roberto, 169n7
Barnwell, H. T., 176n69
Barthes, Roland, "Écoute," 12, 84
Bastien, Pascal, 108, 178n7, 179n34, 179n37
Batcho, James, 12
Bayley, Peter, 63
Beaugendre, Antoine, 112
Bée, Michel, 178n7, 179n40
Béguin, Katia, 133, 137, 182n15, 182n21, 182n23, 183n39, 185n7
Béjart, Madeleine, 72
Bellefonds, marquis de, 126
Belleforte, baron de, 106
Belle-Isle, Brittany, 75
bells, in Paris, 14, 20, 170n28
Bergerac, Cyrano de, 45
Berryer, Louis, 76
Berthod (Berthaud), Claude Louis, *La Ville de Paris* (1654), 14, 22, 23
Besse, Pierre de, 111
Blanc, Judith le, 173n66
blind musicians, 3, 39, 41–43
Blot, Claude de Chavigny, baron de, 51, 136
Boësset, Antoine, 36, 47
Boileau, Nicolas, 131
  L'Art poétique (1674), 21, 32
  Satire IX, 35–36
  Satire VI "Les Embarras de Paris", 12–13, 187n2
Boisrobert, 149
Bossuet, Jacques-Bénigne
  in Condé's circle, 131
  funeral oration for le Grand Condé, 67, 143, 174n36
  Lenten sermons (1662), 4, 63–68, 75–76, 91–92, 174n20, 176n72
  Sermon on Death, 65, 174n20
Bourbon, Louis Armand de, 148
Bourgoin, Charles, 150
Bourqui, Claude, 72
Boutin, Aimée, *City of Noise*, 169n14, 170n35
Brantôme, Pierre de, 130
Bray, Alan, 137
Brice, Germain, *Description nouvelle ... de Paris* (1684), 22
Brienne, Louis-Henri de Loménie, comte de, 62, 74
Brinvilliers, Marie-Madeleine-Marguerite d'Aubray, marquise de, 179n47, 180n51
Brossette, Claude, 152
Bruneau, Antoine, 99
Burke, Peter, 92
Bussy, Roger de Rabutin, comte de (Bussy-Rabutin)
  correspondence with the marquise de Sévigné, 48, 49, 56
  Histoire amoureuse des Gaules, 156–57, 159
  possible author of Chausson/Guitaut song, 154–59
  resentment of Guitaut, 131, 141, 149, 182n13, 186n44
  seeks appointment as Chevalier de l'Ordre du Saint-Esprit, 157–58
  writes obscene version of Easter hymn, 156–57, 186n36

Cagnat-Deboeuf, Constance, 176n72
Callières, François, 171n5
  Des bons mots et des bons contes (1692), 25–27
Calvin, John, 180n56
Canto, Charles, 62–63
Certeau, Michel de, 135
Chaduc, Pauline, 179n46
Challe, Robert, 122

Chamillart, Guy, 77, 87
Chansonnier Maurepas (songbooks)
    Chausson/ Guitaut song, 2, 95, 96
    indication of tunes to songs, 56
    mazarinades, 61
    origins of, 27–29
    parodies of Lully's operas, 54
    song relating to Chausson, 106
    songs by le Grand Condé, 151
    songs relating to sodomy (homosexuality), 95, 116, 121, 149
Chantilly, chateau de
    archives of, 95, 138, 145, 152, 155, 158, 183n44
    Condé's estate at, 131, 184n49
Chapelle, Claude-Emmanuel, 45
Châtillon, Gaspard de Coligny, duc de, 135–36, 183n36
Chausson, Alexandre, 105
Chausson, Jacques
    accused of singing blasphemous songs, 103–4
    allusions to after his death, 120–24
    execution, 4, 96, 110–13
    interrogation document, 165–68
    judgement on, 106–8
    nickname, 101–2
    possible author of Chausson/Guitaut song, 159–60
    referenced in songs, 113–16, 120–21, 145–47
    trial of, 98, 99–106, 147
    use of name to designate homosexuals, 118, 121–23, 181n73, 181n77
chaussoneurs, 118
Chausson/ Guitaut song ("Grands Dieux!")
    attempted suppression of, 163
    authorship of, 152–60
    origins of, 95–98
    outrage expressed in, 145
    tune sung to, 1
    version in Chantilly library, 95–96
Chéruel, Adolphe, 176n86
Chevaliers de l'Ordre du Saint-Esprit, 125–30, 157
Choisy, abbé de, 61, 62, 175n38
Clairambault, Pierre, 27, 28
Coirault, Patrice, 35
Colbert, Jean-Baptiste, 68, 71, 73, 75, 77–78, 81, 82–83, 87, 88, 176n68
Coligny, Maurice de, 185n7
Coligny-Saligny, Jean de, 131, 132, 149
Colletet, François, 17

Mémoires, 119–20, 181n66
comédie-ballets, 72
commedia dell'arte, 35
commerce of songs, 38–39
Comminges, François de, 149
communality, and songs, 54
Condé, Louis de Bourbon, Prince de (le Grand Condé)
    author of songs, 151, 186n23
    awareness of street song, 5, 150, 152
    Bossuet's funeral oration for, 67
    correspondence with Guitaut, 137–41, 183n44
    favorites of, 134–37, 183n40
    homosexual preferences, 133–37
    investiture as Chevalier de l'Ordre du Saint-Esprit, 125–26
    literary salons, 133
    marriage, 132–33
    military prowess, 132
    and Nicolas Fouquet, 68, 74, 79, 90
    preferment of Guitaut, 4, 96, 131–32, 149
    and the siege of Lerida, 150, 185n18
    songs celebrating, 36, 151
confessors, at executions, 110–12, 179n46, 179n47
Conti, prince de, 125, 147–48, 155, 163
Corbin, Alain, 20, 170n28, 170n43
cordon bleus. *See* Chevaliers de l'Ordre du Saint-Esprit
Corneille, Pierre, 45, 71, 175n48, 182n19
Cornette, Joël, 174n13, 176n65
Cotgrave, *A Dictionarie of the French and English Tongue*, 25, 40, 41, 43, 44, 101, 171n63
Coulanges, Philippe-Emmanuel, 54–55, 79, 161
Couperin, François, 34
Couvreur, Manuel, 173n58
Coypeau, Charles. *See* Dassoucy
Craveri, Benedetta, 182n22
Créquy, Charles de, 185n15
crime, on the Pont Neuf, 22–23
Cris de Paris (Cries of Paris), 15, 35

Dangeau, Philippe de Courcillon, marquis de, 123
Darnton, Robert, 169n9, 171n60, 171n67
Dassoucy, Charles Coypeau
    Avantures burlesques (1677), 44–47
    compared to Chausson in song, 120, 147
DeJean, Joan

INDEX

How Paris Became Paris (2014), 20, 21, 170n45
Libertine Strategies (1981), 45
De La Force, Piganiol, 178n20
Denney, Peter, 14
dentistry. *See* tooth pullers
Desfontaines, Abbé, 123, 124
Deshayes, Catherine, 51, 179n51
Desmares, Joseph, 50
Dessert, Daniel, 75, 176n69, 176n71
Des Valons, Octave Julien, 105
Dewald, Jonathan, 133, 137, 180n54
disabled musicians, 3, 33, 34, 39
Dostie, Pierre, 176n69
Du Bellay, Charles, marquis, 106, 179n32
Duchêne, Jacqueline, 182n13, 184n54

Enghien, duc de (son of le Grand Condé), 125, 141
Époisses, marquis d', 131
Evelyn, John, 19
executioners, 108–9
executions
    in 17th century Paris, 106–13
    and songs, 97–98, 178n7

Fanchon (singer), 33
Farge, Arlette, 12, 14
Félibien, André, 68, 69, 91
Ferguson, Gary, 177n2, 182n9, 184n5
Ferrand, Michel, 101
Fesnau, M. de, 147, 148
Fleuret, Fernand, 100
Forestier, Georges, 72
Foucault, Joseph, 76, 80, 87
Foucault, Michel, 163, 177n2, 187n7
Fouquet, Nicolas
    arrest and trial of, 73–92, 175n38, 176n68, 176n69, 176n83, 176n88, 177n91
    entertainment at Vaux-le-Vicomte, 68–73, 91
    patron of the arts, 71–72, 163, 175n47
    songs inspired by, 25, 77–78, 86–89
Freidel, Nathalie, 176n69
French Revolution, 24
friendship between men, 137, 183n40
Fronde (1648-53), 24, 49, 60, 82, 113, 131, 136, 138, 149
Fumaroli, Marc, 175n47, 177n93
Furetière dictionary, 31

Gassendi, Pierre, 45
Gatrell, V. A. C., 178n7, 178n9, 180n55

Gétreau, Florence, 172n13, 172n53
Ginzburg, Carlo, 99
Gittard, Daniel, 185n7
Godefroy, René, 103, 120
Goldsmith, Elizabeth, 176n83
Goudal, Jean, 183n31
Gourville, Jean Hérault de, 74, 86, 182n14
Goyon de Matignon, Thomas, 123
Gramont, Maréchal de, 131, 148, 149, 182n10, 185n13, 186n46
Green, Eugène, 65, 174n24, 174n25
Grignan, François Adémar de Monteil de, 54, 55, 158
Grignan, Françoise-Marguerite, comtesse de, 48, 49, 53–54, 54
Grisy, trial of, 120, 181n68
Guedron, Pierre, 47
Guérard, Nicolas, "L'Embarras de Paris" (c.1700), 18, 19
Guiche, comte de, 156, 159
Guillaume, François, 108
Guillaume, Jean, 108
Guillaume de Limoges ("Le Gaillard Boiteux"), 34–35
Guillorel, Éva, 171n72
Guitaut, Guillaume de Comminges-Pechpeyrou, comte de
    appointed Chevalier de l'Ordre du Saint-Esprit, 96, 126, 130, 132, 154
    correspondence with Condé, 137–41, 183n44
    estrangement from Condé, 141, 142
    favorite of Condé, 131–32, 143
    friendship with the marquise de Sévigné, 141–42
    house destroyed by fire, 141, 161–62
    as page boy, 131, 148
    physical courage of, 184n46
    and the trial of Nicolas Fouquet, 90
Gutton, Jean-Pierre, 174n12

Hamilton, Tom, 77, 165, 176n75, 178n23, 178n30, 179n43, 179n49, 179n50, 179n51, 185n16, 187n5
Hammond, Nicholas, 187n5
    Gossip, Sexuality, and Scandal in France, 171n69, 175n61, 178n2, 183n25, 185n6, 185n8, 185n10, 185n11
Harlay de Champvallon, François, Archbishop of Paris, 50
Hawcroft, Michael, 82, 176n69
Hennig, Jean-Luc, 180n56
Henriette d'Angleterre, 68, 147

Henri III, 130
Henri IV, 20, 21
Hérault, Jean. *See* Gourville, Jean Hérault de
Hernandez, Ludovico, 165, 178n23, 184n1, 185n9
homosexuality (sodomy)
　17th century attitudes to, 99, 116, 163, 177n2, 184n5, 185n15
　penalties for, 103, 163, 187n5
　scholarly interest in, 137
　songs relating to, 95
Howell, James, 23
Hus, Jan, 123

instruments, musical, 38, 41
Isherwood, Robert M., 171n59, 186n34
Italian Brotherhood, 148, 163

James, Ian, 169n4
Janequin, Clément, 15, 170n34
Jeanneret, Michel, 118, 180n63
Joly, Benigne (père), 112, 116
Jouhaud, Christian, 175n54
　Mazarinades, 171n57

Kay, Sarah, 25
Kettering, Sharon, 183n40
Kühner, Christian, 137, 183n45, 184n50

Labelle, Brandon, 9, 10–11, 169n1, 169n10
Lachèvre, Frédéric, 159, 165, 180n53, 180n60, 180n61, 186n29
"La Coquille" (song), 113–14
La Fontaine, Jean de, 68, 69–71, 77, 91
Lagniet, Jacques
　engravings of street musicians, 33
　"L'Apollon de la Grève", 37
　"Le Savoyard", 42
Lagny, Jean, 185n18
La Grange, Madeleine de, 131
La Mare, Nicolas de, 170n54
Lambert, Michel, 47
La Mesnardière, Hippolyte Jules Pilet de, 157
Lamoignon, Guillaume de, 76
La Moussaye, Amaury-Goyon de, 135
La Parisière, Jean César de, Bishop of Nîmes, 123
La Raliere-Fenestraux, 149
La Toison (councillor), 86, 90
La Vieuville, Charles II de, 102
Le Brun, Charles, 68
Le Brun de la Rochette, Claude, 99, 116
Le Cerf de La Viéville, Jean-Laurent, 52–53

Leclerc, Michel, 33
Le Coigneux de Bachaumont, François, 101
Leighton, Angela, 169n15
Lenclos, Ninon de, 134, 183n31
Lenet, Pierre, 49, 184n46
Le Nôtre, André, 68
Le Petit, Claude
　execution, 32, 117, 119–20, 181n67
　Le Bordel des Muses, 117–18, 152, 153
　Paris Ridicule (1668), 14–15, 116–17, 153–54
　possible author of Chausson/Guitaut song, 152–54
　present at Chausson's execution, 119
　sonnet on Chausson's death, 4, 114–17, 153, 159, 180n53, 181n65
Lerida, siege of (1647), 150, 186n18
L'Estoile, Pierre de, 112, 179n49, 180n56
Le Tellier, Michel, 77, 157
Le Vau, Louis, 68
Lever, Maurice, 179n32, 183n25, 185n13
libertinage, 133
listening, as a psychological act, 12
Lister, Martin, 18, 170n40
literacy, in Paris, 172n55
literary salons, 133, 182n22
Lithgow, William, 23
Lockwood, Richard, 63, 174n16
Loret, Jean, 60, 68, 126–27, 181n7, 186n24
Louis XIII, 148, 149, 185n11
Louis XIV
　appointment of Chevaliers de l'Ordre du Saint-Esprit, 125–26, 158
　appropriation of artistic control, 71, 163
　assumption of full power, 59, 62, 162–63
　Mémoires, 63, 73, 174n13, 176n65
　sermons addressed to, 63–68
　and the trial of Nicolas Fouquet, 71–72, 77, 88–89, 175n38
Louvre chapel, the Oratory, 63, 65, 174n23
Lully, Jean-Baptiste
　composes music for Fouquet's entertainment, 69, 72
　court composer, 47
　homosexuality of, 116, 121, 180n56
　parodies of, 53–54, 173n66
　Le Bourgeois Gentilhomme, 72
　Psyche, 53
Luynes, duc de, 185n11

Maillé-Brézé, Claire-Clémence, 132–33, 182n21
Maillet, Marc, 33

Malebranche, Nicolas, 131
Mandrou, Robert, 172n21
Manicamp, 156, 159
Marais, Mathieu, 179n36
Mariot, Marie, 105
Maucroix, François, 68
Maurepas, Jean-Frédéric Phélypeaux, comte de, 27
Maurepas songbooks. *See* Chansonnier Maurepas
Mayenne, Seigneur de, 150
Mazarin, Cardinal, 4, 60–62, 74, 75, 116, 174n7, 175n38, 186n18
mazarinades, 24, 60, 171n57
McIlvenna, Una, 98, 178n4
McKenzie, Andrea, 178n7
Ménage, Gilles, 54
Mercier, Louis-Sébastien
   on executions, 109–10
   on the influence of street songs, 97
   on literacy in Paris, 172n55
   on the Pont Neuf, 21–22, 171n55, 184n4
   on singers, 32
   on the sounds of Paris, 16
Merlin-Kajman, Hélène, 175n54
Merrick, Jeffrey, 178n2, 181n68
Mesmes, Jean-Jacques de, 101, 145
Milliot, Vincent, 170n29
Minard, Charles, 33
Molière, 45, 181n67
   Les Fâcheux, 72–73
Mongrédien, Georges, 176n68, 176n69
Monmerqué, 183n34
Montagu, Sir Edward, Earl of Sandwich, 104–5
Montespan, marquise de, 67
Montpensier, Anne-Marie, duchesse de, 60
"mouches" (spies), 163
Mousnier, Roland, 183n40
Moyes, Craig, 73
musical culture, 173n62
musical instruments, 38, 41, 127
Muze historique, La (gazette), 60, 126–27

Nancy, Jean-Luc, *À l'écoute (Listening)*, 10, 13, 169n5, 169n6, 170n22
Nantouillet, marquis de, 106
Newman, Karen, *Cultural Capitals*, 170n45
nicknames, 101–2
Noguès (judge), 86
noise, 11–18, 69–71, 74, 170n21
Notre-Dame church, Arques-la-Bataille, 65
Noudelmann, François, 25

opera, songs parodying, 52–54
orality, 10–12, 25–27, 43, 79–84, 137–38, 143, 169n9
oranges, in 17th century France, 147–48, 184n4
Ordre du Saint-Esprit, 96, 125–30, 145, 154, 181n3, 182n9
'Orlande de Lassus', 33, 38
Orléans, Philippe, duc d', 68, 147, 184n6
Ormesson, Olivier Lefèvre d'
   celebrated in song, 87–88, 177n114
   rapporteur at the trial of Nicolas Fouquet, 76, 78, 79–86, 90, 91, 177n101
   snubbed by Louis XIV, 88–89

page boys, 105, 147–50, 178n29, 185n15
Palais de Justice, Paris, 77
Paris
   17th century sounds, contemporary accounts, 12–18
   construction projects (17th century), 20–21
   Pont Neuf, 18–27
patronage, of the arts, 71–72, 163, 175n46, 175n54
Patterson, Jonathan, 180n57
Paulmier, Jacques
   employed by Lord Montagu in England, 104–5
   execution, 96
   interrogation and trial, 100, 105–6, 165–68, 185n9
   judgement on, 106–8
   link to Fesnau, 147–48
   nickname, 102
Pellisson, Paul, 72, 75, 77, 175n65
Pepys, Samuel, 104–5, 185n15
Perceau, Louis, 100
Percheron, M. A., 172n15
performance, of songs, 96
Petitfils, Jean-Christian, 89, 175n47, 176n69
Phélypeaux, Jean, 24
Phélypeaux, Jean-Frédéric. *See* Maurepas, Jean-Frédéric Phélypeaux, comte de
Phélypeaux, Jérôme. *See* Pontchartrain, Jérôme Phélypeaux, comte de
Philippot "Le Savoyard", 32–47
   blindness, 39, 40–43, 45
   depicted by Dassoucy, 44–47, 172n53
   engraving by Jacques Lagniet, 42
   published songs of, 3, 35–37, 102, 172n16
   self-depiction in songs, 39–44
   song in praise of le Grand Condé, 151
   subject matter of songs, 36–41

Piro, Edme, 179n47
Pitts, Vincent J., 176n69
Place de Grève, Paris, 108–9, 112, 113, 116, 117, 125
Place Royale (Place des Vosges), 20–21, 54
"plebeian noise," 14
Pocock, Gordon, 170n19, 170n26
Pogu, Thomas, 180n64, 181n67
Poilly, François, "Chevaliers de l'Ordre du Saint-Esprit,", 128
Poirier, Guy, 178n2
police force, established under Louis XIV, 28, 162, 170n54
Pomeau, René, 181n80
Pomponne, Simon Arnauld de, 49, 79, 85, 90
Poncet, 86
Pont au Change, 21
Pontchartrain, Jérôme Phélypeaux, comte de, 24, 27–28
Pont Marie, 21
Pont Neuf, 18–27
  availability and performance of songs, 25
  circulation of *mazarinades*, 60
  communal entertainment space, 3, 21
  construction of (1606), 20–21
  crimes and criminals on, 22–23, 171n55
  "L'Embaras de Paris" (c.1700), 18, 19
  Marquise de Sévigné on the songs of, 49
  Samaritaine hydraulic water pump (Pont Neuf), 19–20, 47
  as social leveller, 21
  and the trial of Nicolas Fouquet, 77
Pont Notre-Dame, 21
ponts-neufs (street songs), 21, 150
Prévot, Jacques, 185n15
Promé, Jean, 35
Proust, *La Prisonnière*, 135
Pujo, Bernard, 182n13, 182n14
pulpit oratory, 63–68
Pussort, Henri, 76, 87, 88

Racine, Jean, 131
raillerie, 25–26
Rees, Jonathan, 2
Régent-Susini, Anne, 65, 174n20, 174n27
Renard, Jacques, 82
"Réveillez-vous, belle endormie" (song), 1, 96
Revill, George, 10, 169n3, 169n11
Reynie, Gabriel-Nicolas de la, 28, 162, 174n12
Richelieu, Cardinal, 36, 131, 149
Rivière, François de Chevery, Chevalier de, 136
Rocroi, battle of (1643), 132

Romey, John, 36, 172n15, 172n24, 172n26, 173n71
Roquesante, 86
Rou, Jean, 118–19, 153, 180n64, 181n65
Rousseau de le Parisière, 124

Saint-Aignan, duc de, 157
Saint-Amant, Marc-Antoine Girard, 45, 150, 185n18
Sainte-Hélène, Jacques le Cormier de, 76, 84, 85, 87, 88
Saint-Foix, Germain-François Poullain de, 128, 154, 181n3
Saint Germain fair, 16–17, 148
Saint Laurent fair, 16–18
Saint-Marc, Charles-Hugues Lefebvre, 152
Saint-Mars, marquis de, 185n11
Saint-Maur, chateau de, 148, 185n7
Saint-Pavin, Denis Sanguin de, 39, 133–34, 180n59, 183n27
Saint-Simon, Claude de, 185n11
Saint-Simon, Louis de Rouvroy de, 63, 182n21
Samaritaine hydraulic water pump (Pont Neuf), 19, 20, 47
Scarron, Paul, 45
  Foire Saint-Germain (1654), 17
Schafer, R. Murray, 169n3
Schildebek, baron de, 117
Schindler, Norbert, 101
Schneider, Herbert, 173n66
Scribe, Eugène, 24
Scudéry, Madeleine de, 173n56
Séguier, Pierre, 76, 79, 80, 81, 82, 83, 141
Sens, Prévost de, 112
Sévigné, Charles de, 50–51, 54
Sévigné, Marie de Rabutin-Chantal, marquise de
  on Bossuet's sermon, 174n36
  correspondence of, 48–57
  on Coulanges, 54
  friendship with Guitaut, 141–42, 162
  on Guitaut's house burning down, 161–62
  musical accomplishments of, 48, 54, 56, 173n56
  on the Pont Neuf, 21
  on salacious songs, 50–51
  on a song parody of Lully's *Psyche*, 53–54
  on the songs of the Pont Neuf, 49–50
  on the sounds of Paris, 15–16
  on the trial of Nicolas Fouquet, 49, 79, 81–83, 84–86, 90, 176n69, 176n83, 176n88, 177n91, 177n95

singers and musicians, 32–5. *See also* Philippot "Le Savoyard"
singing
    of blasphemous songs, 103–4
    prohibited in public, 23–24
Smith, Bruce, 25, 169n13
Smith, Mark M., 169n3
sodomy. *See* homosexuality
Soman, Alfred, 100, 179n31, 187n5
songs
    anthologies, 27
    blasphemous, 103–4, 152
    and communality, 55
    on the *cordon bleu* ceremony, 126–28
    execution ballads, 97–98, 145–47, 178n7
    as form of resistance, 24–25, 28–29, 91
    genres of, 172n21
    and morality, 25–27
    parodies of opera, 52–54, 173n66
    relating to sodomy, 95, 113–18, 122–23
    and social class, 31
songwriters, need for anonymity, 28
Sorel, Charles, *Histoire Comique de Francion* (1623), 41
sound, and social class, 14–16
soundscapes, 10, 25, 169n3
sound studies, 10
Sternberg, Giora, 181n3
street fairs, 16–17
Swann, Julian, 176n66

Tallemant des Réaux, 33, 148–49, 179n32, 183n25, 184n51, 185n13
Talon, Denis, 76–77
Telliez, Romain, 174n12

Thommeret, Loic Y., 176n69
Titon du Tillet, Évrard, *Le Parnasse françois* (1732), 54
tooth pullers, on the Pont Neuf, 44, 172n41
Toulougeon, comte de, 136
town criers, 62–63, 174n12
Treaty of the Pyrenees (1659), 131
Treuvé, Pierre, 141
Tristan l'Hermite, 45, 185n15
Tucker, Holly, 174n12
Turenne, Henri de La Tour d'Auvergne, vicomte de, 74, 155–56, 157

Vallière, Louise de la, 67, 92, 148, 175n36
Vatel, François, 69
Vaux-le-Vicomte, Fouquet's entertainment at (1661), 68–73, 91
Vendôme, duc de, 156
Vermandois, comte de, 148, 163
Versailles, chateau de, 141
Verthamon, Antoinette-Élisabeth de, 132
Verthamont, M. de, coachman of, 33
Viala, Alain, 175n46
Vigean, Marthe de, 134, 183n30
Vivonne, 156
Voltaire,
    allusion to Chausson, 123–24, 181n79
    attitude to homosexuality, 181n80

Welsh, Ellen R., 176n69, 177n91
White, Khadijah, 170n21
Wissmann, Torsten, 170n21
women singers, 33
Wootton, David, 181n80

www.ingramcontent.com/pod-product-compliance
Lightning Source LLC
Chambersburg PA
CBHW021947290426
44108CB00012B/985